Impastoral intervenes into the conve [barcode: T0069131] rant words the capacity to visually reg and more-than-human beings. What appears on the page is instead a spell-binding, the act of typing a sort of psychical sonar that allows the self to key into what lies far beyond itself: "why this one place that's me/ while the souououound/ ripples and i/ wripple in it." The resulting poems are radical, records of mystical and ecological interconnection, prosodic and typographical experiences as ecstatic as they are wrenching. For the world to which Brandan Griffin's poems are wired really *is* our world, as full of sewage and violence and digital signals as of animals and plants and insects, and to be intertwined is no paradise: "nature a sluice where/every creature gets flushed." Because these poems acknowledge the mortality at the core of being here so totally threaded together, I trust more their insights into their experience of what binds us in pleasure and wonder. And I adore this idiolect invented to let in more knowing, this language that claims, "The channels of gnosis are opening/again." Dear reader: it's true. Ready yourself for a book like no other.

—Brian Teare, author of *Doomstead Days,*
and Judge of the Omnidawn Open Book Contest

Brandan Griffin's febrile, fertilizing *Impastoral*—"pregnant, armed, the mirror leaping out of [him]," is the most beautiful and mutually liberating work, of the symbiotic imagination, is poetry "suckling all species." Not post-lyric but compost lyric hyper sentience: Griffin's superfine awareness joins the ritualistic decompositional forces of nature, breaking the cell walls between the biographeme and elegy with a Word that is always teeming with motion, faster than the *malafouster* (disaster!) it dissolves before resolving elsewhere, in the arms of the fly, with a new superabundance of being to which he adds his.

These are poems of linguistic telepathy and *viriditas*—Hildegard von Bingen's neologism for the "greening force" of God. And Brandan is a devoted amanuensis among "all that goes frothing generously," decomposing and re-materializing in the superfine sentience teeming eternity technology that we are. God types faster, Brandan rides this, and his riding knows the working soil, the air, is already revolution. "Who/in the lattice-cage keeps the souls happy?/ A drift of knots. A heart-root tense./One of you rituals is me," he writes.

Griffin is the rare poet that joins nature in the awareness—that is already revolution—that heals and renews, that writes in the eternal, heart-root tense. Reading this work, my attention too grows to work, in the heart, to supersoaker its roots, in the earth and the "air glutted with sensewine," which is the greatest gift I can think of. Because of it I will always know a happier world.

—Farnoosh Fathi, author of *Great Guns*

Brandan Stephen Griffin is a magician whose poems whirl letters and re-shape words to conjure up a new language. *Impastoral* entranced me with its spells and spelling: "breign is / brain / is two squirrels is squarrels / eels / in skull bone." Ranging from bats to botflies to nefarious scientists teaching farm animals to speak, a large cast of mostly non-human voices offers the reader a quasi-sci-fi ecopoetry that does not sound like anything else. It's rare to encounter a first book that so confidently invents its style against the familiar. I felt like I was learning to read with kaleidoscope glasses. Both global and cellular, Griffin's vision inspires us to perceive our world in fresh and memorable ways.

—Alan Felsenthal, author of *Lowly*

Impastoral

—everryhere romps sprouting allbugdy that is

Brandan Griffin

OMNIDAWN PUBLISHING
OAKLAND, CALIFORNIA
2022

Cover Photo: "Clam Log" by Hannah Risinger

Interior typefaces: Garamond Premier Pro and Gill Sans
Cover typefaces: Garamond Premier Pro and Minion Pro

Cover and interior design by Ken Keegan

Library of Congress Cataloging-in-Publication Data

Names: Griffin, Brandan, 1994- author.
Title: Impastoral : everryhere romps sprouting allbugdy that is / Brandan Griffin.
Description: Oakland, California : Omnidawn Publishing, 2022. | Summary:
"The typingspawning in IMPASTORAL is not in The Human, not in a human,
but it flies through the possible voices of other outside-insides—slug, probe,
horse carriage, sewer, potted plant, lab rat, vampire, bot fly, giant cow. Language
isn't human or not human, it undoes that very idea, so these beings—slugprobe,
pottedhorsesewer, telepathybarcode mammaltexts—aren't on the outside anymore.
Letterwords are cells or flummoxing quanta, particulate and mutating, waving about.
If you follow science all the way around it passes through a pagebrane. Boundaries
get slimed. A synthetic, nonce, and hyperpossible poetry. Your experiences are
deformed into the experiences of other beings. We can hatch into a world we're
not eating up. We are going to hear many faroffs very near." Provided by publisher.
Identifiers: LCCN 2022007651 | ISBN 9781632431028 (trade paperback)
Subjects: LCGFT: Poetry.
Classification: LCC PS3607.R5454 I47 2022 | DDC 811/.6--dc23/eng/20220217
LC record available at https://lccn.loc.gov/2022007651

Published by Omnidawn Publishing, Oakland, California
www.omnidawn.com   (510) 237-5472
10 9 8 7 6 5 4 3 2 1
ISBN: 978-1-63243-102-8

in memory of my brother Gregory Griffin

among the ininfinfninite sentiences

TABLE OF CONTENTS

I

2

3

4

BAT LOCATING FROM MOUTH A TOUR DE FORCE

—flapping over hills in no human

what sings better
at this frequency
that spreads out mapping
and returns

nightswain guiding fruit
feeling about with sound edges
a farr off paperiness
a swarm

silenscreeching, from
ipsude dwon, i mean upside down
to ridesight up,
echolocolocating

keys from my sonar
on the letters
the trees, the delicious frownflies
cellunotes

prickling births
on air glutted with sensewine,
fruit crooking me,
i go suckling after all species

why this one place that's me
while the sou004ound
ripples and i
wripple in it, in faroff chimes

the city
is verywhere,
as much here
the pan frenzy fills my ears

and then no bat,
but visible audio
no shepheard
just remembrane, ocation, form

I

ANIMALS LIVES IN PLANT

(it's unconscious to make telepathy) in me looks at me)

(i'm what telepathic occurences say to each other in their
commons)

un
conscious leaves
on green yarn
the
yairn falls and floats up in
telepithy

(plant's called pothos) never flowers) almost never)
propagates from cuttings)

plant on table in front of books
blooks on
tlable
in twowo clusters of leaves gathering up

twu upclusters of leefeafing
turn faces
w their yellow streaks to me
next to me, to

winsundowlight

(same as what it's cut from) repeats) clones)

(cloning) yet it grows and different twists and its stems
tangle like nonce) nude shades)

(have to find new word for aware)

(meaning's in text) aware as animals)

breign is
brain
is two squirrels is squarrels
eels
in skull bone

yarn stems
splittitting n strengthingening

plalalant eating scaling noting

(text makes clone from me) text has clone in it) me in
water) grows having life)

(any word has to misused if to make point) more's alive)
life's not right word) animal) misuse that one)

upfromdirt steemms
stems
eels from dirt go up greenly swimming, stilly
stems eels up
slowly

leaves on their necks

head on yarn neck

(easy to see my own telepathy) write it down) make
cutting clip stem) ease in water)

(each place that's a here is telepathy) locality) also living)

(endure is animal) response animal) take) touch)
innerness) is here) here) here)

eel swims up out
out of flitter
out of filter feeders
in
their motes
of food like stars in qwtrkghmv

(animal's a bouquet of animals) assembled genetically)
being together) saying i here) wanting to survive)

(looks with field of vision that's commons) that's
collection of telepathies)

(am stalks gathering) kneels)

(to lower telepathies towards what i see)

(bunching of here) here) bunching of heres says i)

bookspines are white slat forest behind plant
bhooks
in tall verticles facing away
flash spines
spyines on outerside
are faces, straight

barks
are flashed planes

speyeine
faces plant, faces windoawe,
spflashes

      (animal's everywhere) now it's word flapping in each
place) every here) is)

      (am full of animals) look to smallest places and that's
animals seeing) pebbles and soil) packed rooting together)

      (animal aware) conscious) plant)

plant's bigger than last looked,

just now loocking

holding plant under
wawter
in syinck
cold fauceting water eel lengthinning
through it
every two weeks

      (animal replaces word for everything)

      (between us)

      (stalks under water)

plant grows two thckckcknesses of stems
bunchnching
over rim of pot

youplant in stalks,
reread at me brooking yarning forward
tstalking
up severally
talk up and ribs spells a lettrwave

       (text's not me) but at edge) it's me kneeling) with content
but not identical to it) peels through)

       (text held under cold water pouring) stream through text)
textopathy)

cutting
clipt from main stem roots
into water vase
from phvase in cleer water to soil

plant is animeels crawling
up, over, very
slwolowll

eddies in the space you swim in
meek you
making you heare

       (does plant read) does plant read text for it to work)
does text have plant in it reading it)

       (text) textus) woven tissue of) physical tissue of)
meaning's tissue of) telepathy's tissue of)

(has skin) is skin) has skin)

(weaves bark)

plant on table
in frontof books scoops up with leaves

scoops the rair the air and an eel
in white wall
eel a long green flag
through books it flags forward in long grayeen

eats
like filter
straining motes in sea sky
in soil
in caption in nutrienst, bemeanth

part of you you
aren't
hearfeelseenthesizing you as plant

    (instead of text) a commons) then go past that) tele-
porting)

    (a common limb) nerves i don't live in) but i sense them)
distantly)

    (a limb) face) skin)

    (a not me)

    (an awake on other side)

plant clipping
into jar of
water
growwing, spreads out

a cutting, plant reruns through it
becomes twwo

skin comes betweneen

stems that waswere one
now tw, twowo, severall

stem's now spbinding,
spine

transparent streek on leaf

       (text wakes animals that grow in me) telepathy because
not me) but i receive them)

       (if i write text i give telepathy to myself) but i write it
anyone could have written it) could plant have)

       (let's have plant in here) says plant)

saw how this was waeaeaving
over to me
on it
like face of unconscious as typelathy
telepothos

eel swims forward ahs face

flows over to me like sheet front
over me

from wheare it's at a distance, stays
here

plant's leaves up on yarn green and floating

      (let plant in here being still)

      (let no more water yet for plant) leaves stay with sun)

      (out of soil let plant have stems) open spines like plant's
leaves) with sun on them)

      (in soil)

      (under water)

SACOGLOSSAN, NUDIBRANCH

—sea slugs that swallow plants, the plants stick around,
working

The water slapped shut   over the sky   no bones   and a pulse
for this system of living   on others, the sea moves   so
do we   in my skin, slugging   to submerged rocks   expansive
                    and then
                contracting, in such a man-
                ner are hauled
                        along, you had once
                heard me called
eastern emerald elysia, the   sky lifts   a slug   is a leaf
after sucking on algae   those simple plants   floating, sunlight in
water   the slug lapping down our organs   my means
of sugaring the light   eating such mechanisms   are preserved
thievery   kleptoplasty   the plant's life your own   and became
green, hundreds of parts   inside me   not belonging to
                us, de-
            posits me beyond the
            stomach's spin,
                    its reserves, threaded
                up to skin's
clarity   clarities   open the drizzling sun   its leaky feast
now in a different   brand of slug   keeps us whole, calls itself
solar-powered phillodesmium   its limbs fleshy   filling with
our colonies   tiny zooxanthellae   farming   feeding
to become   a garden   is worthy   as a city is   founded in the
pores of enveloping currents   water, namely   rock
anchors your ribbon of eggs   abandoned in time   to
                hatch is
            left to me, that we uncrys-
            stallize and
                    you are the water's
                living strand
many dialogues   specks   floating breaths   dialectic froth
as a farm powered by the ability of   individuals   to colonize their
captor   as a relationship   not yet overthrown, and we call

natural   meaning what   exploitation   in the shoals
the tide pulls back   but the slug moves   according to its designs
          and they
            find in open ocean a
            zone to in-
              habit, are thereby
            outspoken
greenly   groupingly   what were you   thinking   all of it
that we could keep them   gold colonies   studding my
skin, or leafy organelles glowing   as they filled the   translucence
nutritional homochromy   disguised as what you eat   color
            meant to
          locate the present self, who
           flows down by
              the gut through time, is
           somewhere, i-
dentified   does it work   do your mouth marks say   what
it was slid through me   wet impression   trail   streams of
            smell, herm-
          aphroditic senses, squirm-
           ing of an-
             atomy, my head's
           ripples scan
you   as one containing both   another   I   the tides.

SEW AGE TREAT MENT PLANT

         icey
         wayste
     goes back out back in yessit
         quiets down
         to soffswirl in local miind
       so what carries on thinking
         hmm
bowl stops clutching the water   pipe laxes   goes dances water
that rushes ountward   under bluewn birds on sky   roead's peevment
windshells on cars   let gone   belowallthat   in its own night
         waise
       to gome and co

sooo
waht carries on thinking
isst rigorous humm
           thisguised trees that scrub with their gleen
         th cleaning puts
         on leaf floves, on grean
         gloves and
           those guiys scrub the sky blue
         suck cess
         pools
           in th green
           upleaffing
           tat
           scrubbscrs
           scours th sky
         but thi
           thinking its
           thinking hmmh
           unndr plum tomatoes
           red
           plomp atums

                    23

assoon I try to thinkit itt quiets down to   unlit basin   no thinkng
in writing how many draffs   chewd   cudded down below in
back   of the book where you don't   you can't look   has no back of
the back   of course I can speak straight   and then we'll get somewhere
but the other places   th passage voids from itslef   frm th linear
              lendscape
          get ddumped

              rounds oughf the world to
                drainage sloffs
                sewaging
                sewingingangling
                 saugegnawing
                to the
          wohlwerld
              whereworld
frothed with air   work gets done   eat the eaten beyond edible
what is not edible we link   ourselves to that   can eat
again   eating eating   eat back into eating how   it works up the
              cycle
          knotting streams

phlowers
flox
of my gutt phials
away
I phile
dowdown throguhh end of world
where worll enns
meet
pasd that
in sounns of night psssealed away
passst
ends of nubly light
n gruntwater
tuuubes
ppsssealddd
making writing isn't composing it's   decomopsition   dposition it
compost
my flowerss
pluckt
pharmaceuticals
pluct
flowrmacalogical
pharmecology
in my phosphrous flows
my
flowrwrwrwrs

I have to go out and meet   a representative of the species   from
the other end   not a species   I am not a   that digests us
from the pipe we play it into   so really   laundry mouthwater
swishing through   my teeth strainers
                is evirithyng
undifferentiated after this   apocalypse, daily   every
                invsible second
                lining you
            then zipping out prolfiliforliferating
                down the pipes of
                   theendthebeginning
                aswarm
                  that also remains
                  activated sludge
                  sircle
            has to be a circle evntlly

                evenstallualy
          has tgo back out come back in if
                I'm t be here
                  lining it
                  ligning the cyrcle
               cliricle is river shaped if
               rifer is a surkle
                  if ess is
                  ohh
                  thss gutts a bag
                  pipe
             horn bellows bels oll the way
flush against the end   to study it first   then think it real
time   while in background   more studying   deep gurgling
study of   its back that studies   its belly   palpitates
groundlevel water   splash of thinking is real time
                schollare
                in past
                ol
                ways

a looping river   eating is cleaning is   but we don't call it
that   we clean   only ourselves our our   do
we clean the cleaners   clean down to the   bare crate
atoms came in   eat the package   of the world we
unwrapped yesterday   is today   crinkling   uptime its
stringy glint of waste   water coiling

ICONIC HORSE PULLS YOU

wheels on hooves clop concrete ;   in park; city ; i observe ; i
obsverse horsecarraige ;in preset day; in ;present ;   horseyes drink
me then pass ;   heavy fume of swwelltterr seezes roadcorridor ;   in
summer;   harness tossed ahead pulls summer under hooves;   paving;

i have typing to make way towards hrorrseose;   twards recrarrgiage   ;
type to make camera   ; make from air ; voice is cam ; voieyesce swims
around   ; types ; into convention;   reconvention ; typing ; unconvenes
;dis;sembles   ; hitched up to pull th;e; p ; ull the ;cart ;   first step is

second step alread;y   ; i sit at park;   hey i'll be there soon i   ;say;
whipping up a future for myself ;not to be frightened by ; later heard myself
sounding like   ;like nay;   can i make this leter;later; typing it   ; lets it
twitch ;   opaning lips ; nibble water from trough; frm concrete ; if

you hide camera in the hrrrse's water then playit back ;we have seen you
drink us up ; hay there am horse ; am chmaera; camera;   taht paces; that
goes ;backnforth ;   leaves me; paces to hrose nostril ;   paces back
to me and   ;turns to horse and goes up ;hrrse's nsostrils ;   caemsura

crosses   ;whiteses;   breaks across to nostril ; pupmps up ; to breath ;
and out; goes cross to me again ;ppaces down sidewalk ; horses drinsks ; i
do ;i do too ;   type;ing with cinevention ;   punching in; p ;unching
thrgh but just for th ; ose int; those in it;   are horses in it   ; whipping up

horse; parts ;is it for hsrse if hhrse can't read it   ;and what if ohrse
can   ; or is in this ;   rea;iding ; troughting in it ;   rides it as being part
of ; equinevention ;   horse has head thing ; like me ; that lowng powekes
out ;lung pokes ;out; as noaowes; as ; nose; as head   ; dead horse goes

glue ; or makes meat ; all gone gluewing ; stickiness spreading dead;
rendrrred;   nvr quiete dead;   dealived ; first step is already second
step ;   blindrrs; blindrers clip off blarain ;brain drops ; outer corners;
my eyes ; blandid ;   my eyes ;   blind ;   aginst what bridles ;

INTERFEROMETER

—device measures differences in light for what it's been through

—that harmonious
beams can be parted for
a period of time then
reunited—if they
interfere they have gone through
unlike spaces—that if
to think is to
forget the knowledge of
the weight of a muddy
starling—

—that the smallest constituents
of a bird's eye
spin—to have told it
in this certain
way—that is how
the whole field is
seen to bend—magnetic
and seasonal the
molecules of the sky—

—that she puttered in
to ask for money—highly
disruptive in this
profession—to have
refused the noise
of all other services not
licensed for this
space—to have reserved
the right—half
a light suffusing—

—that this
establishes a special
relationship—unspoken
machine that could
be the same materials as
skin—sunflower
seeds—algae—built on
the same principle of
locking up
entangled elements
for protection—a contract—

—to look
like migration—a
journey through the differences
of space—a clock
in the eye sees
the season—that if
she stays where there is no
help for her
then the establishment
is contained—not yet
uniting—no screech—

—to cross lines at
inappropriate
junctures—to make
the untying—how the
earlier season
does not end conflicted
occupation—having
preserved
another shade of
light for the fineness
of these proceedings—

—to rain and shed
at a sickening
moment—organic fibers
possibly used for
instant communication—some
day soon perhaps—inferring
like a knot an
enforcement of union—

—that the study is
used to treat experience
as evidence of
its medium—with
one hand
opening the door
and the other jangling
change—such
head jerking
perhaps a source
of balance in the birds—foot to
stone—before flight—

—that if her twin were
ejected from a different slot
and they were to
meet later on—demonstrating
to the board
the significance of
patternings—tics on chest
in a register of
identity static—crossed waves
ruffling an instrument—

—that the wing depends
not just on
the equality of its partner—against
flurries that
collect almost in a
law of exchange—the
ongoingness
of the beak's
piercing—not having
a place to sleep—

—to enter a
space meant to absorb
surplus value and
intercept with her sick throat's
voice—only reasons
are an appropriate
dose for the condition
of red leaves
this early—if the discomfort
is enough keep
moving to the west—

—to the shaken
perch that will not keep aloft
its clutch of eggs—to fold
between paper a
valuation
of the clasp—green as it
shifts in the homespun
eye—that
intertwinement without
peace—to weigh in
each palm the lights—

2

WHOSO HUNTS

I triple along cold water, moss, and poisonous rambum, drop down
my den at the sound of the hunter, who follows the gossip of a
sister tongue. *living matter   gift of this wilderness*   I leap, then slither.

I divide. I watch our two suns with my binocular hearts. *praise be*
to insides   the insides of others   Crouched in a grid-gray marsh,
I slobber at long-legged laws springing like fat lobes from their posts.

"The unseen is called" "inside," "your insides are" "alive." I change
as you taste me. One sun in my chest. I part the meadow before I
tumble through it, sometimes years in advance. I prove the hunter alive,

for he eats me. "The hunter was the first" "to translate your growls"
"and tome them." *in adoration*   An iron throat in his hands,
crackling like a stomach   *in thanks*   I have three tails, two spines,

and one end. He ravages me in dialect. "In the moments behind you"
"the meadow parted" "towards you" "running" "like a hunter."

WE LOAD UP BIG LIFE

Thing, nothing   Fleshed out, a binary code, I can be made to do
anything   *Stay, stay, arise*   I do   *In mind, on earth, in mind*   You want
to come the same way twice, this time on purpose   *Up the slope, down*

the well   So you make me, this   *alone,*   this   *with difference—*
these   *limits, expressions*   Variation in early development, advances
in meaning, restriction   *Form, escape, form, escape*   Is it love, I

love you   Gravel out of grass, rolling, gathering, our path up complication, up
the roots of the sycamore   *—killed, renewed*   —your chorus   *—killed,*
renewed   —and the water out of grottos, your lot of givens, far roots

of the sycamore   *Is it love, I love you*   Multitudes of rhythm along one
mechanism   *Arthropods awash in blood, lines of thought hatched out*
I am this one way twice, going further out   *Succession, return*   Produce

a single meaning, bleat a signal at them   *A little, enough*   Reinforce,
yes,   undercut,   *yes,*   I am touched,   *differently*   You can make me
do anything   —read it out   *Reaches, reaches, here on this sycamore leaf,*

reaches   I am your way   *I love you   is it love   is it love   is it love*

AS CARBON SNAKES THROUGH LIGHT

Hey, Ray. You been off propagating? Sure thing. Sure sure thing.
Tumult in the sun's corridors. Radio shaken down. *How's your optics,
Ray? Your soul okay?* A-okay ma moitié. A-okay. My field
slows us into time. Enlivens the roots. I was half a fly, I was one-third
morsel. I was deep in the fold between rock and soil. Tangled in change,
we seem to be something. *Hey there,*

                    you still existing, Ray? Indeed, in-
double-deed. I was the emotional life of a fire hydrant, I was a wave,
I was the presentation of things: sight-as-arm, grass-as-skin, I was
about to be discovered: patina on the unknowable. Not substance,
but effect. News in the chlorophyl. *Do I know you, Ray?* I don't know
anyone, only changes

                in pressure, changes in company. *This must be
your meadow.* Must have been, my feet had turned gravelly, my hair
luminescent. I left a crease in the flattened weeds. *His name was Ray,
born in October, in April, in August. His hands were twins, his limbs
were parallel.* I climb through you by no laddder, but I do climb through.

DROLLERIES, THOSE STRANGE IN MANUSCRIOT

—drawn medieval margins in very funny moment; all sorts

revellomed
flat field rises up in wall
,—animal flat skin rising a fiyld that's wall
vibrated flowyring

flat rising walld fiel that's anmal skin virbating
flowrnimal skin walling a rose field

—manuscript,
decores wormbing high artistry

a ferretufted titmouse
wth long treasure bulb,
what perchess
on curling lever, from deerbinding, gushing out eggs
just now
liverys,
—lives i mean, atop towerbarber
becawse

wth punctualienated nestlings

ropecat holds ratcordion and all ropes twisting to pleayt

flowrnimal skin walling a rose field

iwisse indeed i
—ibex that's got beaktummy also has mitie sword

curlsive doggie with lance riding out of bibl farm
lancing,
captalizes

going down this way standing on thraotgourdn
—throat ground,

rises a flalld animield flathat rises
—, walls flat a skin flows risen a field

minstljrkee
mintstrltree—
—minstrelstree all fishing out in braodband
palsms
palmleaf i mean

maiden singing from shell in textwting
text twig

rump is face it gooesethother way is pointy

pwointy bridgedock stretchss to errceive
beanstork,
allbuild all laboard th bouncing ships afoxes
the spiny floxes
peourple,
as pinque as bloo

as falt skin a wall fields up rising flat
riots
in sbooky ghosdex

wheezal's trumpet neck
and hooded monkgooese landing skim in robing
over water
to fixate distance

cobbabled together
flin waiell rising flowd up roses a rsiing

unvelloming back to be baby again
codex rises
drawn up flatty fyield flewwors

historiated muskitoe tying
hairing
highairing some violet manutubes, with golden gnobs

snrailabbit
snarlarailabit
hops
from hiding shell,
den,—
furlined with babyblinds

nailsarabite, snarials, snails arbbit
hopening
softsliming, ctoony
—ctottony
lalabbit, rara, bibi
t

roises
or lilies off th field
don't go into soil but hayang on groundwall
walpepp

goatspder webbing up barnbnding
barn binds
webs of garny bote spider goesth hoofing,
goas down silkilky fmountain
—msilk,
pagey hay catches illustrating goaoaot horizon eye
eight of em

fisheerd tam ayil
yail
yam tail
fearish fishion, pawter walk in waughter perk
—, bubbling startleye sensing
standsdsin
wayter, water way i mean, water park, it's fish deer
with yamtail

hay flingung flangs up roase vellum
wall fling vasing a book

theh're all loving
hawkbery loavesth hawkelbeary
—loves, bverryly
flies dancindincing,—dancing,
flew

s'got twighome, banananest in calws
claws, picking up phruit phone, saying
seige
desn't matter
they flume here immedictly

SILVER NUMERAL, LEAPING

Numbers?   Skin, until it frays like water.

A fury of rain couldn't smother

the furious puddles.   Count them.

    A salmon heaved itself

from stream to stream, over dry banks,

choked then breathed again.

                    Count its insides,

    beats,   pulses. The organ of water

retains our coldest wants.   Ones.

Taut sensations,

crowding, bounded, tally

into a ribbed arm,   floating, gilled,

grabbing at the next fleshy liquid,

    shattered into glittering scales.

Our legs as numb

as numberless water.   Do you remain

countable, do you remain?   Closed

like an umbrella.   Spreading like a pool.

ALL THAT GOES FROTHING
GENEROUSLY THERE

—geyser thread—that's twang of commons—clear
polyp strands plume up—materials—if have wet
lucence—vent—boil up pluming—geyser vent feathering up
   in matter—
   what is—aware—

      wh
      ocea
      an
      owsheathing
      slides in
      venting
      plumes

—slops ocean—almost no light except sub torches—
all over with lit up space—video makes light there—
   —how's there difference—logic asks why not all
one white haze—

      wo
      ne of you
      plumming
      up
      blubl plumbs
      to
      bree
      thze

—each with its life—pluming—but how's being-this
not being-that—how's awareness end—and then another's
   picks up—how many levels of transparence—

      vi
      d
      eoing

vwide
eeyo
of sleeping rock
fssh

fswifshing
gill
sleeps
in
vwalve in wvave

—what's in salt jellies—all us clicks slopping together
in prism case—
    coral gapes spouting up flows—

vwadeo
wades vent
open
s
flows owout

continent valve kee
ps
mapping
floowr floa
ts past
shelvf

—wakes up and coral glass inserts in head—so that
one can be there—not yet bleached—one gets dunked into skull
    in glass fishy or log—
    or one log rammed into skull as seen-through jelly
because one's there—

cr
acking
watr
in earth
blowl

bo
wl of earth
vents

vi
olett streams
fill whir
orld
underraw
t
er
swa
ys thrgh max dnsity

—vein whines it's here—gel plane flown blue through—
organ in blurry organ waves—
    bauble—each stem a polished a tall window—it
sways—each us
    perches in salt—

        crorcal carrall core
        ll
        mouthingr
        ock
        it
        mouw
        thsro
        ck
        dryeenks

        anemo
        ne's
        daisy's
        gol
        den eye hole
        sucks
        in

o
paque
no
unit un
it

no unlit

—sub's air helmet isn't ocean—carrying glugs of sky—
at noon on waves—wind tips that's ocean
elsewhere—

trennsparince trins
peers
p
ierces
bag of petalls
b
agging rightnow

opti
ca
ll
lusion
deisy glrows in
bag no
light

—how can difference be at all—what's
look—what's be there—cuttlefish emerging from
shadow suit—it drags ocean—sky knocks on waterlid with
time—cuttlefish
isn't black tux—ocean following—silk jacket—

in beag in
bgagg
some kindof
thru
ness thrashrashes in
baag

th
fattt cell eye
is clowse
d

—no differences—but differences—summed up in
what's same—like white—no different from
any colors—though it
looks different—all it flashes up—

gbagaggb
th bag
no liy
ght
yet light
enter
s

GET THUS, SPREADS BOBBING

Spire of bamboo in glass, a pollen-furred column,
the middle level. *Where's Me?*
Loafing with microbes, surely. Drunk
on mud lust, absolutely. *Who*
in the lattice-cage keeps the souls happy?
A drift of knots. A heart-root tense.
One of you rituals is me. Indoctrinating
water, live syrups pumped through fibrous shapes.
I live in a control bush, outer edges flowering.
Me the flourish, *Me* the sacs spilled out.
You thrive on such dimples, you thorny limbs,
jugular roots.
    Am contolled by what, most likely?
Most likely dirt, an air-tank loaded
with gravel. *Most likely roots.*
At the crook of the center I heard it,
an echo of notated laughter, I couldn't keep up.
Ring me, ring me, don't swallow me
yet. You were off on the scent waltz,
bounding the crest of stance and distance.

BOTFLY: AN ALCHEMY

—mother fly lays egg in you

A lamp under the skin, barely large enough to feel
growing   in the arm stream, I'm   clear as egg
laid inside the surface of living.
It's in the arm   I'm the arm
I'm in the arm,
esoteric   person nest, first term.
Larva, also called an   alembic, its hot glass skin
smuggled over

on a mosquito.
Mary the Jewess, first alchemist, invented it.
Hermetically
sealed, vapor collection
someday leading to a more refined version called a
retort,   the perfumes in my   long tapering neck
my first word.
Which they want to know for identification purposes.
Could be the soul is   there, guard box   on darkling gulf

once a foreign growth   the mosquito sinks its mouth in
alchemically.
Coming at my birth from over here with implements.
These lights that pass at regular intervals
are feelings   I have
inscribed your name on this gold brick
but it crumbles   in the music   go softly

warm but distant,
I have the history of phosphorus.
Evoporated from bones   in electric heat
toxic. Had flown to symbologies in reckless arcs,
stood nowhere   from here   perched
like the glass stem of leaden wine,
towards surfaces.
I came to life carrying numbers in my belly,

a man made of gold led me to the fire and bade me drink,
a man made of silver
bade me speak.
Glowing   yet still cold   in this wind circle.
Though it was in his power to start the world
from the beginning
God chose   to begin it now, halfway,

switching on mid-flight, an urge
to walk away   walked out of it,
pulled back his hood, the monk
was an automaton.
Alternating numbers adapted and the fly
appears to move
having such natures, such discipline   antique forms
to speak   to Nature, speak   of no names, shed the fallen
and unify

the updraft of fields.
Among the lodestones.
Among these falsified memories. Plenum,
corpuscles in their smallest
configuration   a world built for angels   to understand.
This habit   of human skin,
pregnant, armed,
the mirror leaping out of me all calculated by their
buzzing wings.

AT NIGHT IT GOES ON LIKE THIS, INVENTING

Against glass

As a fern's mechanism may be called

Firn, meaning snow as it settles into the glacier, meaning

We began to see our DNA

Not as a rope, but a stream, forking and evaporating

Where did my blood end, was this my skin

Now I am transmitting to you about

The argument you're living in the too-late

Yet still believing in the noise of alternatives

If time's made of invention

If we're in fact a technological animal

Even so, the many directions our lives can bend

The future just a

Tingling in your skin, your nose pressed against

Glassiness, in a world of towers, windows

Tinted like a screen, their

Smoothness, as if a logarithm of air, uncorking the secret

Which, according to glass, is endless division

The world a barrier only light can pass through

So argues glass, the

Cubicles, atoms empty enough

To fit workers in

Clarity, clarity you call your world

Stripping it down to

Edges, planes

The echo that never comes back

Though some obscurities continue through the night

Dreams of other meshings you can hear

Chirring, me stirring among them

You and I are demons to each other

Creepy crawlies living on the paths the other

Could not take

Disturbing the glossiness of the spheres

Ghosts, plasms of what we digest

Plant and animal matter

Me in a mischief of time, haunting you

Starting to tell you a future it's already

Too late for, the city

Of veins, the monstrosities whose gentle

Feeding sustains us, their pals, here

The new vampire is blue

Is an open system, an IV, a trans-

Fusion, my blood thumps down its throat

And keeps hidden, we're like two lungs, our body

Isn't meat, not a vehicle, not the rigs of blood

Hanging beside you, not the miscroscope slide

You're siphoned into, where for you

A hospital is a doctor exploding

Into a factory, while here we're

Tendrils, antidotes

No longer requiring sterility to perceive

The fineness of small things

This crawling in your pores

Certain roots experience it too, bacteria

Converting nitrogen to ammonia, fixing it

To the soil

The hand that brings down breath

Our brains swapping out, morsel by morsel

For fungal systems

Fibers, lacy and spongy tissues, filling in

Along our old pathways, then

Swerving to the side

It was a kind of upload

We swung into boggish telepathy, spores

Sucked down the ear

Distant mushrooms pinging like language nerves

The sparrows, wet in a puddle, were a kind of keyboard

Asking questions for me

Our tongues minted irregular coins

Sputtered them out, secretions with no

Standard value, like sand dollars, marbled pheromones

In a not-yet-realized economy

Its jittery surplus energy, all subsistence

It was moving now, flexing in the air like pollen

Blowing past the idea of ownership

These pebbly coins, seeds of plants that would

Flower in a different world

That might have been yours, but as always

We continued as only one fragment

In an ecology of possibilities

That went on surviving, adapting, a seething forest

Decay flowering in the zombies

That had once animated your fear

Of matter, that your flesh

Doesn't need you, that you don't need

Yourself, are only

Nature, nature a sluice where

Every creature gets flushed

While here zombies let themselves decompose, hungry

For brains they don't have

We need them, are crammed in our skulls, overcrowded

The feasting zombies open space

So proportions regrow, reconfigure

Brain sinews reweave, a taut softness, a rewiring

Of attunement's flesh

A negotiated exchange, they eat us, adjust us

We live in partnership with the dead

Our skin falls

Over muscle and bone, the layers of fat

The hair squirming from follicles, tangling, falling out

These processes no longer

Dumped into advertising

Claims to exterminate wrinkles, corpulence

Changes in odor over time

Instead these transitions spice us

The sorcery of genetic timelines, an inheritance

We haven't plumbed

No definition except through

Mutation, I swallow a possible core

And let it run through my system

Appearance cured

In salt, swamp, the faceless wind mummifying

Then un-mummifying, intuiting new chemistries as we die

Can you hear us through the glass

Clouded over with your fingerprints

You can't breathe it

But still you try, wanting to see

How a window is the gene of light

Copied, unmutating

In your history clarity first meant radiance, a glut

Cloaking its source

Though it's come to signify purity, to

Purge, the window emptying, getting out of your way

Getting in it

You try to breathe the window and your throat

Splits open like a cape

The window does the seeing for you

Projecting like the eyes of a stranger

Who arrives in your world

Before you do, out of the ancient backlight

But we, in this other place

We were ready

Our first visitor lowering from the stars

In a column, its mass

Of green sails blazing with interstellar radiance

Its roots, billions of them, thinned out, stretched to

Probability by the journey, each

A filament, whisping back to a previous world

It had touched along the way

Of course it's trees that become travellers

Quiet enough

Not to ruin the world they leave

Enough patience for spaceflight, which is, in

The long run, stillness

All expectations burnt off like a flimsy atmosphere

We were lucky by this point

To have cellulose phonemes, pores that mouthed

At the rate of seasonal change

We began a long, rhythmic congress with our visitor

Planning shifts in surface I can barely

Understand, though I can

Taste your future

How you fled

Cutting clarity into that open night

Every new planet a desert

Torched to glass by the descent of your rockets

Sifting those desolate conquests for signs

Of the stranger, whose traces

Circled back, eventually,

Here, your old, hot world

The strangers had arrived while you were gone

Found the planet could not be healed

And you sunk down from the radiant night

The other worlds falling away as always

What is it about this place, the homeliness

And repulsion you feel

Afraid to give in to the relief that maybe

It's all there is for you

Though no longer your property

What do you call an accidental ambush of the stranger

The guest become host

When you are lost

Do you keep moving or wait for help to come

Facedown, bubbling the seedy mud

Attempting to thrive

Your skull softens under my saliva's fizz, my decaying teeth

You must peel back the hatch of your head

To the soft muscle, so I can eat

Its hard, glaziered corners

The secret of glass breaking

The field brightening slightly

Also by Stephen Leather

Pay Off
The Fireman
Hungry Ghost
The Chinaman
The Vets
The Long Shot
The Birthday Girl
The Double Tap
The Solitary Man
The Tunnel Rats
The Bombmaker
The Stretch
Tango One
The Eyewitness
First Response

Spider Shepherd thrillers
Hard Landing
Soft Target
Cold Kill
Hot Blood
Dead Men
Live Fire
Rough Justice
Fair Game
False Friends
True Colours
White Lies
Black Ops
Dark Forces

Jack Nightingale supernatural thrillers
Nightfall
Midnight
Nightmare
Nightshade
Lastnight

TAKEDOWN

STEPHEN LEATHER

TAKEDOWN

HODDER &
STOUGHTON

First published in Great Britain in 2017 by Hodder & Stoughton
An Hachette UK company

1

Copyright © Stephen Leather 2017

A CIP catalogue record for this title is available from the British Library

Hardback ISBN 978 1 473 60552 7
Trade Paperback ISBN 978 1 473 60553 4
Ebook ISBN 978 1 473 60554 1

Typeset in 11.5/15.75pt Plantin Light by
Palimpsest Book Production Limited, Falkirk, Stirlingshire

Printed and bound in Great Britain by Clays Ltd, St Ives plc

Hodder & Stoughton policy is to use papers that are natural, renewable
and recyclable products and made from wood grown in sustainable forests.
The logging and manufacturing processes are expected to conform to the
environmental regulations of the country of origin.

Hodder & Stoughton Ltd
Carmelite House
50 Victoria Embankment
London EC4Y 0DZ
www.hodder.co.uk

For Abby

I

Caleb McGovan sat back in his seat as the aircraft began its roll-back and the easyJet flight attendants went through the usual pre-flight rituals. He had heard airline safety drills so many times in his life that he could have recited the script word for word from memory, but it was less conspicuous to pretend to pay attention than to read a newspaper ostentatiously while it was going on. Around him there was the usual excited buzz of chatter from people setting off on vacation, one or two of whom were already well into the holiday spirit after a session at one of the airside bars in Departures. Apart from one particularly boisterous hen party, all in matching outfits including pink feather boas and 'Horny Hens on Tour' T-shirts, the other passengers were couples or families. McGovan might have been just another holidaymaker, except that he was travelling alone and did not have the air of a man with pleasure on his mind. One look at his closed and slightly forbidding expression was enough to stop the person in the next seat to him trying to strike up a conversation.

As soon as the flight safety briefing was over, he closed his eyes and cat-napped throughout the rest of the four-hour flight to Turkey.

★   ★   ★

Three other flights had just disgorged their passengers at Dalaman airport, and McGovan joined the seemingly endless queue of tourists snaking its slow way through Passport Control. The Turkish immigration official gave his passport no more than a cursory glance before waving him through. While the other passengers were spilling from the arrivals hall to hail taxis or were being picked up by their hotel and resort shuttle buses, McGovan walked straight past the taxi stands and out across the car park in front of the terminal. A four-by-four was parked at the far side and four men wearing Arab dress were waiting for him. They exchanged only a few words before they all climbed into the four-by-four and set off. McGovan was squashed into the back seat between two others as they drove east while the setting sun sank slowly over the Mediterranean behind them. It was a gruelling, all-night drive, heading away from the Turquoise Coast, then skirting the forbidding ranges of the Taurus Mountains, capped by the towering Mount Tahtali, which flanked the Mediterranean coast all the way to the Syrian border far to the east. There were other smaller airports much closer to the border but none with the anonymity that came from using a bustling tourist hub like Dalaman, where almost every passenger passing through it was a foreign holidaymaker.

As dawn broke they were still three hours' drive from the Syrian border. Apart from a few isolated tourist sites, almost the whole of south-east Turkey was a military zone, and as they drew closer to the border the driver of the four-by-four took a circuitous route, turning off the highway for the back roads, keeping well away from the Turkish army bases. They drove through dense forests, where the scent of black pine, cedar and juniper filled the air, and crossed an arid plateau where shepherds and their scrawny flocks paused to watch them pass in a cloud of dust. Steering well clear of the border posts, they eventually took a rock-strewn dirt road, a smugglers' track leading up into the high mountains.

Eventually they crested a rise and McGovan saw the track running on ahead towards a steel-mesh and barbed-wire fence. Death's head warning signs in Turkish and Arabic hung from it at intervals, showing that the fence marked the Turko-Syrian border. The smugglers' track ended at the fence, but an even fainter, narrower path continued on the other side, zigzagging away down the far side of the ridge. The four-by-four ground to a halt beside the fence. There was silence broken only by the metallic ticking of the engine as it began to cool. McGovan looked at his companions. Although he had been travelling with them for hours, he was still not sure whether they were acting as his guides or his guards. They stared back at him in silence. 'What now?' he said at last, in Arabic.

'This is where you get out,' one said. 'Crawl under the wire and walk due south for a mile where, *inshallah*, another of our vehicles will be waiting in a *wadi* to collect you.'

McGovan paused a moment, in case they had anything to add, but they remained silent. One of the men next to him opened the door, got out and made a gesture with his hand, as if wafting away an irritating fly. McGovan shrugged his shoulders and followed him. The man climbed back into the vehicle, the engine roared into life and the four-by-four slewed around, spraying sand over him as the wheels slipped and skidded, then sped back the way it had come.

He watched it go, then took a careful look around. Satisfied that he was alone in the sweep of desert landscape, he drank some water from his flask and urinated against a rock, then moved towards the fence. From the fresh tyre tracks running parallel to the wire, Turkish Army vehicles patrolled this area frequently and he had no desire to be stopped and interrogated.

When he reached the wire, he lay flat in the dust and wormed under the lowest strand at the point where the smugglers' track intersected with the fence. The compacted earth, scored by the marks left by the elbows and feet of countless others as they had wriggled under the fence, showed that he was far from the first to cross the border there. He picked himself up on the far side, brushed down his clothes and took another careful look around him. Then he set off, moving away from the fence and heading due south.

The sun was high in the sky and the heat was pitiless. The mountains and the desert were shimmering in the heat-haze, but there was no other movement, apart from a pair of vultures circling on the thermals high above. The sun-bleached animal bones he saw at intervals as he picked his way among the rocks, suggested that they never had to wait too long in this unforgiving landscape for their next meal.

He walked for perhaps twenty minutes, picking his way along a narrow dry riverbed cutting through the steep scree slope that marked the Syrian side of the border. Further down he could see the riverbed broaden as it disappeared into the mouth of a *wadi* and, as he drew nearer, the glint of sunlight reflecting from the white metal roof of a Toyota

Landcruiser showed him that his escort for the next stage of his journey was waiting for him.

As he approached, four more men, who had been sheltering from the sun in the shade beneath an overhang of rock, stepped into the open and stared at him impassively. Once more all were dressed in black Arab robes. Two wore *keffiyeh*s but the others wore hoods with crude holes cut for their mouths and eyes. There were few words of greeting. One merely grunted and pointed to the back seat of the Landcruiser, where McGovan again found himself wedged between two burly, silent Arabs as the Toyota bounced and buffeted its way down the rough, rock-strewn bed of the *wadi*. The men on either side of him smelled as if neither they nor their robes had seen soap and water for many weeks, but his years serving in the British Army had inured McGovan to far worse.

They drove for more than an hour, coming to a halt at a checkpoint flying the Islamic State flag. 'The Black Standard' was claimed to date back to the time of Muhammad in the seventh century. It was inscribed with the Shahada – 'There is no god but Allah and Muhammad is the messenger of Allah' – above the seal of Muhammad, both etched in white Arabic script against the black background of the flag.

The ISIS men manning the checkpoint were armed to the teeth with what McGovan's well-trained eye immediately recognised as brand-new American M-16 assault rifles and M-203 grenade launchers. All were no doubt part of the endless shipments of US military equipment that had been poured into Iraq during Operation Iraqi Freedom and its aftermath. McGovan's weather-beaten face creased into a

sour smile as he savoured the irony of the title. America's
desire to lash out at someone, anyone, in the wake of 9/11
and its professed intention to replace Saddam Hussein's
brutal dictatorship with an American-style democracy had,
directly or indirectly, caused the deaths of an estimated
half a million Iraqi citizens, most of them civilians. Now
the country was dissolving into civil war, inflicting yet more
misery on its long-suffering population.

Despite the unprecedented levels of manpower, equip-
ment and resources devoted to the Iraqi Army since the
American conquest, the Iraqi troops that the Americans
had trained in their thousands had evaporated, like water
in the desert, on almost every occasion when the going
had got even slightly tough. In addition, 90 per cent of
their American-supplied military equipment – just like
90 per cent of the billions of dollars the US had poured
into the country as military aid or bribes to buy the loyalty
of Sunni tribesmen – had also disappeared. Some had gone
into the pockets of corrupt American contractors and mili-
tary personnel, while the rest had been funnelled through
Iraqi middlemen to reappear in the hands of hostile Iraqi
forces, and the jihadists who were now turning the weapons
against the Americans and their Iraqi stooges. Bought or
stolen from the American-trained Iraqi troops, or carried
by deserters joining ISIS from the Iraqi Army, some of
those weapons had now been brought across the border
into Syria.

The guards manning the second ISIS checkpoint exchanged
greetings with the Arab occupants of the Toyota but directed
baleful, suspicious looks at McGovan. 'The *faranji* must be
hooded and bound before you can go further,' one said in

Arabic, glaring at him. 'It is forbidden for all unbelievers to see the route or the houses we use.'

One of McGovan's escorts reached under his seat and pulled out a black cloth hood, which was placed over McGovan's head and tied with a cord around his neck. His wrists were secured behind him. The cloth sack was even more foul-smelling than his escorts' body odour and the thick cloth made the heat beneath it even more intense, but McGovan ignored the stench and the sweat trickling down his face, focusing only on what he would need to say to the ISIS commander whom he would soon be meeting. Before he had set out to travel to Syria, he had been left in no doubt that if he did not convince the commander of his bona fides, the journey he was now making would be the last he ever took.

The Landcruiser drove on for another twenty minutes, and McGovan felt the vehicle making frequent changes of direction, presumably in an attempt to disorient him. Eventually it pulled up and the engine was switched off. He heard more challenges and greetings in guttural Arabic, then the car doors were opened. He was hustled out and taken inside a building, where the hood was removed and his wrists untied. He stood blinking for a couple of minutes, getting a sense of his surroundings. He was inside a low, mud-walled building, a goat-herder's hut from the smell, which was now evidently doubling as an ISIS safe-house. A few ISIS fighters, yet more anonymous bearded figures in long black robes, with black hoods or *keffiyeh*s, kept watch over the surrounding desert from the narrow windows, while others leaned against the wall, directing malevolent stares at him. The look in their eyes told him that if their commander was not satisfied with any of the answers McGovan gave in response to his questions he would not leave the building alive.

After a few minutes' silence, broken only by the buzzing of the flies that swarmed around him, a door at the rear of the building opened and the ISIS commander swept into the room, flanked by two massive bodyguards. The commander, who looked to be in his late forties or early fifties, was dressed like his men, in flowing black robes, but he was bare-headed and the fringes of his greying beard were dyed with henna – McGovan knew that was usually the mark of a *hajji* of South Asian origins. However, whatever his origins might have been, he spoke to McGovan in flawless Arabic, first making the traditional greeting, '*As salam aleykum.*'

'*Wa aleykum as salam,*' McGovan said. His accent was nowhere near as good, but it was passable.

'We already know your name and much about you,' the commander said. 'I am known as Saif al-Islam.'

'The Sword of Islam,' McGovan said, nodding. 'A good name for a warrior.'

'Indeed so, and one whose blade will not be sheathed until, inshallah, the Caliphate has been established and history will turn again, overthrowing the empire of the United States and the world Jewish government.'

McGovan said nothing in reply, and after a few moments, Saif al-Islam gestured towards a low table at the side of the room. The two men sat cross-legged on the floor, facing each other across the table. They sat in silence at first, scrutinising each other, while the commander's men brought them cups of bitter cardamom-scented coffee and fresh dates.

'So, Englishman,' Saif al-Islam said at last, 'you claim to have come to join our jihad.'

McGovan nodded. 'I can help you in your fight, I'm sure of that.'

'We have many foreign fighters here,' said Saif al-Islam, 'many from England, but also from around the world.'

McGovan nodded again. 'It's good that so many Muslims are prepared to help their brothers where help is needed,' he said.

'You realise that we do not pay our foreign fighters? We can give you food and arms but we are not interested in mercenaries.'

'I am not doing this for money, Saif al-Islam. In fact I don't want to take part in the fighting here. I've come to seek your help to stage a high-profile attack inside the UK.'

'You do us too much honour,' the ISIS commander said, with what might have been a mocking smile. 'We are only simple fighters. We are used to waging a guerrilla war in the desert, but we have no experience –' again the mirthless smile '– or, at least, very little, of waging war on the streets of Western cities. Tell me, what or who would be the target of such a high-profile attack?'

McGovan shot a glance towards the circle of ISIS men standing around the walls, all well within earshot of their conversation. He took a piece of paper and a pen from his pocket, wrote a few words on it and slid it across the table.

Saif al-Islam regarded him with amusement. 'You do not

trust my men, Englishman? Yet I would trust any of them with my life.'

McGovan inclined his head. 'But you know them, Saif al-Islam, whereas I do not. And I am a cautious man. The fewer people who know of my plans, the less chance there is of them being compromised.'

As if to reinforce his words, as soon as Saif al-Islam had glanced at the note, McGovan took it back and burned it with his cigarette lighter. The commander's expression did not change. 'Before we can talk further about this,' he said, 'I need to know more about you. As the Prophet has ordered us, we fight in the name of Allah and in the way of Allah. Why would you, a *faranji*, a Westerner, and a Christian,' his lip curled, 'wish to join our jihad against your own people?'

'I no longer consider myself a Christian,' said McGovan. 'I fought for the British in Iraq and in Afghanistan.' He saw the ISIS fighters stir and the hatred on their faces. One spat on the ground and began to stride towards him, fists clenched, but was stopped in his tracks as Saif al-Islam held up a warning hand.

'Let the *faranji* speak first,' he said, 'and then we will decide what to do with him.' He turned back to McGovan. 'Most of my fighters have lost friends and family,' he said, 'brothers and fathers on the battlefield, of course, but also wives, mothers and children killed by bombs, shells and bullets. No one who fought for the Americans and their friends in those countries can expect any sympathy or forgiveness from us.' He paused for a few seconds, holding McGovan's gaze. 'And no mercy either.'

McGovan nodded in acknowledgement. 'I fought there

because at first I believed what I was told, that we were there to protect the people from their brutal rulers, end the torture and the killings, and give them the chance of the peace, prosperity and freedom that we in the West enjoy.' He gave a bitter laugh. 'It was all a lie, of course. It was never about helping the people. It was about oil. Sure enough, we removed one set of brutal rulers, but those the Americans installed to replace them were little if any better than those we had deposed. And, worst of all, we Westerners, British and American alike, showed ourselves to be no less capable of brutality, torture and killing. For that I hang my head in shame.'

'As you should,' said Saif al-Islam.

'I lost all faith in my religion, and in my country,' said McGovan. 'As you know only too well, hundreds of thousands of Iraqi people have died, not because they were fighting against us, though some were, but because they happened to be in the wrong place at the wrong time. Some were killed by their own countrymen because they were Sunni, or because they were Shia, or because they were Kurds, but many more were killed because they chose the wrong moment to walk down the street, drive in their car or even attend a wedding when American and British bombs, missiles, drones or heavy weapons were raining destruction on our supposed enemies. And the dead were always described as "terrorists", of course, even when they were women, older people or tiny children. The officers and politicians never admitted their errors. Never apologised for the civilians they killed.'

Saif al-Islam stared at McGovan with unblinking eyes.

'Even after most of the forces were pulled out, when

they realised that they were fighting a battle they could never win, still the pain and suffering continued. Thousands crippled and poisoned, an economy that cannot support its people.'

'We are aware of the damage that your country did to ours,' said Saif al-Islam. 'But what has turned you against your own people?'

'Shame,' said McGovan. 'I am ashamed of what they made me do. The men and boys we captured were held in military prisons of which the very existence was denied, and many of those held there were tortured over and over again, for months and even years. Some were water-boarded, taken to the point of drowning, then revived, at least a hundred times. Others were beaten to a pulp, abused, sodomised, and some were murdered. Or they were handed over to different torturers – Iraqis who had last practised their skills on behalf of Saddam Hussein, and Afghanis every bit as cruel as the Taliban we were supposed to be fighting. Some victims, hooded and manacled like prisoners from the Middle Ages, were flown out of the country for even more extreme interrogation and torture by short- or long-term allies, like the Jordanians and Libyans, whose brutalities in the infamous secret prisons they operated were not restrained by even the faintest pretence of Western values.'

'You were there?' asked Saif al-Islam. 'You took part in the torture?'

McGovan held Saif al-Islam's gaze. 'Yes. I was at Abu Ghraib.' He saw the ISIS commander's eyes narrow in recognition of the name. Abu Ghraib – Arabic for the 'Place of Ravens' – was also known as Baghdad Central Prison even though it was twenty miles west of the Iraqi capital. The American military had controlled it from 2003, after the invasion of Iraq, until they handed it back to Iraqi forces in 2006. When Saddam Hussein ran Iraq, the prison kept as many as fifty thousand men and women jammed into its twelve-by-twelve-foot cells, with torture a daily occurrence and weekly executions. When the Americans took over, they retiled the floors, cleaned the cells, repaired the toilets and filled it with suspected terrorists, mainly civilians scooped up in random sweeps and at military checkpoints, or on the word of often anonymous tipsters. And while the executions stopped, killings and torture were again a regular occurrence at Abu Ghraib.

'I saw innocent people tortured and killed there,' said McGovan, quietly. 'I looked the other way while these atrocities were taking place and then I helped to sanitise the prisons and torture chambers. I hid the evidence, cleaned up the blood and even buried some of the victims. I have not had an undisturbed night's sleep ever since. It has burned into my conscience and it has changed me as a man, to my very core. I owe it to those people to take revenge, to force my fellow Britons to understand what has been done in their name and what the consequences will be.'

'And you are now, what?' asked Saif al-Islam. 'Now you are no longer a Christian. Now you say you have stopped being a crusader.'

'I am a Muslim. I converted while I was in Iraq.'

'You were allowed to become a Muslim?' Disbelief was written across his face.

'I did it in secret. I was schooled by an imam who was

held there for two years. I watched as the Americans tortured him and the British stood by and did nothing. I saw them beat him and humiliate him, and all the time he just smiled. I used to speak to him afterwards, to see if there was anything he wanted, and he said he already had everything he needed because he was serving Allah and that was all that mattered. He taught me about Islam and about Allah, and now I'm a Muslim and will be until the day I die.'

There was a long silence. 'Very well, Englishman,' Saif al-Islam said. 'If what you say is true, then we fight on the same side and for the same cause. But the attack you seek to make will be at the risk of your life. Even if you succeed, you are unlikely to emerge alive. Does that not concern you?'

McGovan shrugged. 'The thought of death doesn't frighten me. And it won't deter me from doing what I believe to be right.'

The ISIS commander gave him one last searching look, then turned to his men, many of whom were still regarding McGovan with intense suspicion or hatred. 'The *faranji* is a true believer in our cause,' he said. 'He is willing to atone for the wrongs he did to our brethren in Iraq and Afghanistan, even at the risk of his own life. While he remains under our protection, you are to guard him as you would guard me.' He turned back to McGovan. 'So if your attack is to take place,' he said, 'what do you need from us?'

'Money, arms and at least a dozen jihadists within the UK from whom I can select a group to support the attack. They must all be men whose loyalty and obedience to you are absolute, and men who would rather be martyred than betray our plans.'

'All such things might be possible,' Saif al-Islam said, 'providing you can convince me that it is the best use of our men and resources.' He allowed himself a brief smile. 'Our Arab friends are generous, but even their generosity has its limits. If the targets you have described can be successfully attacked, that would, of course, be a great blessing to us and the cause we serve. But many men before you must have dreamed of such a thing and none has ever been successful, or even come close.'

McGovan could tell the ISIS commander was tempted but was still more than a little suspicious of him. 'That is undoubtedly true,' he said, 'but perhaps they did not possess the resources or manpower you can command, and lacked the skills that I possess. Skills I am prepared to put at your disposal.'

Again there was the briefest flicker of a smile from Saif al-Islam. 'And yet, for all the particular skills you may possess, your most valuable asset in such an attack might be the colour of your skin. You may be able to pass without challenge in places where men such as we . . .' he waved a hand languidly around the circle of his men watching them '. . . would be subject to instant suspicion.'

He studied McGovan from beneath his eyebrows. 'However, there remains the question of trust. We know who you are and what you may be capable of,' he said, 'and your words seemed to be spoken from the heart, but that does not mean we can be certain that we can trust you.' He thought for a few more moments. 'My men will now take you back to the Turkish border, where others will be waiting to escort you. Return with them a week from today and I will tell you my decision.' He turned his back and strode out of the room as McGovan's escorts replaced the foul-smelling hood over his head, tied his wrists behind him and hustled him outside to the Landcruiser.

2

McGovan spent the next week maintaining his cover as a tourist. He stayed at a modest hotel in a small resort town two hours east of Dalaman on Turkey's Turquoise Coast. Unlike his fellow guests, he did not use the swimming pool during the day or frequent the bar in the evenings, and those other guests who had noticed him at all would have been hard put to describe him other than as an aloof, monosyllabic Englishman who had spent most of the week sitting on the terrace with his nose in a book or running up a viciously steep track through the pine forests cloaking the hills that fringed the sea.

At the end of the week, he checked out of the hotel and rendezvoused with his escort in a supermarket car park on the outskirts of the town. He was taken back to the Syrian border by the same route as before, but this time, having once more slipped under the border fence and made his way down to the *wadi*, he was driven to a different safe-house, much deeper inside Syria and very close to the border with Iraq. The same ISIS commander, Saif al-Islam, was waiting for him. 'I never sleep more than one night under the same roof,' he said, in explanation for the change of safe-house. 'The *faranji* have spies and informers everywhere, and the skies are full of their aircraft and drones. So we move by night and go to earth before the dawn.'

'Infrared surveillance cameras can still see you in the dark,' McGovan said.

'Indeed so, and many martyrs are already in Paradise as a result, but as you see, may Allah be praised for His mercy, I have been spared for the great task, the holy jihad we pursue.' His eyes had been raised Heavenwards as he spoke, but he now switched his shrewd gaze to McGovan's face. 'Now, to the point. In order for us to be sure we can trust you, you must carry out a trial task for us.'

'You want to test me?'

'Of course. You wouldn't be the first spy who has tried to infiltrate our ranks with stories of conversion. We need to separate the wheat from the chaff.'

'And if I refuse your test?'

'Then you will treated as chaff. Are you refusing?'

McGovan smiled easily. 'I had expected to be tested, and I will carry out any task you ask of me. I am more than happy to prove my commitment, and my worth. What's the task?'

'The US Army training team,' Saif al-Islam said, watching him closely, 'is based at an Iraqi Army base near Mosul. You are to kill the leader of that team. If you succeed, we will give you the help you seek.'

McGovan thought for a few moments, then nodded. 'First I will need all the intelligence information you have on the target and the base where he is operating. I'll need mapping of the area, aerial photography of the compound, if possible, details of which forces, Iraqis, Americans or

British, are mounting the guard on the base, the ORBAT – the Order of Battle – of the training team on the base, and the VRN. Sorry,' he said, as he saw the ISIS commander's blank expression. 'Acronyms are an occupational hazard in the armed forces and it is a habit I've found hard to shake, I meant the registration number of the vehicle he uses. Once all that is assembled, I'll need three or four days to prepare. I'm assuming you can obtain weapons, plastic explosives, timers and so on.'

'We have already assembled everything you need,' Saif al-Islam said. 'But you will not be making the attack in three or four days, you will attack the base tomorrow night.'

McGovan frowned. 'I'll study the intel and mapping, then tell you if that schedule is possible.'

'No,' Saif al-Islam said. 'You will not. I will tell you what is possible, not the other way round. And I'm telling you that you will do it tomorrow night. That is your test. Accept or decline.'

McGovan glanced round the room at the dozen ISIS men, who still stared unblinkingly back at him, each with an M-16 or M-203 slung over their shoulders, and then he spread his hands in a gesture of surrender. 'Very well. It shall be tomorrow night. Inshallah.'

He spent the next twenty-four hours studying every scrap of information they could put in front of him. To an untrained eye, the Iraqi Army base appeared a daunting target. The outer compound of the sprawling site was surrounded by a barbed-wire fence, punctuated by four watchtowers. Each was manned by armed guards, and at

intervals between the watchtowers arc lights illuminated
the fence at night. At the heart of the base was an inner
compound, with a steel-mesh fence topped with coils of
razor wire. The outer fence was patrolled by Iraqi guards,
but the inner one was guarded by American troops.
American and British soldiers both operated from within
that compound.

'Not easy, is it?' one of the ISIS soldiers said to McGovan,
peering over his shoulder at the surveillance images of the
compound he was studying. One of ISIS's British Asian
jihadists, the man had a strong Black Country accent, which
sounded utterly incongruous in the heart of the Syrian
desert.

McGovan turned to him. 'It's easy if you know how,' he
said.

'What – even though there are two barbed-wire fences
and all those armed guards to get past?'

McGovan gave him a cold smile. 'You're not a trained
soldier, are you, my friend? The base may look daunting
with all those watchtowers, barbed wire and guards patrol-
ling it, but if you think about it, who will be guarding those
fences? It won't be crack troops, will it? And you can be
certain they won't be dedicated to the task they've been
given. The men on guard duty will be the ones who happen
to have pissed off their commanders recently. They won't
want to be there either, because it's dark and it's cold, and
they'd rather be in bed asleep, or playing Warcraft on their
PCs. They'll be staying under cover as much as they can.
And because there's a barbed-wire fence, they'll be relying
on that to keep out intruders. If we fire a rocket into the
base, all hell will break loose, of course, but I guarantee

that I can be in and out through both those fences without any of the guards hearing a sound or seeing anything but dust blowing over the desert.'

Just before sunset the following night, once more escorted by four ISIS fighters, McGovan climbed into one of their four-by-fours and was driven towards the Iraqi border. The only weapon he carried was a pistol, though he was as effective with that in close-quarters combat as any less well-trained soldier armed with an automatic rifle. He wore a light pack on his back, containing two sophisticated IEDs. A trained demolitions expert in the special forces, he had put the devices together himself, moulding the plastic explosive into pieces of right-angled steel section to create devastating shaped charges that would concentrate the force of the blast in one direction. Both devices were triggered by pressure release switches, designed to activate if pressure was placed upon them or if existing pressure was taken away. He then checked the detonators, tested the firing circuits and loaded everything into his pack.

Night had fallen before they reached the frontier and they crossed into Iraq without incident, once more using one of the many smugglers' tracks on which everything, from food and drugs to explosives and heavy weapons, was traded across the porous borders.

The Iraqi Army base they were targeting was another three-hour drive beyond the border. They reached the area just after midnight and left the four-by-four in dead ground, a dip in the desert floor that hid it from view unless you were standing almost directly on top of it, then made their way onwards on foot. The arc-lights around the fence were illuminated, but they cast small, intense pools of light directly below them, which made the areas of fence between them seem even darker by comparison. The guards in the watch-towers were motionless, bored and inattentive. Some appeared to be dozing or were perhaps even fast asleep. The only creatures patrolling the fence were not soldiers, but the prowling feral dogs that were as ubiquitous in Arab countries as crows in an English cornfield.

McGovan lay in cover, assessing the guards and estab-lishing the routine of their patrols – or at least the routine of those who ventured beyond their shelters – but he spent as much time watching the movements of the wild dogs around the fence line. Well inside the outer fence, close to the inner one surrounding the American and British area of the base, he could see refuse bins overflowing with garbage. If he could see them and smell the stench on the breeze, the feral dogs would certainly be well aware of them. As he watched, he saw a steady stream of the braver animals, bellies to the ground, squirming under the barbed-wire fence, then padding across the compound towards the bins.

McGovan nudged one of the ISIS fighters in the ribs and breathed in his ear, 'Those animal tracks are going to be our way in as well.'

While two of the fighters remained outside the compound to give them cover, the other two belly-crawled forward with McGovan and slid under the wire after him as the prowling dogs backed away, eyeing them suspiciously. One emitted a low growl, resenting the interruption to its evening routine, which caused one of the guards to glance in that direction and sweep the beam of his torch across the compound. McGovan and the ISIS fighters had already flattened themselves to the ground and lay motionless, almost invisible. After a moment, the guard, convinced that whatever he had seen or heard was only the dogs arguing over a choice bit of refuse, turned away.

A moment later, McGovan saw a flare of light and the red glow as the guard lit a cigarette. If he needed any additional sign of the guards' carelessness and unpreparedness, the cigarette had provided it. The flare of flame from the soldier's lighter would ruin his night vision for some minutes and smoking the cigarette would distract him from his duty. If the guard heard a noise, he was as likely to think it was his sergeant out on an inspection as an intruder breaking in, and would be more concerned with getting rid of his cigarette end before he was put on a charge than anything else.

McGovan waited for five more minutes, then continued to creep forward, belly-crawling across the outer compound, the two ISIS fighters at his heels. They paused again in the deeper shadow cast by a Portakabin while McGovan studied the ground ahead. Two American soldiers were patrolling the inner fence, but their body language showed their boredom and disinterest. They clearly thought their sentry duty was a pointless waste of time and stayed close to the warm yellow light from the guard post at the entrance gates to the inner compound, patrolling no more than ten or twenty yards away from it before turning back towards their shelter.

The two ISIS fighters who had slipped under the wire with him now remained by the Portakabin, covering the American guards, while McGovan crawled forward alone. The steel mesh of the inner fence was tight to the ground and there were no animal tracks leading beneath it to aid him, but he pulled a pair of wire clippers from his belt and began cutting through the wire next to one of the stanchions supporting the fence. Each strand snapped with a faint click, but it was virtually inaudible even to the two ISIS men watching from close behind him, let alone to the Americans near the gates.

He eased the clippers into his belt, folded back the section of wire he had cut, then wriggled through the gap. He paused to rearrange the wire so that, to a casual glance, it appeared to be untouched, then crept across the compound to the vehicle park. It was the work of a moment to identify his target's Land Rover and he went to work at once. He fixed one of the IEDs, activated by a pressure-release switch, under the driver's seat, then coupled it to another IED, which he installed on the underside of the petrol tank. As an insurance policy, it would guarantee that anyone travelling in the Land Rover when the IEDs were detonated would be killed. If anyone now put weight on the switch or lifted the seat away from it, the IED would activate with devastating effect.

He took one last look around, making sure he had left no visible traces that would trigger an alarm, then crept back into the shadows. He made his way back through the inner fence, once more carefully replacing the cut wire behind him. With the ISIS fighters again at his heels, he wriggled under the outer fence. They linked up with the other two fighters, who were waiting in cover a few yards outside the compound. They stole into the darkness, and within half an hour, they were back in the four-by-four and driving fast across the desert towards the Syrian border.

The four-hour return drive meant that the sun was already climbing the sky well before they reached the border. They followed a track up a rough incline, and emerged onto the plateau of rock, gravel and coarse, gritty sand that stretched all the way to the border. As they scanned the plateau, they saw a plume of dust to the south-west ahead of them: a vehicle driving a course that would intersect with theirs. McGovan's escort exchanged worried looks and a few words of muttered Arabic, but they could see no option other than to carry on. To turn back would place them in greater danger from Iraqi patrols. The driver changed direction, taking a side-track running further to the north of their previous route, but almost at once they saw the other vehicle change its course too.

As the minutes ticked by, the outline of the other vehicle became clearer. It was a squat, broad-based vehicle with a jagged black outline projecting above its roof. 'It's a Humvee,' McGovan said, 'an American armoured vehicle, though the chances are that it's being driven by an Iraqi Army patrol, not the Yanks.' He pointed. 'Drive to that low ridge ahead of us and stop,' he said to the driver. 'It'll give us the advantage of the ground overlooking them, if nothing else.' The man scowled at him but did as McGovan had suggested. McGovan had spotted a shallow dip just to the right of the place on the ridge-line he had indicated, which would provide enough cover to protect a man lying prone. The four-by-four came to a halt and they waited in an atmosphere of rising tension as the other vehicle closed with them. They could now see it clearly and, as McGovan had said, it was indeed a Humvee, with Iraqi Army insignia. The jagged shape mounted on the back had resolved itself into an M-2 Browning .50 calibre heavy machine-gun, the operator sitting behind it, keeping its barrel pointing straight at them.

Still as stone, McGovan watched it approach, willing it to move closer and closer before stopping. Their training required SAS men to know the range and capabilities of every weapon they were likely to encounter, whether in the hands of their allies or their enemies. He knew that the M-2 had an effective range of 1800 metres, over twice the range of the M-16s that the ISIS fighters were carrying, and more than eight times the range of the M-203 grenade-launcher fitted to one of the M-16s. Had the Humvee been driven by an American patrol, they would have stopped no closer than 800 metres away and used a loudhailer to order the occupants to get out of the four-by-four and flatten themselves in the dirt, or be cut apart by machine-gun fire. The Iraqi patrol in it, though, were less circumspect, and whether through overconfidence or incompetence, they did not pull up until they were just a couple of hundred metres from the four-by-four.

McGovan's keen gaze missed no detail. He saw that the machine-gunner manning the M-2 was only partly hidden by the armoured shield in front of him, which covered his body from the breastbone downwards, but left his upper chest and his face below his steel helmet exposed. The Iraqi commander had climbed out but remained standing close to the side of the Humvee, shielded behind its open armoured door, with only his lower legs exposed. The rest of his team were still inside the Humvee.

'Let me handle this,' McGovan said, turning to the ISIS fighter sitting next to him. 'Give me your rifle.'

The ISIS fighter glared at him. 'Why should I give you my weapon?'

'Because if you don't, we'll all die. That heavy machine-gun you see on the back can fire over five hundred rounds a minute and each one will slice through this vehicle's soft metal skin like a knife through paper. It will shred everyone inside it to pieces, whereas your rifle rounds won't even penetrate the Humvee's armour. So I'll get out and talk to them. When they see I'm a Westerner, they'll hesitate, thinking I might be special forces on a secret op. That hesitation is all I'll need to take out the machine-gunner. But if you keep me arguing any longer, they're likely to shoot first and ask questions afterwards. Then we're all finished. Okay?'

The fighter hesitated a fraction of a second longer, then handed over his weapon. McGovan clambered past him, opened the door and jumped out, holding his rifle at the vertical in one hand, wide of his body. At once, the Iraqi commander shouted in Arabic, 'Drop your weapon! Get down on the ground!'

'We are British special forces,' McGovan shouted, lowering his arm to bring the rifle down by his side. 'SAS! We're on the same side! Don't shoot!' He stepped away from the vehicle into the open, and saw the barrel of the machine-gun move to cover him again.

'Drop your weapon! Get down on the ground or we fire!'

McGovan spread his arms wide in a what-the-hell gesture, then fell to his knees at the edge of the shallow dip in the ground. He saw the machine-gun barrel swing back momentarily to cover the occupants of the four-by-four. At that moment, he dived forward, bringing up the rifle in one fluid movement and fired a short, unaimed burst at the machine-gunner. As the man swung the barrel round and his weapon began to erupt in rapid fire, the deafening rattle was echoed by the *thwock-thwock* sound as some of its rounds buried themselves in the sand, and the crack and whine as others ricocheted from the rocks to howl away.

McGovan barrel-rolled sideways, then brought up the rifle again, firing from a point several metres away and this time stilling his breathing with a slow exhale and squeezing off two carefully aimed shots. The first hit the machine-gunner dead centre in the chest, an inch or so above the armoured shield, and the next struck him under the chin as he was thrown backwards by the first. He was stone dead even before his body had tumbled from the back of the Humvee to the ground. His fingers, clamped to the trigger in his death agony, caused his weapon to stitch a tracer line of rounds across the sky before it jammed and fell silent.

McGovan had already rolled and fired again. The Iraqi Army commander's body was still protected by the armoured door of the Humvee, but his legs from the knee down were visible beneath it. McGovan again inhaled deeply as he took up the first pressure on the trigger, squinting down the sight, then released the breath in a slow exhale and squeezed the trigger home. He felt the recoil into his shoulder and saw the man's right knee blown apart by the impact of the round. He slumped to the ground at the side of the Humvee, lying fully exposed in the open. He was now disabled, incapable of walking and in agonising pain, but McGovan knew that none of that could be guaranteed to prevent him firing his weapon. He squinted through the sight again, aiming at the bridge of the man's nose, and drilled a single shot through his brain.

McGovan switched targets again as the other Iraqi soldiers jumped from their vehicle and opened fire. Their shooting was nervy and inaccurate, their months of American and British training forgotten in the nervous terror of real combat in which one error might be their last. By now the ISIS fighters had leaped out of the four-by-four, and added their own weight of fire to McGovan's, including rockets from an RPG-7 and grenades from an M-203. One of the ISIS men was hit, gut-shot by return fire, and slumped to the ground, but by then two more Iraqi soldiers already lay dead.

Their last man, the driver, panic-stricken by the sight of his comrades being wiped out, made a frantic attempt to save himself, flooring the accelerator, slewing his vehicle around in a storm of dust and debris, then roaring off across the desert as a fresh torrent of rounds from the ISIS fighters rattled against the armoured bodywork.

McGovan was already on his feet and sprinting for the four-by-four. 'After him!' he shouted at the ISIS driver, as he dived into the back seat. 'If he escapes, we're all dead.'

One of the other fighters, still clutching the RPG-7, threw himself into the four-by-four as the driver hit the accelerator, but his other comrade, tending the wounded man, was left staring after them as they sped away. The Iraqi Humvee had a minute's start on them. In other types of desert terrain its weight and power would have seen it pull away from them, but the four-by-four was a lighter and faster vehicle over the rocky ground they were traversing and was soon rapidly overhauling it. McGovan snatched the RPG from the ISIS fighter, loaded a high-explosive, dual-purpose round, capable of penetrating five centimetres of steel armour-plating, then snarled at the driver, 'When I say stop, hit the brakes as hard as you can. Got it?'

He met the driver's eyes in the rear-view mirror and waited for his nod of agreement, then knelt on the seat and leaned out of the open rear window, bracing his arms against the frame and locking his knee against the back of the driver's seat, as the four-by-four bounced and jolted over the desert floor.

The grey shape of the Humvee, half hidden by the dust cloud it was raising as it stormed along the rough desert road, was now no more than a quarter of a mile ahead and the distance between them was still shrinking. It was impossible to shoot accurately from such an unstable, bouncing platform, and McGovan raised his gaze from the sight to scan the terrain ahead, searching for a straight, level section where he would have the best chance of a clean shot. He saw what he was looking for some way ahead and waited, counting down the distance as they approached it.

'Ready . . . ready . . . STOP!' he shouted. The driver hit the brakes hard, sending the four-by-four slithering and sliding to a halt. Even as it was still rocking on its suspension, McGovan was taking aim at the Humvee's front offside tyre, clearly visible in half-profile as the vehicle swerved around a bend in the track ahead. He wasn't confident that the RPG round would penetrate the Humvee's armoured bodywork or bulletproof glass windows unless fired at right angles to them, so the tyre and wheel were the percentage target. He squeezed the trigger and the RPG round launched with a soft pop, a flash of flame and smoke. Despite the size of the projectile he barely felt the recoil against his shoulder.

The round armed itself automatically after flying for twenty yards or so, then sped to its target. It detonated right on the aiming point, blasting into the front wheel of the Humvee. The explosion ripped the wheel from the vehicle and sent the Humvee careering across the track, where it smashed into a boulder on the far side with a sickening impact. Despite its two-ton weight, it was thrown into the air for a few seconds before it crashed down into a ditch running alongside the track. It hung on its side for a moment, then toppled slowly on to its roof.

As the four-by-four slewed to a halt alongside, McGovan leaped out and sprinted towards it. The Iraqi Army driver was semi-conscious, hanging upside down from his seat belt, blood dripping from his head where he had been thrown against the side window. There was no pity in McGovan's eyes, only an icy determination that there would be no witnesses to tell the tale of what had happened. His expression blank, McGovan jerked open the door on the other side of the cab, slid his rifle barrel in through the opening and put two rounds into the man's head at point-blank range. He reached into the cab and ripped off the sleeve of the man's army shirt and walked to the back of the Humvee, where he forced open the fuel cap and soaked the cloth in the diesel spilling from the upside-down fuel tank. He retreated a few yards, held his gas lighter to the sleeve and waited while the flame heated the diesel to its combustion point. When it burst into flame, he tossed the burning sleeve into the spreading pool of spilled diesel and ran back to the four-by-four as the fuel ignited and the Humvee was engulfed in flames.

McGovan got into the four-by-four and they drove back across the desert to pick up the other two fighters. The wounded man was by now grey-faced and probably beyond help as they drove flat-out, aiming to have crossed the Syrian border before the inevitable Iraqi Army sweep for the killers of their comrades began. McGovan was a trained patrol medic and could have treated the ISIS fighter's wounds, but he ignored his groans and the spreading stain from the blood pulsing out of his stomach wound, keeping his gaze fixed on the terrain around them, searching for any sign of further army patrols. His wounds left untreated, the injured man was continually jolted and thrown around in the back of the four-by-four as it bucketed over the rocky ground that stretched for miles on either side of the frontier. He had bled to death long before they reached the safe-house inside Syria. He was carried off for a martyr's burial while his comrades were debriefed by their commander.

When they had given him their account of the firefight with the Iraqi soldiers and McGovan's role in killing them, the commander embraced him. 'You have shown yourself a worthy brother to us,' he said. 'You shall have everything that it is in my power to give you to help you achieve your own aims.'

McGovan remained in the safe-house with the ISIS fighters throughout the next day. An hour before sunset, the commander received a radio message. He listened in silence, removed the headphones and smiled. '*Allahu Akbar,*' he said. 'The *faranji* unbeliever, the American officer, is dead. His vehicle blew up while he was climbing into it in the compound this morning. Two of his traitorous Iraqi guards died with him. There will be much fear among the training teams from now on. They will not feel safe anywhere. We move to a different safe-house after dark, and tomorrow we begin planning your attack in Britain.'

McGovan spent much of the next day with Saif al-Islam, as he laid out his requirements for cash, weapons and equipment. They discussed the potential fighters the ISIS commander could offer him. After hearing Saif al-Islam give details of each man, including how they had come to join ISIS and what skills and experience they had, if any, McGovan rejected most, but eventually he had a list of a dozen names. Some were already based in Britain and others were UK passport holders who, although now fighting as jihadists in Syria, could return to Britain with few questions asked, entering the country through the Channel Tunnel on Eurostar trains where immigration controls and passport checks were likely to be less stringent than at UK airports.

The following night McGovan began his journey back to Britain through Turkey. As soon as he arrived in London, he booked a room in a military club north of Oxford Street for an indefinite period. As he reflected to himself, after he had finished checking in and was moving away from the desk towards the stairs, there could be no better cover for what he was planning than to be an ex-military man, staying in a military club, surrounded by other serving and former soldiers. It was the last place that any agency searching for terrorists would be likely to look.

As soon as he was settled in his room, he searched the

internet for news reports of the American soldier's death in Iraq but, as he had predicted to Saif al-Islam, the incident had made barely a ripple in the British press. There was only a tiny paragraph on an inside page of the *Daily Telegraph*. The deaths of all four members of an Iraqi Army patrol did not rate a mention.

3

The robbery had been planned to perfection, but not by the men who carried it out. They were hired hands, brought in for the job with no idea of the big picture. They were being paid a flat fee, plus a share of the proceeds, and were all happy with the arrangement. There were four in the initial group. They gained access through the next-door building, easy enough because it was a regular office block with no special security arrangements and deserted at weekends.

They opened one of the lifts on the ground floor and pressed the button to send it up to the top of the building. One had a key he used to open the doors. Once it was open the lift was automatically locked in place, a safety feature they were using to their advantage. They had ropes and abseiling equipment with them and two of the men lowered themselves to the basement, where they unhitched themselves. The men on the ground floor took a Hilti DD350 industrial power drill from a large black nylon kit bag and carefully lowered it to the men below. It was a big drill for a big job: they had to bore through half a metre of reinforced concrete.

The first hole took just under an hour. The men took it

in turns to operate the equipment, wearing masks to keep the dust from their mouths and noses, and heavy-duty earmuffs against the noise. The drill made quick progress through the concrete but slowed markedly each time it hit the reinforced steel bars that threaded through the wall. Eventually it burst through into the vault. The man operating the drill switched it off and pulled it out. He knelt down, peered through the hole and grinned as he saw the rows of metal safe-deposit boxes. The man with him patted him on the back. 'Let the dog see the rabbit,' he said, slipping his mask over his mouth and nose. He took over the drilling, starting a second hole that overlapped slightly with the first. It took just forty-five minutes to break through, and the third another forty minutes. By the time they had finished, the three holes formed a gap twelve inches deep and two and a half feet wide. The four men who had carried out the task were carrying a few more pounds than was good for them and weren't anywhere near slim enough to squeeze through. They packed up the drill and cabling and two climbed back up the ropes, hauling the equipment after them.

As they left the building, their kitbags hidden in a wheelie-bin, two more men arrived, wearing grey backpacks. They were smaller than the first four, wiry and shorter than average. Their small stature belied their strength: they were both former SAS and as hard as nails. They abseiled down the lift shaft and examined the hole that had been drilled into the vault. 'Tight fit, but it'll do,' said one. He took off his backpack and went through head first. He had to breathe in and wriggle a bit but he managed it. His colleague passed through the two backpacks and followed him.

They stood up and surveyed the 999 safe-deposit boxes. They were graded in size, the larger ones at the bottom, the topmost ones only a couple of inches deep. Each had a number, and two locks. The owner of each safe-deposit box held one key, the company the other. Both keys were necessary to open the box. That was the idea, anyway, but the drills the men had in their backpacks meant that it was a matter of seconds to open any of them. Unlike the massive drill that had been used to bore through the wall, the smaller models came with their own power supply. One man took a folded piece of paper from the pocket of his overalls. 'Seven six two,' he read out. It was on the right of the room, a medium-sized box at about waist-height. The other man pressed the trigger of his drill and pushed the bit against one of the locks. It ripped through it in seconds. He did the second lock, then opened the flap. His colleague pulled out a slim metal box, placed it on the floor and opened the top. Inside were three men's watches, several small red boxes, a stack of notebooks and a black thumbdrive. The man took out the notebooks and the thumbdrive and put them into his backpack. As an afterthought he took out one of the watches – a gold Rolex GMT Master – and slipped it onto his wrist. 'What do you think?' he asked.

'I think with what you're being paid for this, you could buy your own fucking watch.'

The man grinned. 'I like this one.' He waved his arm around the strong room. 'Make it look good.'

'How good?'

'Fifty, at least.'

The other gunned the drill. 'And we get to keep the ill-gotten gains, right?'

'The guys outside take the gear and sell it. We'll get our cut down the line. The important thing is that it looks like the jewellery and cash were the prizes. Catch you later.'

'Not if I catch you first.' He began on another lock as his colleague threw his backpack through the hole and wriggled after it.

4

Charlotte Button poured Pinot Grigio into a large glass and carried it with a plate of spinach risotto to the sofa. She flopped down, took a long drink of wine, and pressed the remote to watch Sky News. She ate her risotto as a pretty blonde girl with augmented breasts and a too-perfect pixie nose went through the events of the day in an annoying sing-song voice more suited to a primary-school teacher addressing a class of eight-year-olds.

The raid on the Manchester safe-deposit company was the third item. The fork froze in the air on its way to Button's mouth. Fifty-eight boxes opened: no idea yet how much money and jewellery had been stolen but several Premier League footballers were thought to have had boxes in the vault. And allegations were flying that the Manchester police hadn't been doing their job properly. Next a grey-haired security expert described the robbery as a 'good old-fashioned caper', which bore an astonishing number of similarities to the break-in at the Hatton Garden safe-deposit company earlier in the year.

Button put down her fork, drained her glass and walked over to the burglar alarm console in the hallway. She activated the perimeter system but kept the motion-sensors and infrared detectors on standby. She opened the cupboard under the stairs and took out a black North Face backpack and placed it by the front door. It contained a change of clothes, a torch, a first-aid kit, five thousand pounds and five thousand dollars in cash, and two passports, one Irish and one British, both with her photograph but neither using her real name. The Americans called them bug-out bags, but at MI5 they had always referred to them as go-bags. Every officer on overseas assignment had to have their go-bag close by so that they could leave at a moment's notice, and even though she no longer worked for the security service, keeping an up-to-date go-bag was second nature to Button.

She took her plate and glass to the kitchen, washed them and put them on the rack. The kitchen door was locked but she flicked the bolts across, top and bottom. She switched off the lights and went back to the hallway. She killed the lights there, too, and in the sitting room, then went to the window and looked outside. Her car was parked in front of the garage, a two-seater Audi. The driveway was gravelled so she'd have heard anyone walking across it, but there was plenty of grass around the house.

She went back to the burglar alarm. The outside lights were normally linked up to motion detectors but she pressed a button to switch them on. She went into the sitting room and looked out. No unusual shadows that she could see. No movement.

She picked up her black Chanel handbag and took out her car keys, slung the backpack over her shoulder and set the alarm. She closed the front door behind her as it was bleeping, jogged over to her car and climbed in, heart pounding. She started the engine, put the car in gear with a shaking hand and drove away, the tyres of the Audi kicking up a spray of gravel behind her.

Less than three hours after Sky News had reported on the robbery, Barbara Reynolds left Heathrow Airport on a flight bound for JFK. Her only luggage was a black North Face backpack and a Chanel handbag.

5

Button had arranged to meet Richard Yokely at midday in Central Park. Specifically Sheep Meadow, the fifteen-acre field on the west side of the park, between 66 and 69 Streets. It was a popular spot for dog-walkers and picnickers, and a favourite site for demonstrators to gather and protest. It was also the perfect place to spot watchers and followers. At eleven o'clock Button found herself a seat in a coffee shop on 67th Street overlooking the meadow, sipped a latte and nibbled a croissant as she read that day's *New York Times*. She saw Richard Yokely arrive at exactly midday. He seemed to be alone, but Richard Yokely was a pro with decades of experience in surveillance and counter-surveillance working for agencies that preferred to identify themselves by initials, including the CIA, NSA and DIA. He was wearing a long black coat over a grey suit, a gleaming white shirt and a yellow tie with pale blue stripes. He was too far away for her to see his footwear but she was sure he'd be wearing his trademark tasselled loafers.

Button left the coffee shop, crossed the road and entered the park. He saw her the second she stepped onto the grass, smiled and waved as if he was an old friend. Yokely was in his very early fifties with short grey hair, thin lips and teeth so white they were either veneers or chemically treated. He air-kissed her on both cheeks and she caught the scent of sandalwood.

'I didn't know you were visiting the US, Charlotte,' he said. 'You should have let me know you were coming.'

'It wasn't planned,' she said. 'All a bit rushed, actually.'

'What's interesting is that the INS doesn't seem to be aware of you arriving on our shores either. But an Irish lady named Barbara Reynolds seems to bear an uncanny resemblance to you and has identical fingerprints.'

'Ah, yes, sorry about that.'

'False papers aren't the asset they used to be, not now we take the fingerprints of any foreigner who flies in.'

'I've been a very naughty girl,' said Button, fluttering her eyelashes theatrically. 'Please don't arrest me.'

'Why the fake passport, Charlotte?'

'It's genuine, issued by the Irish authorities.'

'You know what I mean.'

She smiled tightly. 'I know, I'm sorry. It was more about leaving the UK discreetly,' she said.

'Are you in trouble, my dear?'

She nodded. 'I'm afraid so.'

'And that's why you wanted to meet here instead of at a perfectly good restaurant?'

'I thought it might be more appropriate, yes.'

'Don't you trust me? After all we've been through?'

'I'm not sure who I can trust just now. I'm sorry.'

'You might at least have chosen somewhere I could smoke,' he said. 'Smoking is illegal in Central Park. Pure madness. It's outside, but you can't smoke. Cross the street to the sidewalk and you can smoke there. The wind will blow the smoke into the park, but that's the rule.'

'Health Nazis,' said Button. 'What can you do?'

'What about the UK?' asked Yokely. 'Can you smoke in Hyde Park still?'

'I think so. But I'm not a smoker.' She started walking across the field and Yokely kept pace with her. 'How much do you know, Richard?'

'I know everything. It's my job.'

'About my position?'

He smiled, like a kindly uncle. 'I know you left MI5 under a cloud. I know you've been accused of using government resources to resolve personal issues.'

'I used the Pool to kill the men who were responsible for the death of my husband,' said Button. 'Shame on me.'

'Charlotte, I would have done the same, trust me. You have my sympathy. But what you did . . .' He shrugged.

'You were never one to shy away from an off-the-books operation, Richard.'

'It wasn't what you did that was the problem,' said Yokely. 'It was the fact you got caught. But that's water under the bridge. What's happened to get you over here under a false name, looking over your shoulder, like a fox who can hear the hounds on her tail?'

'I'm in shit, Richard. Deep, deep shit.' The wind tugged at her hair. 'I kept records of everything I was asked to do, obviously.'

'Obviously.'

'After what I did, they couldn't keep me on, but they could hardly drag me through the courts. Not with what I know.'

Yokely chuckled. 'You know where all the bodies are buried. Figuratively and literally.'

'So, basically, they had two choices. Lose me, or use me. And my insurance policy against anything bad happening to me was a file. A very big file. I made three copies of that file, and stored those copies in safe places.' She smiled thinly and corrected herself. 'In what I assumed were safe places. Did you read about the safe-deposit robbery in Manchester?'

'Sure. A professional job, perfectly executed.' Realisation dawned. 'Ah. You had a box there.' It was a statement, not a question.

'There were nine hundred and ninety-nine boxes in that vault. They broke in without being discovered, they had all weekend to work, and they opened fifty-odd.'

'Because they were interested in just one? Yours?'

'That's what I'm assuming,' said Button.

'It could be a coincidence,' said Yokely. 'Have you been told officially that yours was one of those opened?'

'I don't need to hear officially,' she said. 'It's the second of my boxes to have been raided. Mine was one of those that was broken into when they raided the Hatton Garden Safe Deposit Company earlier this year. That time they broke open seventy-two boxes and one was definitely mine.'

'But didn't they arrest the men responsible?'

'They did indeed. But I'm pretty sure they were just the fall guys. I doubt they did the planning. Hired hands, I'm guessing.'

'And you think, what? The government?'

'Possibly.'

'I'm sure they wouldn't be stupid enough to try to hurt you, Charlotte.'

'There are some very stupid people in our intelligence services,' said Button. 'A lot of very bright people, but we have more than our fair share of idiots. And one of them might well have decided to have a go at me.'

'Your nemesis, Jeremy Willoughby-Brown?'

'I'd hardly call him my nemesis, Richard.'

'He did get your job at Five. And he was responsible for you leaving.' He sighed. 'Charlotte, I really need a smoke. Can we please go to the sidewalk? I give you my word we're not being followed.'

She nodded, and they walked across the grass towards 68th Street. 'I don't think it's Jeremy. He got what he wanted, my job. He wouldn't gain anything by killing me.'

'So who would?'

'A dozen people whose careers would come to an abrupt end if the file were ever made public,' said Button. 'Politicians and civil servants. The Pool was always acting in the interest of the greater good, but things were done that . . .' She sighed. 'Well, you know what I mean.'

'I do indeed, Charlotte. Sometimes the ends justify the means.'

'Morally, yes. But not legally. And a number of people would sleep easier if the file and my good self were laid to rest. I could go to the papers with the file I have left. But I'm reluctant to pull that trigger, obviously.'

They crossed the road and Yokely took a small cigar case from his coat pocket. He selected a cigar and lit it, taking care to blow the smoke away from her. 'You were never a smoker?'

She shook her head. 'My father smoked a pipe and I hated it. Hated the smell. It's funny – sometimes I forget what he looked like but if I walk past a pipe-smoker it hits me.'

'Smells can be like that. They're a direct link to memories.' He held up the cigar. 'I'm fairly sure that within my lifetime possession of one of these will be a criminal offence. At least, it will be here in the US.'

'So long as I can still get a decent bottle of wine, I'm happy,' said Button.

Yokely took another drag on his cigar as they walked south, the park to their left.

'I need protection, Richard. I need someone to watch my back. Just for a while until I get a grip on what's happening.'

'I thought you were in the protection business, these days. Your company, what's it called?'

'It's called Executive Solutions but it's still known as the Pool.'

'Because you're in at the deep end?'

She laughed softly. 'It was always called the Pool. Partly because we had people we could call on as and when required, but partly because so many of them seemed to come from Liverpool. The thing is, yes, I could get a couple of my guys to follow me around. But that's not the sort of protection I need. I need government-standard surveillance. I need to know the chatter, Richard. I need to know what's being said about me. I need to know if I'm being watched as I move through an airport. I need to know if I'm in danger.'

'You want the NSA looking out for you?'

'That would be nice. And I'd like it known that I'm being watched over.'

Yokely nodded. 'The idea being that if the world knows Charlotte Button is under the NSA microscope it's likely to leave her alone?'

'Just for a short time, until I get my ducks in a row.'

'Those ducks being?'

'I have one more copy of the file in what I consider to be a safe place. In view of what's happened at Hatton Garden and in Manchester, I need to make sure it isn't compromised, and I have to put other copies in other places. Clearly safe-deposit boxes aren't safe, despite the name.'

'There is an alternative, Charlotte. You could give me a copy.'

'I did think about that, Richard, but it's perilously close to treason.'

'We're on the same side.'

'Of course we are. But the information in that file is classified. And passing it to another government, even an ally, could be taken the wrong way.'

'You could give it to me personally.'

'To be opened in the event of my death?' She laughed again. 'No, I'll handle it. But until then, I need someone watching my back. Will you help?'

'Of course I'll help.' He put a bear-like arm around her and hugged her. 'You think I'd let anything happen to my favourite ex-spook?'

'Thank you, Richard. You're a sweetheart.'

He released his grip on her. 'Actually, it's fortuitous that you turned up when you did. I have a favour to ask of you.'

'A favour?'

'Let's call it a quid pro quo.'

'I'm listening.'

6

Lex Harper studied the menu, unable to decide between *pad thai* or the *khao pad*. Noodles or rice. The menu was idiot-proof and consisted of a plastic photograph album into which had been slotted a couple of dozen pictures of the dishes on offer. Each had a sticker, with the description in English and Thai and the price. The waitress, a pretty teenager with her hair in plaits, stood patiently with her notepad. Her name was Som and she was the daughter of the owner, still at school but helping her mother in the evenings.

'What do you think, Som? *Khao pad* or *pad thai*?'

'I like *pad thai. Pad thai mu.*' Thai fried noodles with pork.

'You've sold me,' said Harper, handing her back the photograph album. 'And another bottle of Heineken.'

He was sitting in a beer bar in a side road off Walking Street, Pattaya's main red-light strip. It was just after six, the street was quiet and there were only two other customers in Noy's, playing pool, the loser buying tequila shots. The bar was open to the air but two large fans overhead gave enough of a breeze to make the evening bearable.

Som returned with a fresh beer, slotted into a foam

cylinder bearing the bar's logo – a bright red lipstick kiss superimposed on a cross of St George. Noy's second and fourth husbands had been English. No one was quite sure how many she had had over the years, but they had all contributed to the upkeep of the bar in one way or another. Harper was just about to take a sip when he recognised the young girl walking purposefully along the street towards him. Her name was Em. Dark-skinned and lanky, she was nineteen years old and one of the top-earning dancers at the Firehouse, one of the busier Walking Street go-go bars. She was in the off-duty bar-girl uniform of tight black top, cut-off denim shorts and impossibly high heels, with a thick gold chain around her neck and an even thicker one around her left wrist. A dragon tattoo wound down her left leg. She looked upset and got straight to the point. 'Khun Lek, Pear is in hospital.'

Thais tended to have trouble pronouncing Alex or Lex and most ended up saying 'Lek', which happened to be the Thai for 'small' and was a common nickname. Harper had long ago given up correcting anyone who mispronounced his name and simply answered to Lek.

'What happened?' he asked. Pear was a dancer in Em's bar, and came from the same village outside Surin, not far from the border with Cambodia. He had known her since she'd started working in Pattaya two years earlier, sent to dance in the bars by parents who were having trouble scraping a living as farmers. He'd met her on her second day on the job and she had been relieved to discover that Harper could speak Thai. She had spent the whole evening sitting next to him, telling stories about her life as a farm kid, then thrown up over him and passed out after her fifth tequila shot. Harper had assumed that the drinks he'd been buying her had been watered down, but there had been a miscommunication with the barman and Pear had been as drunk as a skunk. From that day on he had always felt responsible for the girl and had often helped her out at the end of the month if she wasn't able to pay her rent or didn't have enough to send back to her parents.

'A customer attacked her,' said Em. 'He raped her. She's very sick, Khun Lek.'

'Which hospital?'

'Pattaya International. ICU.'

Harper was already off his stool and heading for the door. If Pear was in the intensive care unit, it had to be serious. He handed Som a five-hundred-baht note and told her to eat his *pad thai*. His Triumph Bonneville motorcycle was parked outside the bar, his black full-face helmet sitting on one of the mirrors. He pulled on the helmet, fired up the bike and drove off.

Ten minutes later he was outside the ICU talking to a pretty Thai doctor with waist-length jet black hair and makeup that would have been more at home on a fashion model. Her nails were painted a glossy Barbie pink that matched her lipstick. 'She's been badly beaten,' said the doctor. 'She has lost two of her teeth, her kidneys are swollen and she's passing blood at the moment. We'll know in a day or two how bad her kidneys are, but it's not looking good.' Her English was perfect but with a slight American accent, probably the result of being educated at an inter-national school and university.

'Is she in pain?' asked Harper.

'We've made her as comfortable as we can but if we give

her any more painkillers she'll be unconscious and we don't want that.' The doctor looked uncomfortable. 'Is she your girlfriend?'

'Just a friend,' said Harper.

'Because there is something else, Mr Harper. I'm afraid she was raped. With considerable violence. Both her vagina and rectum are quite badly damaged.'

Harper cursed under his breath.

'We have contacted the police and they will be sending an officer with a rape kit to gather evidence,' said the doctor.

'Can I see her?'

The doctor shook his head. 'I'm afraid not. She's too sick for visitors at the moment. She's in no immediate danger now, though, and we'll be moving her out of the ICU tomorrow.'

'That's good to hear,' said Harper.

'But there is something else, I'm afraid . . .'

He cursed again, wondering just how bad it was going to get. 'There's the matter of Khun Pear's bill,' said the doctor. 'That's why she gave us your name. She said you would settle her account.'

'No problem at all,' said Harper. He unzipped his hip-pack, counted out twenty thousand baht, then handed it with a Visa card to the doctor. 'Take that on account and put whatever you need on the card.'

The doctor smiled and handed it back with the money. 'That's all right, Mr Harper. You can pay when she checks out. But we'll need a copy of your passport.'

Harper took his passport out of the hip-pack and gave it to the doctor. The hip-pack was around his waist pretty much all the time. It contained two of his many mobile phones, his passport, two credit cards and money. Always money. The pack, with the heavy gold neck chain he always wore, was his guarantee of a fast exit from any country, at any time, should the need arise. He had a more substantial escape kit stashed under the bed in his Thai apartment and another bug-out bag in a specially made concealed compartment beneath the floor of his SUV, but the hip-pack had everything he needed for a high-speed escape.

The doctor took the passport and headed down the corridor, her white coat flapping behind her to reveal an extremely shapely pair of legs and the red soles of fake Christian Louboutin high heels. At least, Harper assumed they were fake – Thai doctors weren't as highly paid as their UK and US counterparts but she might have been from a wealthy family. Or maybe she had a rich husband.

Harper waited until she'd turned a corner, then slipped into the ICU. A machine was beeping quietly in time with Pear's heartbeat. There was a bandage across her forehead and a plaster across her nose. Her eyes were almost hidden by puffed-up skin. Her lips were cracked and swollen and there were bandages on her arms. A tube ran from a bandage on her wrist to a clear bag hanging from a metal stand.

Harper touched her arm gently. She flinched and groaned but didn't open her eyes. 'Pear, baby, it's me. Lek.'

Pear's eyes fluttered open and she tried to smile but the effort made her wince. 'Lek, I'm sorry.'

'Don't be silly, baby. There's nothing to be sorry about.'

'I have no money.'

He patted her arm. 'Don't worry, I've taken care of it.'

'I'll pay you back.'

'You bloody won't,' said Harper. 'Now, who did this to you? Em said it was a customer.'

'It was a Russian. Valentine. He owns a bar in Walking Street.'

'Tell me what happened.'

'I went with my friend Ying. She dances at the Cellblock. She wanted to see Russian girls dancing so we went to Red Oktober. They have pretty girls there. Valentine was giving us drinks and I got drunk very quickly. When I woke up I was upstairs in a room and there were two men with me. Valentine and another man.'

'What was his name?'

'I don't know, Lek. I'm sorry. I forgot. He was a friend of Valentine's. A Russian man.' She shuddered. 'They'd taken my clothes off and Valentine was taking pictures as the other man had sex with me. I shouted at them, told them not to take my picture. Valentine laughed and slapped me. I started screaming and then they . . .' She shuddered again. 'They did this to me.' She sniffed. 'I thought I was going to die, Lek.'

'This room, where was it? Above the bar?'

'I don't think so. I think it was a short-time hotel. I don't remember.'

'Don't you worry,' he said again. 'Just get better, okay? I'll take care of everything.'

She nodded and slowly closed her eyes. 'Thank you, Lek. You're a good friend.'

Harper leaned over and kissed her on the forehead, then hurried out, just in time to see the doctor coming down the corridor with his passport. If she'd seen Harper disobeying her instruction not to disturb the patient, she didn't show it, just smiled, thanked him and returned the passport. She also gave him a business card with her mobile phone number. 'You can call me anytime to ask how Pear is,' she said.

'She's going to be all right, though?'

'She needs a lot of rest. And I worry that she will always have the scars. But other than that . . .'

'If you think a plastic surgeon will help with the scars, get one in,' said Harper. 'I'll pay whatever it costs.'

'We'll see about that once she's out of ICU, but I will be able to recommend someone, yes.'

'Do you know where she was when this happened?'

'I don't.'

'Did she come here in an ambulance?'

'No, a taxi. One of her friends brought her, I think.'

Harper thanked her and headed out of the hospital.

7

The Cellblock didn't usually start to get going until ten at night and the best girls didn't bother turning up until eleven. They knew they'd be taken out by a customer within an hour or so of going on stage so there was little point in clocking in early even if not doing so meant the management docking a few hundred baht from their pay. Most of the girls didn't care about the salary the bar paid, anyway. They earned most of their income from customers in hotel rooms, anything from two thousand baht from a Pattaya regular to five or six thousand from a newbie who didn't know the going rate.

The Cellblock was done out as if it was a prison, with an upper area of barred cells in which girls would dance and a lower area like a concrete exercise yard. Harper didn't want to miss Ying so he got there at eight and sat in a corner nursing a Heineken. There were two other customers and half a dozen girls pretending to dance on concrete podiums, shifting their weight from foot to foot as they checked their smartphones. Over the next hour a dozen or so more arrived, mostly wearing crop tops and shorts, flip-flops slapping on the floor. They would disappear through a curtain into the changing room, emerging a few minutes later in high-heeled boots, thongs and little else.

Several of them eyed Harper as they walked by but his body language and blank eyes betrayed him as a local, which meant they didn't bother trying to hit him up for a drink. That was the third way the dancers made money: they earned commission on every drink a customer bought them. A girl who hustled could easily get twenty drinks a night – usually cola or water masquerading as tequila – which meant a thousand baht or so in her hand. Harper had enough mates in the Pattaya bar business to know that a hard-working girl with a sweet mouth could earn more than two hundred thousand baht a month – close to fifty thousand pounds a year.

He was on his second beer when Ying walked into the bar. He almost missed her – with no makeup, her hair tied back and her figure disguised in an oversized T-shirt, she looked more like a farm-girl than one of the Cellblock's top-earning dancers. 'Hey, Ying, over here,' he called.

Her eyes widened when she saw him. 'Lek, you know about Pear?'

'That's what I want to talk to you about.' He patted the seat next to him. She slid onto it and almost immediately a chubby waitress with bad skin appeared, nodding expectantly. Harper didn't bother arguing, just ordered a drink for Ying. He knew the rules: if a girl sat with a customer she had to have a drink. The waitress pointed at herself and smiled, showing uneven teeth. Harper shook his head. He didn't mind buying Ying a cola but the waitress was pushing her luck. She held out her right hand so that he could see her palm. On it was written in felt-tip pen – BUY ME A DRINK?

Harper shook his head. No.

She held out her left hand, fingers splayed. CHEAP CHARLIE. She waited until he had read it, then spun on her heels and flounced off with her nose in the air.

'What happened last night?' Harper asked Ying.

She had high cheekbones and skin the colour of mahogany, big almond eyes and full lips. With her large breasts and long legs she was the sort of girl Westerners flocked to, though most Thais wouldn't have considered her pretty. 'We went to Red Oktober,' she said, her lips just inches from his ear. 'We wanted to see Russian girls dancing, and a man started buying us drinks.'

'His name was Valentine, right?'

She shook her head. 'Valentine wasn't the man who bought the drinks. His name was Grigory. Valentine owns the bar.' Her hand was stroking his thigh as she talked, from habit rather than any wish to arouse him. It was her bar-girl instinct kicking in.

'You know him?'

She shook her head again. 'No, he told me he was the boss. I joked about working for him but he said he only has Russian girls in his club.'

'And who was this Grigory?'

'Just a customer.'

'And he was a friend of Valentine?'

Ying nodded. 'They were good friends, I think. They kept talking to each other in Russian, and laughing. We'd been there about an hour and my boyfriend rang. He wanted to see me. He was gambling and he needed money.'

'So you left her?'

The waitress returned with Ying's cola, then flashed her CHEAP CHARLIE hand and flounced off again.

'She was okay, Lek. She seemed happy. A bit drunk, but you know Pear. She drinks a lot.'

Like most of the girls in the industry, Pear used alcohol and drugs to get through the night, partly for energy and partly to numb the pain.

'If I'd known what was going to happen, I wouldn't have left her.'

Harper sipped his beer. 'Do you know where they took her? Pear said she was in a room somewhere.'

'I don't know,' she said. Tears were welling in her eyes. 'It's my fault, isn't it?'

'No. It's Valentine and Grigory who are responsible.'

He paid for the drinks, then headed down Walking Street and along a darkened side street to BJ's, one of Pattaya's seedier bars, with half a dozen scantily dressed girls sitting outside touting for customers. 'Is Ricky in?' he asked one.

She pulled open a stained curtain. Harper ducked and walked through, wrinkling his nose at the stale smell of God knew what inside. BJ's was called BJ's because that was the speciality of the house, the act taking place in one of a dozen small booths around the edge of the bar, while a few plump girls went through the motions of dancing on a podium in the centre. To the right there was a Jacuzzi in which two even plumper girls were lathering themselves as a couple of elderly men in matching Chang Beer vests ogled them.

Ricky was standing at the cash register. His face lit up when he saw Harper. 'Fuck me, Lex, long time no see.' He walked over and hugged Harper. He was a big guy, well over six feet, a former merchant seaman, who had retired to Pattaya three years earlier. He had a good pension and several property investments back in England. The bar was more of a hobby than a business, which was why he'd staffed it solely with the sort of girls he liked – short, plump and dark. He couldn't care less whether it was busy or not. It was his own personal playground and that was all that mattered.

'Beer?' asked Ricky. 'On the house?'

'Sure,' said Harper, slipping onto a stool. Ricky joined him, waved at the barman, mimed a beer and held up two fingers. The barman nodded. Ricky had never bothered learning Thai but his sign language was understood the world over.

'What can you tell me about Red Oktober?' asked Harper, as the beers arrived.

'Russian go-go on Walking Street,' said Ricky. 'Pretty girls. A lot of Russian and Latvian blondes. Teenagers most of them.'

'Underage?'

'Borderline, but they're paying off the cops big time to let non-Thais work so I don't think anyone's bothered about how old they are.'

'And who runs it? A guy called Valentine?'

'Valentin,' corrected Ricky. 'Valentin Rostov. But he's the figurehead. It's Russian Mafia money. Have you got a problem with him, Lex? If you have, you need to stay well clear. They're vicious bastards and they're protected.'

'He put a friend of mine in hospital.'

'A girl?'

'Yeah, why do you ask?'

Ricky looked pained. 'Because he's got a bit of a reputa-tion for liking the nasty stuff. We've warned our girls not to go there. He knocked around a girl from Electric Blue a few months ago. And a girl from Dollshouse before that. He's got a thing for anal, especially if the girls don't like it.'

'For fuck's sake, Ricky.'

Ricky held up his hands. 'Don't shoot the messenger, mate,' he said. 'What do you expect me to do? Go to the cops? Then I'll be the one taking it up the arse. Valentin Rostov is protected. There's nothing can be done.'

'What's he look like?'

'Big. Probably former military. Crew-cut. Scar across his left cheek. Jagged like it was done with a bottle. Diamond earring.'

'The gay ear or the straight ear?'

Ricky laughed. 'An earring in any man's ear is fucking gay, mate. But this is a big diamond. Real, by all accounts. A couple of carats.'

'And he's got a friend called Grigory?'

'That I don't know. There's a lot of Russians drink there, obviously. And Indians. The Indians like the Russian birds and the Russian birds aren't fussy.'

'I doubt they're given much choice, right?'

Ricky nodded. 'Fair comment.'

It was an open secret that many of the Russian girls working in the go-go bars were little more than slaves, trafficked into the country, their passports held by their bosses until they had paid off the cost of their flight, visa and assorted bribes. The local girls could always choose whether or not to go with a customer, but the Russians had to do as their pimps told them. If a Thai girl was unhappy with her bar she could quit and find another place to work. That wasn't a luxury afforded the Russians.

'Be careful, Lex,' said Ricky.

Harper grinned. 'Careful is my middle name.'

'Yeah? I heard you were christened Alex Mad Fucking Bastard Harper, in which case Fucking would be your middle name. At least if you can't be careful, be lucky.'

'I always am, mate,' said Harper. He patted Ricky's shoulder and headed out into the night.

8

Harper waited until midnight before visiting Red Oktober. Two busty blondes in evening dresses were standing at the entrance and flashed him beaming smiles as he walked between them. The entrance led to a flight of red-carpeted stairs, a large Russian bouncer, with a shaved head and an earpiece in his left ear, at the top. Harper flashed him a smile and the Russian pulled open a glass door. Techno music blared and the temperature dropped a good ten degrees as Harper walked in. A dozen sofas were spread around the room and there was a bar with a dozen stools to the right. Stunning girls in evening dresses sat at tables with customers while others wearing thongs did some impressive pole work at three podiums. Unlike the Thai dancers, who rarely did more than shuffle around the poles, the Russians girls put their hearts and souls into it with gymnastic performances worthy of an Olympic medal.

Harper spotted Valentin immediately. Ricky had been right: the diamond in his left ear was huge and the scar on his cheek had obviously been done with a broken bottle. It made sense to use a bottle because Valentin was a big bastard, and hard with it: broad-shouldered and with a chin that looked as if it could shrug off a punch from anyone less than a world heavyweight champion. The Russian was pouring whisky from a bottle of Johnnie Walker Blue into a large glass with his right hand while he massaged the backside of a teenage blonde in a tight blue dress with his left. He was sitting next to a smaller man, and laughing at something he'd said.

A Thai waiter motioned for Harper to sit at an empty table but he went to the bar and took the stool one away from the man who was sitting next to Valentin. He ordered a Heineken, then swivelled around to get a better look at the bar. Most of the customers appeared to be Indian or Thai in contrast to the regular go-go bars, which tended to attract Westerners. They seemed to be big spenders too – the Russian dancers were drinking colourful cocktails and there were opened bottles of champagne on several tables.

'Hello,' said a voice to his side. Harper turned to find himself looking into the eyes of a stunning brunette. Almost immediately his eyes dropped to a gravity-defying cleavage threatening to burst out of a skin-tight white dress. 'What's your name?' she asked. His eyes clawed back to her face and he saw that she was smiling in a way that suggested she was used to her breasts getting most of the attention.

'Gerry,' said Harper. 'From Wales.'

'Wales?'

'Near England.'

'You are here on holiday?'

'Been here a week. Having a great time. Lovely place, innit?'

The girl nodded. 'But very hot.'

'You're on holiday?'

She laughed. 'No, I work here. Do you want to buy me a drink?'

'Sure.'

'A cocktail is six hundred baht.'

'Money no object, I'm on holiday.'

The girl ordered a drink from a waitress, then turned back to him. 'I'm Alena,' she said. She offered him her hand.

Harper kissed it. They chatted for the best part of half an hour, with Harper playing the part of the naïve tourist and Alena apparently hanging on his every word while she sipped her cocktail. He bought her another, and another, then asked her about Red Oktober. 'I've been thinking I could run a bar in Pattaya,' he said.

'It's not easy,' she said.

'Who runs this place?'

'Valentine,' she said, indicating the man with the diamond earring. 'He's the boss.'

'Let me buy him a drink,' said Harper, slurring his words.

'He only drinks Johnnie Walker Blue.'

'Then I'll buy him a Johnnie Walker Blue.' He slid off the stool, making it look as if he was a lot drunker than he actually was. He walked unsteadily to Valentin and tapped him on the shoulder. 'Hi, mate, my name's Gerry. From Cardiff. Have you heard of Cardiff?' He held out his hand.

Valentin shook it. 'Of course. Wales.'

'And where are you from, Valentin?'

'Moscow,' said the Russian.

'That Putin's a laugh, isn't he?' said Harper, slurring his words again. He let go of Valentin's hand and clapped the other man on the shoulder. 'What's your name, mate?'

'Grigory.'

'You from Moscow, too, mate?'

Grigory's eyes hardened. 'My friend and I are in the middle of a private conversation, if you don't mind.'

Harper stepped back and raised his hands. 'Sorry, right, sure, yes, no problem. Just wanted to say hello, that's all.' He flashed an exaggerated double thumbs-up. 'Great bar!' He backed away unsteadily, and knocked over his Heineken. He grinned lopsidedly at Alena. 'Better be getting back to the hotel. My wife will be wondering where I am.' He paid his bill and headed out. As he went through the door, Alena was already moving in on another customer.

9

Valentin and Grigory left the bar when it closed, at about four o'clock in the morning. Harper had waited for them in one of the beer bars on the opposite side of the street, drinking water but buying drinks for the girls and playing them at Connect 4, the children's game where the aim was to get four coloured discs in a row. The girls had played for years and were experts and Harper was lucky to win one game in ten.

The two Russians were clearly drunk and walked unsteadily down one of the side alleys that led to a car park. Harper paid his bill and followed them. The car park was mainly full of pick-up trucks but in the far corner there was a white Lamborghini and the Russians headed for that.

Harper jogged over to a line of waiting motorcycle taxis and gave the rider at the front of the queue five hundred baht. 'Follow that car,' he said, in Thai. Valentin and Grigory had climbed into the car and Valentin had started the engine. A uniformed security guard blew a whistle and waved instructions for Valentin to avoid scraping any of the other vehicles.

'The Lamborghini?'

'Sure.' Harper climbed onto the back of the bike. 'Just don't let him see you. Find out where he lives and there's another five hundred for you.' The Lamborghini edged carefully out of the car park.

'Yes, boss,' said the driver, gunning the engine. He was wearing a purple vest with the number 56 in Thai on the back. Motorcycle taxis were a quick and cheap means of getting around the city, especially at rush hour. They were also an efficient way of following other vehicles: no one ever paid attention to the motorcycle taxis or their customers.

The Lamborghini headed south, parallel to the sea. Valentin drove erratically. The fact he had senior cops on his payroll meant he wasn't worried about being stopped for drunk-driving. Twice he went through a red light and he didn't indicate before turns. Harper patted his driver on the shoulder. 'Don't get too close,' he said.

'No problem, boss.'

The car reached Jontiem and headed east, up a hill over-looking the bay. It stopped in front of a pair of large metal gates covered by a CCTV camera. The gates opened, the car drove through, and the gates closed again. There was security wire on top of the wall but the only camera he saw was the one at the gates.

Harper asked the driver to take him back to his apart-ment, in a high-rise block close to Beach Road. He had just walked into his sitting room overlooking the sea when he felt a vibration inside his hip-pack. He took out his phone and read the three-word text message from a UK number: *You have mail.*

Harper cursed under his breath. The message was from Charlotte Button and nine times out of ten a message from her meant him being on a plane within hours. If he were going to deal with the Russians it would have to be now. Either that or he'd have to walk away. He thought of Pear, battered and bruised in her hospital bed, and put his phone away. He walked through to the kitchen and took a pair of wire-cutters from the toolbox under the sink. He put them into a nylon kitbag along with three old towels from the bathroom.

The wall had been about ten feet high, and he had noticed several ladders belonging to his apartment building's maintenance staff in the underground car park. Harper figured they wouldn't miss one for a few hours. There was a false back to his underwear drawer in the wardrobe and he slid it back to reveal a Glock pistol with three filled magazines. He put the gun and clips into the holdall and went downstairs to his truck. He put one of the smaller ladders into the back, his holdall on the front passenger seat, then drove down to Beach Road. He parked outside an internet café owned by a middle-aged former go-go dancer called Rose. She was open pretty much twenty-four/ seven though when Harper walked in her brother was minding the shop. There were two customers, a drunken Scandinavian tourist on Skype and a bar-girl browsing through online photographs of Louis Vuitton handbags, presumably preparing to hit up a sponsor for a gift.

'Hi, Kung – okay if I use a terminal?' asked Harper.

Kung was engrossed in a Thai soap opera and waved a languid hand at the line of computers without looking up. 'Help yourself to a beer if you want one,' he said.

'I'm good,' said Harper. He sat down at a screen at the far end of the room. He went first to Google Earth and called up a satellite view of the house in Jontiem, then spent several minutes studying the layout. There was a main villa built in an L-shape around a large pool, plus two smaller houses that he reckoned were for the staff and possibly bodyguards. The rear wall faced the back of the house and was clearly the best way in.

He googled Valentin Rostov but all that came up were a couple of Facebook pages, neither of which belonged to the man he'd followed back to the villa.

He logged on to the Yahoo Mail account he used to contact Charlotte Button. She was the only person other than himself who knew the password and could access the email account they used to communicate with each other. They never actually emailed: they communicated by leaving messages in the draft folder. Deceptively simple, it was an almost foolproof system, far more secure than any phone or email link.

Using a chain of listening stations, like Yorkshire's Menwith Hill and GCHQ, both in the UK, and the National Security Agency in the US, the British and American intelligence agencies could intercept every single landline and mobile phone call, made anywhere in the world, and any email. Button and Harper's messages for each other in the drafts folder could not be monitored or recorded by anyone trying to eavesdrop on their communications. To increase security still more, their standard operating procedure was to delete each one as soon as it had been read. The technique had been developed by al-Qaeda terrorists to evade high-tech surveillance of their communications by Western intelligence agencies, but Button and Harper had adapted it for their own use.

When Harper logged in, he discovered that a single, two-word message had been added to the drafts folder: *Paris. ASAP.*

Harper deleted the message and wrote another: *En route, Madame.* He went online looking for flights to Paris and booked himself a business class seat on the 9.50 a.m. Air France flight that would get him into Charles de Gaulle airport at just before six o'clock in the evening.

He dropped a hundred-baht note in front of Kung, who waved his thanks without looking up, then went back outside to his pick-up truck. He drove out to Jontiem and parked off-road a hundred metres from the villa, switched off the engine and sat, gazing out over the sea, as he waited for his night vision to kick in.

It was just after six o'clock in the morning when he placed the lightweight ladder against the wall and used it to reach up to the security wire. He clipped away a section and let it fall to the ground. Broken glass was embedded in the concrete running along the top of the wall and he put the folded towels over it before climbing up and hauling the ladder after him. He slipped over and placed the ladder carefully on the ground, then shrugged off the backpack and took out the Glock. He crouched low, getting his bearings, then crept on the balls of his feet over the grass to the main building. The lights were on in the large room that overlooked the pool. Music was playing. Pitbull. Harper glanced at the two smaller buildings in the compound. Both were in darkness.

He worked his way along the villa to a back entrance. There was a roofed area with a Thai kitchen, a barbecue and a door that led inside. The rear of the house was in darkness and Harper padded over the marble floor, the Glock in his hand. He crept down a hallway that was wreathed in dim shadows. There were two closed doors on the left and the hall turned right, opening into the main living area, a double-height room with a huge chandelier hanging from a wooden arch. Two massive sofas were placed at a right angle to each other. Valentin was sitting with his back to Harper, who could see the diamond in the man's ear. Valentin was talking loudly in Russian and waving a glass above his head. Grigory was sitting on the other sofa, his feet on a large marble coffee-table, side on to Harper.

He stayed put for a couple of minutes until he was sure that there was no one else in the villa, before walking quickly to Valentin. Grigory saw him at the last minute but was slow to react. He hadn't even got to his feet by the time Harper had slammed the butt of his gun against the side of Valentin's head. There was a satisfying crunch and the Russian toppled sideways without a sound. Now Grigory jumped up but Harper already had the gun trained on him.

'What the fuck do you want?' the Russian snarled.

'To give you a taste of your own medicine.'

Grigory frowned. 'What the fuck do you mean?'

'I mean I'm going to hurt you so bad you'll wish you'd never been born.'

'Do you know who I am?'

'I know you're a Russian prick who enjoys beating up little girls and fucking them up the arse. Now get down on your knees.'

'Fuck you. You think I'm scared of your gun?'

Harper kept the gun trained on Grigory's face as he

slowly walked around the sofa. 'Scared or not, it can still blow your fucking brains out.'

'If you were going to shoot me, you'd have done it already.'

'Good point,' said Harper. His foot lashed out and caught the Russian in the groin. He yelped and bent double just in time for Harper to smash the gun into the side of the man's face, cracking his jaw and sending two teeth clattering across the polished wooden floor. Grigory straightened up, blood trickling from between his lips. He opened his mouth to speak but Harper transferred the gun to his left hand and punched him in the solar plexus with his right fist, putting all his weight behind the blow. Grigory fell back, arms flailing, his bloodied lips opening and closing, like those of a stranded fish. He hit the floor hard and lay still. Harper went over to him and kicked him in the side. 'Come on, you nasty Russian fuck. Wake up. You'll miss all the fun.'

10

Harper arrived at Bangkok's Suvarnabhumi airport at just before eight o'clock in the morning. He was travelling light, just a small backpack, and the hip-pack. He'd hired a taxi, a driver he regularly used, who could at least be relied on not to take drugs, drink whisky, or use his mobile phone behind the wheel, which was more than could be said for the majority of the city's taxi drivers. He walked up to the Air France desk and handed over his passport. The woman sitting there was less than five feet tall with glossy black hair and a mischievous smile, but the second she took his passport Harper realised something was wrong. She looked at it, then at a list on her desk, then back to the passport and back to him. She frowned and looked at the list a second time, then beckoned to a man in a grey suit. He came over and took the passport from her. He read the details inside and his eyes flicked to the list. He gave Harper a beaming smile. 'I'm so sorry, Mr Harper, we have a problem with our computer at the moment. I'll have to run this through the computer in our office. Please wait a moment.' He walked away with the passport while the check-in girl flashed Harper a comforting smile that suggested she was sorry for the delay and that she hoped everything would soon be sorted.

Harper smiled back. He had two choices. He could turn and walk away, but they already had his passport and he doubted he would get far. Or he could stand there, smile and see how it panned out.

'Khun Harper?'

He turned. A Thai policeman was standing behind him. Like all Thai cops he had a big gun on his hip and cold eyes that said he'd used it more than once in his career and would happily use it again. 'Yes?' Harper said.

There was another cop to his right, younger and taller, and three more not too far away.

'Please come with us.' The officer motioned with his hand for Harper to move away from the desk.

'Sure, no problem,' said Harper, shouldering his backpack.

'Please give me your bag,' said the officer.

Harper's jaw tightened but he knew there was no point in resisting so he forced a smile and handed it over. The officer gave it to the younger policeman, who went over to the check-in desk and retrieved Harper's passport. As the three of them left the check-in desks, the other three officers fell into step a few yards behind.

They took him to an escalator and up one floor, then along to a door with a keypad. The officer tapped in a four-digit code and pushed open the door. It led to a long corridor. He opened the third door along and motioned for Harper to go inside. A uniformed police colonel was sitting behind a table, smoking a cigarette in clear defiance of the NO SMOKING sign behind him. He wore a tight-fitting brown uniform, gleaming boots, and a scattering of colourful medals on his chest. Police Colonel Somchai Wattanakolwit. He grinned up at Harper and waved his cigarette at the empty chair opposite him. 'I gather you've been a naughty boy, Lek.'

Harper shrugged but sat down and didn't say anything. He had known the colonel for the best part of five years, and had got drunk with him several times, but the relationship was more one of symbiosis than friendship. Harper made regular contributions towards the colonel's retirement fund and in return the colonel didn't pay much attention to what Harper did or didn't do in the Land of Smiles.

The officer took the backpack and placed it on the table, then left and closed the door behind him.

Somchai smiled as he flicked idly through Harper's passport. 'Apparently a *farang* broke into a house in Jontiem and attacked two Russians. Attacked them so badly that they are both in hospital. One of them has lost his spleen and the other will be lucky if he ever eats solid food again. Both are black and blue. They were given a serious beating. Very serious.'

'Pattaya can be a dangerous place, if you're not careful,' said Harper.

'The attacker seems also to have forced beer bottles up their backsides, doing a considerable amount of damage in the process.'

Harper had to fight to stop himself grinning.

The colonel also seemed to be having trouble keeping a straight face. 'The description they give matches you, my friend. Especially the bit about the attacker being cruel, sadistic and probably psychopathic.'

Harper raised a quizzical eyebrow. 'I'd say that description would fit most of the expat population of Pattaya, wouldn't you?'

Somchai chuckled. 'A fair point, my friend.'

'So what's led you to stop me boarding my plane?' He looked at his watch. 'A plane that is due to leave in just over an hour and a half.'

'A young lady called Pear,' said Somchai. 'Who coincidentally happens to be in the same hospital as the two Russians. In the same condition too, more or less.'

Harper folded his arms but said nothing.

'It seems you played the good Samaritan and paid the young lady's hospital bill.'

'Let's get to the point, Somchai. Because I really need to be getting on that plane.'

Somchai smiled and leaned forward. 'The Russians don't know your name yet, Lek. In fact, at the moment they seem to think you're a Welshman called Gerry. But they're not stupid. Do you have any idea who they are?'

'They beat the shit out of young girls, I know that much.'

'Valentin Rostov and Grigory Lukin are very well protected, Lek.'

'I thought I was protected, Somchai.'

'You are, Lek. Which is why you and I are having this conversation and you're not dead in a ditch somewhere. You and I are friends. But these Russians, they pay a lot of money for protection. And they pay people much, much higher up the food chain than me. Money flows uphill, Lek, and shit flows down. That's the way of the world. At the moment I have been told to look for the man who put the Russians in hospital. I'm still looking. But if someone else puts a name to the face . . .' He shrugged.

'You won't be able to protect me?'

'The best thing might be for you to get on that plane and not come back, Lek.'

'Are you threatening me?'

The colonel chuckled. 'Of course not, my friend. It's just a warning. And you should be grateful for that.'

Harper nodded. 'Message received and understood. And thank you.'

'No problem. You have a safe trip.' He slid Harper's passport across the table. 'And, please, be careful. I don't have many *farang* friends and I'd hate to lose one.'

11

The plane touched down in Paris on a cool spring evening and Harper caught the city train to Châtelet – Les Halles and set off to walk to the hotel. He had checked the draft folder and Button wanted to meet him there at ten so he was in no hurry and strolled casually, enjoying the contrast of the cool air after the fierce heat and humidity of Thailand. He crossed the rue Saint-Honoré and cut down a narrow street leading to the rue de Rivoli. It was now almost eight o'clock and the streets were crowded with hordes of rubber-necking foreigners out for an evening stroll while being pestered by a retinue of tour guides, souvenir sellers, ticket touts, street hawkers, pickpockets and others who, in one way or another, earned their living from the tourist trade. As he moved through the streets, he was aware of the constant background chatter, a babel of different languages.

Relaxed though he was, Harper never completely switched off. Without being conscious that he was doing it, his eyes were constantly checking the streets, the buildings and the street furniture for potential danger-points or for cover if attacked, and assessing the body language of the people coming towards him. It had saved his life on more than one occasion, and had become such an ingrained habit during his time in the army and his subsequent off-the-books career that it was now as much a part of his routine as a shower and a shave in the morning.

Harper's normal practice whenever he was in England was to stay in cheap, anonymous hotels and pay cash for his room. Even in countries where the law required all foreign visitors to deposit their passports with the desk clerk when they checked into a hotel, there were always places operating on the fringes. They were the sort of hotels in the seedier quarters of big cities that catered to those who, for whatever reason, preferred to keep the law at arm's length and hired rooms by the night or even by the hour, depending on the particular requirements of their clientele. In such hotels, no ID was required before checking in, cash was the only acceptable form of payment and a blind eye was routinely turned to any laws that might affect business. But Harper was sure he wasn't on the radar of the French police so he had decided he could treat himself to a decent room for his meeting, especially as Charlotte Button would be picking up the tab. The hotel he had chosen, Le Meurice, was one of Paris's dozen or so elite, ultra-luxurious 'Palace Hotels'. It was a tourist's wet dream, on the rue de Rivoli between the Place de la Concorde and the Louvre, with views over the Tuileries Gardens, but Harper's mind was on his mission, Alert for any signs of surveillance or pursuit, he barely took in his surroundings. He was convinced that no one was following him, but as he stepped past the liveried doorman into the hotel's lobby, he drew back against the wall next to the doors, waiting and observing those entering behind him, to make absolutely sure he was secure before going to the desk and checking in.

The duty manager, a chic stick-thin Parisienne in her mid-forties, escorted him through the hotel, giving no more than a hint of a raised eyebrow at the small pack that was his only luggage and which he kept firmly in his hand, resisting a bellboy's attempts to carry it for him. He showed no interest in the Louis XVI furniture and the over-the-top nineteenth-century bling of the hotel's fixtures and fittings as she led him through the lobby and took the private lift to his seventh-floor Belle Etoile suite. He was still paying no more than cursory attention as she showed him the terrace with a spectacular view that encompassed almost every Paris landmark, from Notre Dame, the Musée d'Orsay, the Eiffel Tower, the Grand Palais, the Place de la Concorde and the Arc de Triomphe, to the Opéra and Sacré Coeur. If she was surprised at his lack of interest in a view that had many guests gasping with delight, she was professional enough not to let it show and her expression remained impassive.

When she had gone, Harper showered and changed into a clean shirt, then ordered a club sandwich from room service. He was just finishing it when his phone rang. It was the front desk, announcing that he had a visitor. Harper said they could send her up and he had the door open for her by the time she stepped out of the lift. As always, Charlotte Button was immaculately dressed in an under-stated but beautifully cut grey designer suit. She had pinned up her chestnut hair and the only jewellery she wore was the gold Cartier watch on her left wrist. 'A suite in Le Meurice,' she said, as she looked around the plush interior.

'What happened to your policy of always flying below the radar?'

'It's Fashion Week so everywhere's fully booked. And it was short notice.' He grinned. 'Come on, it's Paris. If you want to meet here we should at least do it in some style.'

'It's France, Alex. And, as I'm sure you must know, the French secret service have a long history of targeting people of interest, usually their industrial competitors. The information they collect is analysed and shared with French industry. It saves them a fortune in research and development and is one of the reasons why the French economy remains competitive even though their executives are more obsessed with their mistresses than their businesses, and a lot of their shop-floor workers are bone idle.'

'Borderline racist, Charlie,' said Harper.

'I love France, and the French, but their intelligence services tend to be a bit over the top. The Direction Générale de la Sécurité Intérieure was caught red-handed a few years ago bugging first-class seats on Air France flights and it's well known in the trade that they target people of interest who are staying in French hotels. So next time maybe go downmarket a bit, same as you do in England.'

'And I'm sure you know that the owners of Le Meurice are just about the only hoteliers in Paris who refuse to cooperate with the French secret service when they want to plant bugs in their guest rooms.' His smile broadened. 'Which is another reason I chose it. Walls might well have ears, Charlie, but not in Le Meurice.' He waved for her to sit down and waited for her to tell him why she had summoned him.

'I need you to do a job for me in the UK,' she said. 'We think a former SAS trooper has gone rogue and is planning something particularly nasty.'

'Do I know him?'

'He was a Para and the end of his time in the Paras overlapped with the start of yours. But he went off to do Selection and joined the SAS while you were out in Afghanistan. Caleb McGovan. Does that ring a bell?'

Harper shook his head.

'McGovan went to Turkey on a charter flight and spent a few days on the Turquoise Coast. He disappeared for a while before reappearing back on the coast. This happened a couple of times and we think in the interim he was making trips into Syria to link up with Islamic State.'

'You keep saying "we" but you don't work for Five any more.'

'It's not come from the British end,' said Button. 'It's the Americans who want it taken care of.'

'Now I'm confused,' said Harper. 'A former British soldier is threatening an attack on British soil, but the Yanks want him taken out?'

'So far as I'm led to believe, the Brits don't know what's going on.'

'So why don't the Yanks tell them, special relationship and all?'

'I gather they worry that the Brits won't handle it . . . correctly.'

'Correctly?'

'They want McGovan dead. And they don't see the Brits carrying out the execution of a British citizen on British soil. And they're a little wary of doing it themselves. Or, at least, of being caught doing it. By using my company, they stay one step removed.'

'So we're doing their dirty work?'

'That's one way of looking at it. The other is to consider that we'll be preventing a terrorist attack on UK soil.'

'That's not really the job of private enterprise, is it, though? That's why we have MI5, MI6 and all those other agencies that use initials. Why not just pass the intel on to them?'

'Because they'd want to know where it came from. And because they almost certainly wouldn't deal with it in the way that the Americans want it dealt with.'

'Sounds to me as if there's something you're not telling me.'

She smiled. 'Alex, if you'd let me finish you'd have the full picture. While McGovan was in the region – in other words, between his outward flight to Dalaman and his return flight to Britain – an American senior instructor working with the Iraqi Army at a base near Mosul was killed by an IED. One Captain Geoff Buckthorn. We – i.e. the Americans – think he was deliberately targeted. The device, with another fail-safe IED attached to the fuel tank, was fitted to his vehicle while it was parked inside a secure compound that was itself within an outer compound at the Iraqi base. The barbed-wire perimeter fence of the outer compound was guarded by Iraqi troops. The fence surrounding the inner compound – it was steel mesh, capped with coils of razor wire – was guarded by Americans. Someone went to an awful lot of trouble to kill Captain Buckthorn. Possibly because his father is a Republican congressman.'

'Ah,' said Harper. 'The plot thickens.'

'Congressman Buckthorn made a big thing about his son being in the military. About his family not just talking the talk but walking the walk. Many of the rich American families are prepared to send ghetto kids to fight their battles, but young Buckthorn was prepared to put his life on the line and so on. The right-wing media lapped it up.'

'And young Buckthorn paid the price. I get it. Now Congressman Buckthorn wants his revenge. But how sure are they that McGovan was behind it?'

'It was a very professional job. Like I said, the compound was being guarded by the Americans.'

'That proves nothing,' Harper said. 'The Yanks are even lazier than the Iraqi soldiers. They'd just be hanging around, shooting the breeze and praying for dawn so they could go to bed. They'd respond to a sniper or a mortar attack, of course, but they wouldn't be out there patrolling the fence line and watching for intruders. You don't need to go looking for rogue special forces to explain what happened there.'

Button made a gesture of annoyance. 'Prior to that attack, the Americans considered there was no group in the Iraqi opposition, or the Syrian for that matter, who had the capability to carry out that kind of attack. It was a complete surprise, Alex, not only to the Iraqis – and, let's face it, plenty of things come as a surprise to them – but also to the Americans. Then they picked up some SIGINT, more background chatter between a couple of ISIS high-ups, that suggested there was something unusual about the incident. It's not just that our target was almost certainly in country when it happened, but the way the attack was

carried out bears all the hallmarks of a special-forces oper-
ation. The Americans compiled a thorough after-action
report, and got Delta Force to replay the incident as a
TEWT – a tactical exercise without troops.'

'I know what a TEWT is, Charlie,' said Harper. 'I had
to do enough of them in the bloody Paras.'

'Then you shouldn't be too surprised to learn that, after
they'd analysed the results of the TEWT, they found enough
similarities to be pretty certain that it wasn't some goatherd
wandering in off the desert who managed to penetrate the
Iraqi base and planted those IEDs. Nor, as far as they
could tell, was it some random jihadi, or even an ISIS
fighter. It had special-forces input written all over it. And
since ISIS doesn't have special forces and since, for obvious
reasons, the British and Americans don't teach Iraqi troops
the most advanced SF techniques, their conclusion can
only be that the expertise was provided by a rogue British
or American special-forces soldier. And the Americans are
pointing the finger at McGovan. And McGovan is now
back in the UK.'

'And you – i.e. the Americans – want him taken out.'

'If we can show that he's been turned by IS, yes.'

'And how much intel do you have on McGovan?'

'He was abandoned at birth and brought up in care. He
pulled himself up by his bootstraps, joined the Paras and
ended up in the SAS. He got married and had a couple
of kids before getting dragged into Iraq and Afghanistan,
where in the gaps between ops he taught himself to speak
Arabic and Pashto. The consequences of too many trips
and too much active service ended with his wife leaving
him and taking the kids. It's a familiar story in the forces,

of course, but it completely gutted him. Seems as if he's a loner now and not good company. I did hear that he'd been involved in clearing up the mess at Abu Ghraib and other less publicised atrocities done in the name of Christianity by our born-again GIs and their British acolytes.' She leaned forward. 'I know this is messy, but it's no messier than jobs you've done before.'

'He's a Brit, and a former Para. It could be me, Charlie. In another world, it could be him sitting here and you two discussing taking me out.'

'But you're not a terrorist, Alex.'

'I know exactly what I am,' said Harper. 'And I have no problems looking at myself in the mirror each morning. But, yes, this is very fucking messy and at the end of the day you're asking me to kill a British soldier on British soil.'

'A former British soldier who has gone rogue,' said Button. 'And who might well be planning a major terrorist atrocity in a British city. I need to know you'll do this.'

Harper shrugged. 'I've never let you down before.'

'On a more positive note, the Americans have made it clear that money's no object.' She looked around the palatial suite. 'Which, considering how much this is costing, is probably for the best.'

She was fiddling with her wedding ring as she spoke. Even though her husband had died some years earlier, Harper had never seen her without it. 'Are you okay, Charlie?' he asked.

She forced a smile. 'I'm fine. Why do you ask?'

'You look tense.'

'That goes with the territory.'

'More tense than usual, then.'

She ran a hand through her hair. 'I've had a rough few days.'

'Is that why we're meeting here, in Paris?'

She didn't answer and looked away.

'Maybe I can help,' he said.

She flashed him another tight smile. 'That's sweet of you, Alex. But I'm not sure you'd be able to do anything.'

'A trouble shared is a trouble halved.'

'Or doubled,' she said. 'It could go either way.' She laughed uneasily. 'Do you think there's wine in the minibar?'

'The prices they charge, there'd better be,' he said. He went over to the fridge, bent down and opened it. 'There's champagne.'

'We're not really celebrating.'

'And white.' He pulled out a half-bottle. 'It's a Chardonnay, with a screw top.'

'In Le Meurice? Now that's a surprise. But I suppose beggars can't be choosers.'

He opened the bottle and emptied it into two glasses, gave one to her and sat down on the winged chair facing her. He raised his glass in salute. 'Cheers.'

She toasted him back. 'You never take life seriously, do you, Alex?'

He shrugged. 'When it matters, I do. But if you can't have a little fun along the way, then what's the point?'

She pulled a face, then drank some more wine. 'You know I left MI5. Obviously.'

'Because of that little shit Willoughby-Brown?' He made a gun with his hand and mimed firing a couple of shots. 'Anytime you want him taken care of, I'll do it for free.'

'This isn't about him,' she said. 'At least, I don't think it is.'

'So, what's the story?'

She took another sip of wine. 'When I left Five, I made it clear that I'd set up what you might call insurance. A file that in the event of my death, et cetera, et cetera.'

'You were scared they might kill you?'

'I know stuff, Alex, a lot of stuff that could embarrass a lot of people and end a lot of careers. Now, my lips are sealed, anyone who knows me knows that, but there are some people who'd rather not rely on my word. I had to make sure I was more dangerous to them dead than alive. That appeared to be working swimmingly until there was a break-in at a safe-deposit vault last week.'

'The Manchester job? I knew that was iffy.'

'Because they only opened fifty-odd boxes?'

'That and the fact that the cops didn't investigate when the alarm went off. And the fact that it was almost identical to the Hatton Garden robbery. And then there's the CCTV footage of the workmen arriving and leaving. I mean, come on, it's the robbery of the century and they couldn't disable one camera?'

'Why do you think that was?' asked Button.

'Red herrings,' said Harper. 'They were all middle-aged and overweight. There was no way any of them could have got through the twelve-inch hole produced by the drill they used. That means the guys who went through the hole into the vault weren't caught on CCTV. Why was one lot of men filmed and the others not? Because they were red herrings, that's why. I knew there was something off about the whole thing.'

'Well, now you know why. One of my insurance policies was in one of the boxes.'

'One of the fifty-odd?'

Button nodded and took another sip of wine. 'They took the thumbdrive and one of my husband's watches. A gold Rolex. To be honest, that's what annoys me more than anything, the fact that one of the bastards behind this is wearing my husband's watch. And just so you don't think I'm being paranoid, I had a similar thumbdrive in a box in the Hatton Garden vault. One of the seventy-two that got opened there. It was my files they were after, I'm sure of it.'

'And who do you think "they" are?'

Button sighed. 'Someone in government, maybe. Someone who doesn't want the file ever being made public. But you know what sort of work the Pool did. There are a lot of people whose careers would die if it was ever found out who did what to whom.'

'And what about me, Charlie? Am I in that file?'

'Redacted,' she said. 'Along with the names of most of the other operatives who were used. This isn't about you, it's about the people who gave the orders and paid the bills.'

'So do you want me to ask around?'

'I'm not sure that'll do any good, Alex. They're probably spooks.'

'The guys who went into the vaults to get the thumbdrives, almost certainly. But the drillers? They'd be good old-fashioned criminals, I'm sure. Like the guys who were pulled in for the Hatton Garden job. And, like criminals the world over, they'll talk eventually. I mean, where's the fun in pulling off the crime of the century if no one knows you did it?'

She smiled over the top of her wine glass. 'There's been no chatter. None at all. I've asked. Quiet as the grave.'

'We move in different circles, Charlie. Let me ask around.'

'If it's not too much trouble, I'd be grateful.'

He grinned. 'How grateful?'

'Not that grateful.'

They laughed.

'You don't know what I was going to say.'

'Yes, I do, Alex.'

12

A man in his late thirties or early forties was among the crowds of tourists emerging from Westminster Underground station on a drizzly London morning. His dark hair was tinged with grey, he was clean-shaven, with no particular distinguishing features, and wore drab clothing that was neither sharp enough nor scruffy enough to catch the eye. The only distinguishing feature about his outfit was the black trilby, tilted down over his forehead, so that the brim cast his upper features into shadow. To a casual glance, his face must have appeared almost as nondescript as his outfit, and only someone watching him closely would have detected his keen gaze as he glanced around him, taking in every detail.

He took a free newspaper from the person handing them out at the entrance to the station and stood with his back to one of the pillars, facing across the road towards Parliament. He stood there for some time, leafing idly through the paper, but his gaze was fixed on the people moving around him, not on the pages he was turning. After five minutes he moved off, but his concentration never wavered, continually alert for anything unusual, any person out of place or paying him too close attention.

The hat he was wearing served two purposes: to obscure his face from the ubiquitous CCTV cameras and also to provide a recognition mark for anyone following him. That might have seemed a perverse act for anyone trying to avoid detection, but he knew even the best-trained followers tended to use a distinguishing feature, like a hat, as a recognition point when tracking a suspect. In a crowded street, if the hat was suddenly removed, the person wearing it could apparently disappear. Also, his jacket was reversible, with a different-coloured lining. It would be the work of only seconds to change his outward appearance, to the potential confusion of any follower.

He walked along Bridge Street, and after strolling right around Parliament Square, he bought a ticket for a walking tour, joining a group of a dozen foreigners who had already gathered around the guide, a woman in her early thirties. Her world-weary, slightly pained expression suggested that of all the job opportunities a master's degree in history from Girton College, Cambridge, should have brought her, tour guide was not the first that came to mind.

She noticed the man at once as he joined the group. Most of her customers were families with children or older couples, and the vast majority were foreign: American, German, Japanese, Chinese, or a score of other nationalities. From the few words he had spoken when buying his ticket, his accent suggested he was English, and a man on his own, especially an English one, was a rarity on her tours. Also, he had no obvious tourist paraphernalia – no camera, guide book or Union flag carrier-bag, full of souvenirs. He was not the only unusual member of this particular party: there was also a group of three young men, foreign-looking, she thought, though she could not have done more than hazard a guess at their nationality. She thought that perhaps they were vaguely Middle Eastern or from one of the former Soviet republics with unpronounceable names, but whatever their origins, they were all serious, unsmiling and, she felt, slightly creepy. Like the other man, they did not attempt to engage with her and their slightly brooding presence had a noticeable effect on the others, who seemed inhibited by their silence and were much less vocal than she was used to.

However, no matter how silent and unsmiling its members might be, it was her job to lead the tour and explain the significance of the landmarks and buildings they would pass, so she began her standard housekeeping notices – 'Follow the orange and white umbrella. Watch out for pickpockets. Feel free to ask questions' – then launched into her introduction to the tour.

Their route took them the short distance to the Houses of Parliament, where they gathered around her for her usual 'Magna Carta and the Mother of Parliaments' mini-lecture, with a brief detour to take in Pugin and the Gothic Revival. She then led them along Whitehall, pausing near the steel gates manned by armed police guarding Downing Street while she explained the difference between a prime minister and a head of state, and fielded the inevitable questions about Winston Churchill and Margaret Thatcher, the only British prime ministers that 95 per cent of her audience could ever name.

As she walked along, she noticed that the lone man was ignoring her commentary and keeping well to the back of the group. He asked no questions, spoke not a word, didn't crack a smile at any of her jokes and appeared to be paying minimal attention to any of the historical sites and statues that she pointed out, though he seemed to take a much keener interest in the buildings flanking the streets they were passing along. They moved on as far as Admiralty Arch, turned back along Horse Guards Road, past Horse Guards Parade, the back of Downing Street and the elegant Portland-stone façade of the Foreign Office, then went along Birdcage Walk to Buckingham Palace. As she carried on with her spiel she saw, out of the corner of her eye, one of the three young men walk across to the man and, after a glance around, murmur something to him. The man silenced him with a ferocious look, turned his back and moved away from him. Clearly chastened, the other man returned to his two comrades and stayed well away from him throughout the rest of the tour.

Dispirited by her unenthusiastic audience, she cut short her usual closing speech about the role of the monarch and, after pausing to allow her group to take the traditional battery of photographs and selfies in front of the palace gates, she led them back down Buckingham Gate and past New Scotland Yard to their starting point. The man did not tip her at the end of the tour and, in fact, she wasn't even sure at what point he had left the group because he certainly wasn't with them when they had returned to Parliament Square. The three young men had also melted into the crowds thronging the square, without tipping her. She frowned as she picked over the modest assortment of coins and the one five-pound note that the rest of the tour group had donated. It didn't look as if she would be able to afford to take a year off to complete her doctorate any time soon. She gave a resigned shrug. It wasn't her job to ponder the motives of those who paid to join her tour, or wonder why so many were such stingy tippers. She glanced at her watch. If she was quick she'd have time for a coffee and a few minutes' rest before she set off again with the next group.

13

Charlotte Button checked in for her Delta flight to New York, using her Barbara Reynolds passport. She waited until she was in the Club Lounge with a glass of chilled Pinot Grigio in her hand before phoning Richard Yokely. 'Harper's in play,' she said. 'I'm on my way back.'

'Yes, I know,' said the American. 'How's the wine?'

'You've got someone here with me now?' She looked around the lounge. A dozen other travellers, mainly suited businessmen, were pecking away on laptops.

'I said I'd watch your back,' said Yokely. 'Your back is watched.'

'And?'

'Nothing so far. Clean as a whistle. Which means either you're not being followed, or you are and they're damn good at it. But my money's on the former.'

'It could just be that they only tail me in the UK, of course,' she said.

'We'll know soon enough,' said the American. 'Now, I have more intel on McGovan. Including an address in London. I'll put it in my dropbox and send you a link.'

'I'll forward it to Harper,' said Button. 'Just to confirm,

Richard, you're not going to have anyone following McGovan, are you?'

'Would that be a problem?'

'I'm afraid so. Harper can get a bit rough, I wouldn't want him crossing paths with your people.'

'My people are good, Charlotte.'

'Clearly. But in view of what you want done, I'd prefer that Harper was left with a clear field. And I'm sure he would, too, given the choice.'

'Message received and understood. I'll call off my dogs. Any news on your insurance?'

'I thought I'd fly back to the States and see how that looks. If I'm still in the clear I'll do a run to the UK and see what happens.'

'Interesting times,' said Yokely.

'Tell me about it,' said Button. She sipped her wine. 'I keep expecting to see you pop out in front of me.'

'Or maybe behind you . . .' said Yokely. He chuckled. 'Made you look, didn't I?'

Button laughed. He was right: she had taken a quick look over her shoulder.

14

The Gulfstream jet touched down at Bangkok's Don Mueang airport and taxied to the general aviation terminal to await the arrival of the immigration officers who would check the passports of those on board. Don Mueang was one of the world's oldest international airports but, since the opening of Suvarnabhumi, it had been rebranded as a regional commuter-flight hub and the airfield of choice for private planes. Half of the private jets using Don Mueang were Russian. Thailand was one of the few countries Russian citizens could visit without a visa and that, coupled with the fact that Russians could buy property and own bank accounts there, meant there was a constant stream of oligarchs flying in and out.

There was only one passenger on the plane: a heavy-set man with a shaved head and a nose that appeared to have been broken several times. His name was Yuri Lukin. He had a gun in an underarm holster and two metal suitcases containing a million dollars in cash. Two immigration officers arrived, did a perfunctory check of his passport and pocketed an envelope of money in exchange for not asking Lukin what the suitcases contained. If the immigration officers noticed the gun, they didn't mention it.

A black limousine and a white Toyota four-by-four had pulled up next to the jet as it had parked, but the passenger stayed in the limousine until the immigration officers had left. Mikhail Mirov climbed out of the vehicle as Lukin came down the steps. He was Lukin's money man in Thailand, a former KGB officer who had realised, as the former USSR fell apart, that there was more money to be made in crime than policing. He was a big man with steel grey hair wearing a pale blue safari suit with short sleeves. Lukin jerked a thumb at the door behind him. 'Two cases,' he said.

Two big men in T-shirts and baggy shorts had climbed out of the four-by-four. Mirov clicked his fingers and pointed at the plane, and as soon as Lukin had reached the tarmac they hurried up the steps. 'How is he?' asked Lukin, taking off his jacket. Sweat stains were already forming under his arms.

'Grigory is as well as can be expected, considering what was done to him,' said Mirov. He held the door open and Lukin climbed into the back of the limousine. Mirov closed the door, then hurried around to the other side of the car. He was already sweating, partly because of the forty-degree heat but mainly because his boss was angry, and when Yuri Lukin was angry people tended to get hurt, and worse.

The two men came down the steps with the cases and bundled them into the back of the four-by-four. 'Are they Valentin's men?' growled Lukin.

Mirov shook his head. 'They're mine. They'll go straight to the bank.'

The limousine drove away from the plane, heading for the exit. 'This hospital, it's good?' growled Lukin.

'World class,' said Mirov. 'As good as anything in Moscow.'

'If there's a better hospital, we move him there.'

'I think he's fine where he is.'

'And what about Valentin?'

'He's out of intensive care. But he was beaten up pretty badly.'

'He pays his own fucking hospital bill, make sure of that,' snapped Lukin. He snarled like a caged animal. 'How the fuck did this happen? Valentin was supposed to be taking care of my son. Fuck him. Why were there no bodyguards?'

'There were, but they were sleeping.'

Lukin's eyes blazed. 'Fucking sleeping? They were fucking sleeping?'

'It was late. Two in the morning. Valentin and Grigory were in the house. The gate was locked. The men assumed they were done for the night.'

'What sort of shit bodyguard assumes anything? They should sleep when their boss sleeps, and even then with one fucking eye open. These bodyguards, they are to be trusted?'

'Former Spetsnaz,' said Mirov. Russian special forces.

'Spetsnaz means fuck-all,' said Lukin. 'Any shithead can join Spetsnaz. They're not like the British SAS or the American Delta Force. If I find these bodyguards were involved, they're dead.'

'Understood,' said Mirov.

'Worse than fucking dead.' Lukin scowled. He wiped his hands over his face. 'Is it always this fucking hot here?'

'Pretty much,' said Mirov. He shouted at the driver to boost the air-conditioning.

Lukin pulled open the drinks cabinet. There were bottles

of Johnnie Walker Blue and vodka. He grabbed the vodka. Mirov reached for a glass but Lukin shook his head, untwisted the cap and drank from the bottle. 'He shoved a bottle up my son's arse,' spat Lukin. 'A fucking bottle up his arse. What sort of sick fuck does that?'

Mirov looked out of the window. There were times when it was best to say nothing.

15

Lukin looked down at his son and shook his head contemptuously. 'Who did this to you?' he snarled. Grigory's face was swollen and there was a plaster across his nose. His lips were puffy and cracked and several of his teeth were broken. His right arm was in plaster and his legs were suspended from a metal frame. He looked as if he had been hit by a train.

'Some fucking tourist,' replied Grigory, the damage to his mouth rendering his words almost unintelligible.

'This tourist followed you back to the villa and beat the crap out of you? For what?'

'I don't know. He tried to shake our hands in the bar. I told him to leave us alone. He was drunk.'

'So a drunk tourist you snubbed in a bar follows you home and does this? Does that make any sense to you? Because it doesn't to me.'

Grigory closed his eyes. 'He mentioned a girl.'

'What? Speak the fuck up. I can't hear you.'

'A girl. He talked about a girl.'

'What fucking girl? If you don't tell me what the fuck happened I swear to God I'll break your other arm.'

Grigory sighed. 'There was this girl. Valentin had some

fun with her. It got a bit rough. The tourist talked about her. Said I'd get a taste of my own medicine.'

'What did he mean by that? What did you do to the girl?'

'We had fun, that's all. Fucked her, got a bit rough with her. It was Valentin mainly. It's how he gets his kicks and he asked me to join in.'

'You and Valentin fucked a girl? Together?'

'I'd been drinking. And he'd had some coke. Good stuff.'

'So, drunk and doped up on coke you fucked a girl and beat her up.' He shook his head angrily. 'And you fucked her in the arse, did you?'

'No, why?'

'Don't fucking lie to me. You fucked her in the arse and that's why you had a bottle shoved up yours.'

Grigory closed his eyes. 'I'm sorry.'

'I bet you're fucking sorry but sorry doesn't fix this, does it? That tourist, he did this to you for revenge. And he did a fucking good job, too.'

'He had a gun. He could have shot me.'

'Might have been better if he had,' said Lukin. 'At least then you wouldn't look like such a fucking idiot.'

'He had a fucking gun,' repeated Grigory.

'Yes, a drunken tourist with a gun. What's wrong with that picture?'

'What do you mean?'

'Tourists don't carry guns, as a rule. Did he say what his name was?'

'Gerry. From Wales. He was drunk. He could hardly stand in the bar.'

'Well, he was sober enough to overpower the two of you.'

'He had a gun.'

'So you keep saying.' He shook his head. 'Have you any idea how stupid this makes me look? It says I can't protect my own family. If they can do it to you they can do it to me – that's the message it sends – and I'll tell you here and now that no one, fucking *no one*, is going to shove a bottle up my arse.'

He stormed out of the hospital – Mirov had to run to get to the limousine first and open the door for him. 'Take me to the villa,' snarled Lukin. 'I want to talk to those so-called bodyguards.'

16

Harper checked out of Le Meurice early the next morning and moved into accommodation that was considerably less grand: a dingy second-floor hotel room with peeling wallpaper and a damp-stained ceiling, rented from an Arab who was happy to be paid in crisp euro notes. The tenement building also housed a derelict bistro on the ground floor, its steel shutters buckled and blackened by fire. The surrounding quarter of Saint-Denis, about ten kilometres north of the centre of Paris, had also definitely seen better days. A few ageing Pieds-Noirs still lived in Saint-Denis, the dusty-footed last remnants of the expatriate French colonists who had run the North African territories then returned, like swarms of starlings flying in at dusk, to settle in Saint-Denis, part of a 'homeland' that many had not seen in three generations. It had not welcomed them with open arms. These days they were far outnumbered by the large North African immigrant population that had followed in their footsteps.

From his window Harper could see the Basilica of Saint-Denis across the rooftops. It had once been a place of pilgrimage, but few who visited it today cared to venture more than a few yards from the basilica for fear of what might befall them in the surrounding streets. The Saint-Denis area scored highly on every index of poverty and disadvantage. It had one of the highest crime rates in the country – fifteen recorded crimes for every hundred inhabitants – and one of the lowest detection rates by a police force widely seen as incompetent, corrupt and racist. As a result, Saint-Denis was regarded by most outsiders as a no-go area. It suited Harper perfectly. The narrow streets made it easy to detect strangers and conduct anti-surveillance drills, while its flourishing sex industry and thriving black market for all sorts of stolen goods made the locals very sensitive to a police presence. People kept themselves to themselves, asked no questions and gave no answers if questioned by anyone who smelled even slightly official.

He spent several hours crisscrossing the city on the Métro, visiting phone shops to buy throwaway mobiles and Sim cards, never more than two of each at one place. By midday he arrived back at his room with a half-dozen cheap handsets and a dozen Sim cards. He sat on the bed and over the next hour spoke to four people, all of whom agreed to drop everything to fly to Paris.

First on his list was the man they called Barry Whisper – a slight, softly spoken figure who also answered to 'Bravo Whisky'. He had been a 14 Int operative during the later years of 'The Troubles' in Northern Ireland and had also plied his specialised trade with the American intelligence agencies for a couple of years. A trained linguist, he spoke fluent Arabic, German, French, Russian, passable Farsi and Pushto as well. An insular, spiky character, he lived alone between jobs on a remote smallholding on the North Yorkshire moors, tending his pigs, goats and the few crops that would grow on his bleak, rainwashed land.

The second call was to another Barry. Barry Big was also from Yorkshire but was Barry Whisper's polar opposite in almost every other way. A loud, hulking figure, he had been a member of the Special Reconnaissance Regiment, based in Hereford and used by the SAS for intelligence gathering and surveillance of potential targets. He now lived in the Dominican Republic because he'd met and fallen in love with a Dominican beauty of half his age. He'd bought a beach bar, and the thought of her there surrounded by amorous customers while he was away for weeks on end drove him mad with jealousy, but he loved his intelligence-gathering work so much that he could never refuse the offer of another job for Harper.

Third on the list was technical and electronics genius Hansfree. In the black humour of the armed forces, he had earned himself his nickname after losing both of his own hands in Bosnia when an IED he had been examining was remotely detonated. He was an intense character in his mid-thirties, always dressed in black, like his hero, Johnny Cash, and wore black leather gloves over his prosthetic hands. He had shown a ferocious determination in rebuilding his life, developing an expertise in electronics that would have made him a fortune in Civvy Street, but Hansfree had loved the military too much to be entirely comfortable working with civilians or corporate career structures. Instead he made a good living working on the margins of society, often for Harper.

Last but not least, Maggie May was a pale, dark-eyed brunette in her thirties. She was a surveillance professional whose career at MI5 had been curtailed after an ill-advised affair with her departmental boss. It had proved to be ill-advised because, in a story as old as civilisation, she had become pregnant whereupon her knight in shining armour had made it very clear that their relationship, 'just a bit of fun between two consenting adults', didn't extend to him taking any responsibility for the child, if she chose to keep it. She did so, and he had her transferred to a dead-end job in a different department. Maggie had taken maternity leave, and when the time came for her to return to work, she quit her job. A single parent, she looked after her son with the aid of her parents, who had no idea of her real work: they thought she worked for a travel agency because she frequently travelled overseas.

All four were pleased to hear from him and all agreed to drop everything to fly to Paris. The fact that he was offering them each a hundred-thousand-dollar signing-on fee was an incentive but Harper knew they weren't just doing it for the money. All four lived for their work and the adrenalin rush that came with the jobs he provided. Life in Lex Harper's orbit was complicated and often dangerous, but it was never boring.

17

'You understand what a bodyguard's job is, don't you?' growled Lukin. 'The clue is in the fucking job description. Body. Guard. You guard the fucking body. You protect it. If necessary you stand between the body and a bullet. Is that so fucking hard to understand?'

The three men standing in front of Lukin were all staring at the floor. They were big men, broad-shouldered, with hands the size of shovels, each a good six inches taller than their boss, but all three were trembling. Lukin was holding a gun and it was clear from the look in his eyes that he was gearing up to using it. They were in Valentin's villa. The maids had cleared up so there was no evidence of what had happened, except for a small area of darkened wood that Lukin suspected was a bloodstain. His son's blood.

'Call yourself Spetsnaz. Special fucking forces? Well, there's nothing special about you.' He waved at the bodyguard on the right. 'You, you big prick. Why the fuck weren't you in the house with my son?'

'They told us we weren't needed,' said the man. His hair was close-cropped, revealing a thick rope-like scar above his right ear.

'What's your name, Shit-for-brains?'

'Peter,' mumbled the man.

'I don't need to know your first name, you fucking prick. I'm not asking you out on a fucking date. Your surname.'

'Volkov.'

'Why was my son unprotected in the bar?'

'There is security in the bar. And they offered to escort Valentin home but he wanted to drive your son. We were waiting for him when he arrived and they were alone. They drove in and said we could stand down.'

'And if Valentin had told you to jump off a fucking cliff, you'd have done that, would you?'

Volkov looked at the floor.

'You, in the middle. Your name?'

'Zharkov,' said the man. He was the shortest of the three but was still well over six feet tall. He was wearing a tight-fitting black T-shirt that showed off over-muscular arms, which suggested steroid use rather than hours in the gym.

'Can you explain how a man gets into the villa without anyone seeing or hearing him?'

Zharkov shrugged but didn't reply.

'He cuts the wire, gets over the wall and no one sees a thing. Is that what happened?'

'There is no CCTV at the back of the house,' said Zharkov.

'And why the fuck not?'

'The CCTV is to check on the vehicles.'

'And whose idea was it not to have CCTV covering the whole wall?'

Zharkov looked at the man to his right. 'Myshkin is head of security,' he mumbled.

'Fuck you,' said Myshkin. His jet black hair was tied back in a short ponytail and he had several days' stubble on his massive chin. 'I organise the rota, that's all.'

'Why is there no CCTV at the back?' pressed Lukin.

'It's not our system,' said Myshkin. 'It was installed when Valentin bought the villa.'

'And why no dogs? Dogs would have spotted the intruder.'

'Valentin doesn't like dogs.'

'Valentin doesn't like dogs or CCTV but he has my son sleeping with the Three Stooges as bodyguards. For fuck's sake.' He shook his head angrily. 'Right. This is what's going to happen,' he said. 'I need two of you fuckwits to help me get the bastard who attacked my son. Only two of you. That means one of you is surplus to requirements. You can decide among yourselves who that one is. Two of you work with me, one of you goes to hospital. And I don't give a fuck which is which.' He sat down and gestured with the gun. 'Get on with it. I don't have all day.'

Myshkin looked across at Volkov and nodded.

Volkov stared back at him impassively.

Zharkov looked at Volkov, then back at Myshkin. 'You were in charge,' said Zharkov, his massive hands bunching into fists.

'Like fuck I was,' snarled Myshkin.

'You said you were the boss,' said Volkov, sullenly.

Myshkin glared at him. 'And I fucking well am, so I'm telling you it's me and you against him.' He nodded at Volkov. 'Okay? You and me, we stand together. Zharkov's always been shit to you.'

Zharkov stepped back and put up his fists. 'You think you can take me, fucker?'

Myshkin nodded earnestly at Volkov. 'Come on, you and me. Zharkov has always hated you. And he fucked that girl you like in Lone Star.'

Volkov glared at Zharkov, who shook his head. 'He's lying.'

'Did you fuck her?'

'What if I did? She's a hooker. I paid her. It's not as if she was fucking me for free.'

Myshkin's fist lashed out and caught Zharkov under the chin. He staggered back and Myshkin followed through with two piston-like jabs to the man's chest, just below the heart. Zharkov's hands went up to defend himself but he was in pain and didn't see the kick until it was too late. Myshkin's foot caught the side of his knee and Zharkov howled as the cartilage snapped, like a dry twig. He fell to the ground, clutching his injured leg and moaning.

Myshkin stepped back, hands up, and stared at Volkov. 'Your call. I'm easy either way. But it won't be me going to hospital.'

Volkov breathed in, grimaced, then turned and kicked Zharkov in the ribs. Hard. Myshkin joined in and for the next thirty seconds the two men kicked and stamped on Zharkov until his arms and legs were broken and his face was a bloody pulp. Eventually they stepped back. Zharkov was face down, unconscious, breathing slowly and heavily.

Lukin waved his gun at the body. 'Take that piece of shit to the hospital,' he said to Mirov. 'Not the one my son's in. Now, you two fuckers need to work hard to get back on my right side or you'll be joining that piece of shit in intensive care. And your first order of business is to find that fucking tourist and bring him to me.'

18

D r Chanika's clicking high heels echoed off the walls as she headed towards her car, a two-seater BMW Z4 that was her pride and joy. She was tired and looking forward to getting home for a long soak in the bath and a bottle of wine. Her shift was supposed to have ended at six but a woman who had swallowed a bottle of weedkiller, after discovering that her husband was preparing to leave her for his girlfriend, had been brought in. That had been five days earlier. The woman had expected to die immediately but weedkiller didn't work like that. Apart from a little nausea she had been fine, for a few days at least, but behind the scenes the poison was systematically destroying her liver and poisonous toxins were building up in her blood. Now it was too late and, barring a liver transplant, she would be dead within the week. All Dr Chanika could do was to try to minimise her pain, and that was easier said than done. Dr Chanika wasn't looking forward to the next few days and she knew she'd need the bath and the wine to stand any chance of getting to sleep that night.

Headlights on full beam almost blinded her. She froze. The car was directly ahead of her. She shielded her eyes with her hand and shuffled to the side.

As she blinked, she realised that a figure was standing between the lights. A man. A big man.

'Dr Chanika?' said the man.

'Yes?' she said hesitantly. 'Who are you?' He wasn't Thai, she was sure of that. He was far too big and his accent was foreign. Russian, maybe.

'I need to talk to you about one of your patients. Miss Pear. She's in intensive care.'

'I'm sorry, are you a relative?' Her eyes were watering in the light's intensity.

'No, I'm just a concerned citizen,' said the man. 'I need to know the name of the man who came to see her. I understand he's paying Miss Pear's bill.'

'I'm sorry, I really can't help you,' she said, turning towards her car. 'You can call the main office tomorrow.'

A large figure appeared to her right, blocking her way. She turned to her left but another man stood there, even bigger than the first. The blinding light meant she couldn't see their faces.

'I need the name, Dr Chanika.'

'I'll call security,' she said. 'Or the police.' She fumbled for her phone in her handbag.

'You could do that, but by the time they get here you'll be in a pool of blood and we'll be long gone. And even if they get here quickly, we'll be back in a day or two. Maybe we'll follow you home. Have you got kids, Dr Chanika? Or a family? Parents? Do you want to be responsible for them being hurt?'

Dr Chanika stopped reaching for her phone. Tears were stinging her eyes.

'I just want a name,' said the man. 'Then we'll leave you in peace. Just a name.'

She wiped away her tears with the back of her hand. 'You can't do this to me,' she whispered.

'Yes, I can,' said the man. 'I can do what the fuck I want. Now stop fucking around and give me the name.'

Dr Chanika felt the strength go from her legs and staggered back, leaning against her car to stop herself falling. She could barely breathe – it was as if there was a steel band around her chest. 'Lex Harper,' she said. 'His name is Lex Harper.'

19

All four of the people Harper had called were in Paris within twenty-four hours, and one by one they sent him a text to confirm their arrival. The last was from Barry Big, who had flown from the Dominican Republic – he had left for the airport within minutes of Harper phoning him. When he had heard from them all, Harper locked the flimsy door of his room, went down the stairs and out through an entrance lobby that was festooned with cobwebs and carpeted with wind-blown rubbish.

He was carrying an envelope containing a dozen or so sheets of photographs and intel that Charlie Button had left for him in the drafts folder. He had collected it from an internet café a short walk from his room on the way to an early breakfast of croissants and coffee. He walked slowly through the streets, carrying out his usual anti-surveillance drills. Once he was certain he was not being observed or followed, he entered a side-street café. He nodded to the Lebanese owner, who had received a cash sum equivalent to the whole of his normal day's takings in return for the use of a private room on the fourth floor of the building, then climbed the stairs.

His team were already there, sitting around a table

drinking mint tea or the café's fearsomely sweet and strong coffee. Barry Big grinned when Harper walked into the room. 'Hey, hey, the gang's all here,' he said, standing up and hugging Harper.

Hansfree was next in line for a hug. His prosthetics were steel claws with rubber bumpers for added grip, and Harper felt them press between his shoulder blades as Hansfree hugged him. He had driven to Saint-Denis in his specially adapted van, using the cross-Channel ferry service. The van allowed him to be independent and he could live in it, if necessary.

Maggie May was next, and kissed him lightly on both cheeks. He caught the scent of her perfume, Dior's Poison, a fragrance that never failed to remind him of her.

Finally Barry Whisper gave him a minimalist hug and a whispered comment close to his right ear that Harper missed. He smiled and took his seat at the table.

'Thanks for coming,' he said. He looked at the machine sitting in front of Hansfree at the centre of the table. It was about the size of an iPhone with a small telescopic aerial sticking out of the top. Several coloured lights on it flashed intermittently, and it emitted the occasional high-pitched bleep. 'What the fuck's that?' he asked.

'Bug detector. State-of-the-art.'

'Looks like something left over from an early *Doctor Who* episode. You sure it works?'

'Absolutely positive,' Hansfree said. 'Looks aren't every-thing, Lex, as you should know better than anyone. It's performance that counts. I picked it up from a very good friend of mine in London and he assures me it's absolutely foolproof. And if my mate says it works then, believe me, it works. It bloody well should do – it cost enough.'

'So we're in good hands,' Harper said. 'Or not in your case.' He winked at Hansfree, who responded with a gesture that, even with a prosthetic hand, was an unmistakable two-finger salute.

Harper began briefing the team on their task. 'The target is a former Para and SAS trooper called Caleb McGovan,' he said. He opened the envelope and took out three photographs of the man. Two were surveillance pictures and one had clearly been taken from his army file. 'From now on McGovan is Tango One. Anyone he meets whom we do not know will automatically become a Yankee. We'll refer to Tangos when they're positively ID'd, and use Yankees for people we've not yet identified. To go back to McGovan, although he's ex-special forces, that doesn't mean he can walk on water. I've checked with people who served with him and he's a good all-round steady guy but you can rest assured that he's no James Bond.' He gave the last few words the full Sean Connery treatment and was rewarded with a few smiles from his team. 'He's special forces but not a spook, so we're dealing with a specialised skill set. We'll have untraceable pay-as-you-go phones, which are to be used only to communicate with other team members during the surveillance phase.' He grinned at Billy Big. 'So no phoning girlfriends on my tab.'

'The thought never occurred to me,' said Barry Big.

'Just to summarise where we are with the task,' said Harper. 'On the positive side we have a one hundred per cent solid ID of Tango One. We also know where he's living. He's based himself in a military club just on the north side of London's Oxford Street. Tango One does not have a private car, but he obviously does have access to the full range of London transport. He is staying within yards of several bus stops, a couple of hundred yards of a tube station and a short walk from Paddington main-line station. There are also black cabs galore in that area, so he can go mobile with minimal advance warning at any time. So, we know the subject's age, sex, location, modes of transport and some of his habits. On the negative side, we don't know as yet the identity of his associates. And we're going to need an ops room somewhere to coordinate everything.'

'I might have somewhere close by,' said Hansfree. 'Let me check.'

Harper nodded. 'Barry Big will be team medic, Maggie will take charge of the admin for the op, setting out working hours, reliefs and downtime, and Hansfree will issue the radios, body sets, batteries and the frequencies. As usual, you'll be on generous expenses with no receipts required, and your fees at the end of the op will be paid cash in hand or into any bank account, anywhere in the world. Anything else, anyone?'

Maggie spoke up: 'I'd say that any pick-up of the subject shouldn't be too difficult, bearing in mind where he's living. There are masses of bits of street furniture, cafés and shops we can use as cover. The follow shouldn't present too many difficulties, providing he sticks to central London where there are always going to be crowds of people about to give us cover. The major problem is going to be housing any Yankees, the unidentified suspects we may move on to. If they're in an area they're not too familiar with, they're usually pretty easy game, but when they get close to home, in an area they know like the back of their hand, then it can be really difficult.'

Barry Whisper had been looking thoughtful for some time and now raised his voice. 'One thing's puzzling me about all this. Exactly what do you think Tango One is planning?'

'I wish I knew,' Harper said. 'And don't think the same thing hasn't been bugging me. He's made a couple of visits to Turkey, landing at Dalaman airport, which is one of the main tourist gateways. We presume he travelled on from there overland and eventually made a covert crossing of the border between Turkey and Syria, but on each occasion, allowing for the time taken to travel there, he's spent just a handful of days inside Syria. So he can't have been training ISIS soldiers while he was there. He simply wasn't in country long enough to be able to impart any useful training, and he can't have been fighting for them because once more, he wasn't there long enough.'

Barry Big cleared his throat. 'So he was either delivering something to them or collecting something from them.'

'Which can only have been money, information, weapons or men,' Maggie added.

'Well, it can't have been weapons or manpower,' Hansfree said, 'because from what you've told us, Lex, he was travelling solo on his way in and out, and probably crossed the border on foot. That leaves money or information.'

'Either is possible,' Harper said, 'but Tango One doesn't have any source of funds, as far as we know, and certainly none substantial enough to justify the risks he's apparently been taking.'

'And why would ISIS divert funds from the campaign they're waging in Syria and Iraq anyway,' Barry Big said, 'just to fund some freelance adventure by a renegade SAS man?'

'They would if he was planning something that would further their own aims as well,' Barry Whisper said. 'But it would have to be big, obviously. A spectacular.'

'I'm with Barry Whisper there,' said Harper. 'But, hopefully, our surveillance will answer that question. OK, we're good to go. Make your own way to London, fix yourselves up with accommodation, and we'll get down to business the day after tomorrow.'

He shook hands with each of them, including Hansfree, then kept watch from the window as they filed out one by one, leaving at five-minute intervals. Only when he was satisfied that they had not been observed did he leave the building himself.

He entered the hallway of his flea-bitten hotel and encountered a prostitute servicing her client in the litter-strewn alcove beneath the stairs. He checked out, strolled back through the streets to the station next to the Basilica of Saint-Denis and caught the Métro to the Gare du Nord. Just over three hours later he was stepping onto the platform at St Pancras station.

20

It was a large apartment, three bedrooms and a huge sitting room with a terrace that overlooked the bay. Mirov was on the terrace, smoking a cigarette. It was early morning but tourists were parascending, towed behind fast-moving speedboats. On the thin strip of beach below, groups of Chinese holidaymakers gathered to be taken on the fifteen-minute trip to the beaches of Koh Larn.

'He's a fucking ghost, this Harper,' said Volkov.

'What do you mean?' asked Mirov. Volkov had kicked down the door to Harper's apartment, then he and Myshkin had spent the past fifteen minutes tearing it apart.

'No paperwork, no photographs, a few bills but other than that there's nothing.' He waved at a bookcase against one wall. 'There's nothing personal. No family photographs, no pictures of him with a drugged-up tiger or friends in a bar. It's as if this was a hotel room.'

'What about his computer?'

'There isn't one.'

'He took it with him?'

'I don't think he has one. There's no printer. No wiring. No desk. If it wasn't for the clothes, you'd think no one lived here.'

'Who the fuck doesn't have a computer these days?'

Volkov didn't answer.

'Okay, we need a phone number for the man, then pay whoever we have to pay to get a list of his calls and texts.' He flicked the remains of his cigarette over the side of the terrace. 'Do you think he's done a runner?'

'I think he's just careful,' said Volkov. 'Whoever this fucker is, he isn't a tourist.'

Mirov walked back into the sitting room and through to the master bedroom. The sheets had been ripped off the king-sized bed and most of the drawers had been pulled out and overturned. Volkov and Myshkin had been thorough and Mirov was certain they had missed nothing. He unzipped his fly and pissed over the bed, playing the stream of urine back and forth as he cursed Lex Harper and the bitch that had given birth to him.

21

Harper checked himself into a small hotel in Bayswater, a short walk from Queensway tube station. An African on the desk was bent over an English language textbook. He flashed Harper a beaming smile and said there was absolutely no problem with him paying in cash – in fact, the owner preferred it. Harper went up a cramped flight of stairs to his room, which was at the rear of the building. There was a single bed, a dressing table next to a sash window, which was smeared with pigeon droppings, and a bathroom the size of a wardrobe with a tiny shower cubicle, a half-size washbasin and a toilet that wasn't much bigger than a bucket. 'Home, sweet home,' muttered Harper, but it was exactly what he wanted: a bolthole that would allow him to stay off the grid. He headed out and spent the next couple of hours having a late lunch. He took the Tube far out into London's dismal industrial hinterland where he walked through a maze of side streets to a panel-beater and accident-repair workshop occupying one of the smoke-blackened brick arches beneath a railway line. It was well into the evening by now, but yellow light still spilled from the half-open door and Capital Radio was playing on a tinny transistor. Harper swung the door open and winked at the balding, middle-aged mechanic swigging from a bottle of beer as he sat in an old leather car seat propped against the wall.

'Bugger me,' the man said. 'Now I do believe in ghosts.'

'It's not been that long, Wheels,' Harper said. 'Eighteen months at most.'

'If you say so, Lex, if you say so,' Tom Wheeler said, 'though I'd have sworn it was longer than that. You need a car?' Tom 'Wheels' Wheeler was a first-class mechanic, who had a sideline in renting out cars to people who were reluctant to use Avis or Hertz. Unlike the major companies, Wheels didn't require his clients to produce a driving licence or a credit card: an envelope full of cash would do just fine.

'What have you got?'

'I've got a brand spanking new Porsche Cayenne, if you fancy something flash,' said Wheeler.

'When have I ever wanted something flash?'

'I've got a ten-year-old Nissan that looks like shit but will do the ton in less than five seconds.'

Harper wrinkled his nose. 'Speed won't be an issue. Comfort's more important – I might be behind the wheel for quite a while.'

'Range Rover?'

'I don't want to be filling the tank every couple of hours, mate.'

Wheeler took another pull on his beer, then grinned. 'I know – I've got a BMW Five Series. She's got a fair number of miles on the clock but she's reliable.'

'Ready to go?'

'Got the money?'

Harper took out a brown envelope and tossed it at Wheeler, who stood up, slid it into the pocket of his overalls without opening it, selected a bunch of keys from the sets hanging on a row of hooks by the door and headed out of the workshop. They crossed the scrap-infested wasteland beyond it to a row of concrete lock-up garages at the back of a block of crumbling flats. Wheeler checked the heavy padlock on the steel shutters of a garage, looking for any scratches or other signs that would show it had been tampered with or picked, then unlocked it and raised the shutters. The BMW was dusty but rust-free, and Harper didn't have to lift the bonnet to know that the engine would be in perfect order.

'Paperwork's in the glovebox,' said Wheeler, tossing him the keys. 'Oh, and there's a neat little secret compartment in the passenger footwell. The previous owner used to bring stuff in from the Continent.'

'Stuff?'

'Not drugs, mate. Guns and ammo from the former Yugoslavia. He was never caught so the plate's clean. Just thought you might be able to make use of it.'

Harper climbed in and pulled on a pair of driving gloves. The interior was clean enough but not too clean, and he didn't want to add any of his prints to the ones that were already there. The engine started first time and he nodded his approval.

'Told you,' said Wheeler. 'As reliable as clockwork.'

Harper flashed him a thumbs-up and drove slowly out of the lock-up, then headed north, away from London.

22

It was eight o'clock in the evening when Harper pulled off the M6 into a service station to the west of Manchester. He flashed his lights as he saw a car cruising around on the far side of the car park. By the time he had driven across, Jony Hasan's silver BMW was already parked in a poorly lit area, well away from the service-station entrance. Harper pulled up next to him.

'Now that's more like it,' Jony said, as Harper got into the car. 'It makes a nice change from those crap motors you're usually driving. You can't go wrong with a Beamer.'

Harper smiled. 'Did you get me the short?'

'Does the pope shit in the woods? Of course I did. Have I ever failed you?' British-born to parents of Bangladeshi origin, Jony was a wheeler-dealer, who operated on the margins of Manchester's sizeable criminal fraternity and, providing the price was right, could supply untraceable weapons. In some ways he was as dodgy as they came, but Harper knew he could trust him absolutely never to grass him up, no matter who was asking the questions, and never to let him down.

The two men climbed out of their vehicles and Jony handed him a Tupperware container. He pulled a packet of cigarettes from the pocket of his black leather jacket and lit one. 'You're usually after something a bit more heavy-duty than a short,' he said, blowing a smoke-ring towards the clouds overhead.

'I'm hoping I won't need to use it,' Harper said. 'It's purely a precaution – in any case, carrying something bigger than this around in Britain is too much of a risk. And you can guarantee it's never been fired, can you, or not in this country at least?'

'One hundred per cent certain,' Jony said. 'Do you want to see its birth certificate?'

Harper opened the container. Inside there was a pistol, with fifty rounds of ammunition in a Ziploc bag.

'Smith & Wesson SD9 VE,' Jony said. 'Nine mil, capacity sixteen rounds plus one up the spout, four-inch barrel, twenty-two-ounce weight. It'd cost you about three hundred and fifty dollars in the States but . . .' He grinned.

'I know, I know,' Harper said wearily. 'We're not in the States. So what's the SP on it in an M6 car park?' As he was speaking, he took the pistol out of the box, checked the action and sighted down it.

Jony pretended to think about it. 'I couldn't let it go for less than seven hundred and fifty.'

'Dollars?'

'Pounds.'

'Bloody hell, Jony! There's supposed to be a recession on. You must be the only retailer in Britain who keeps putting his prices up.'

'What can I say, bruv? It's just the laws of supply and demand at work,' Jony said, grinning.

'Well, in that case I can supply you with six hundred

and you're not getting any more than that,' said Harper.

'All right, then,' Jony said, with a show of resignation, 'but only because it's you.'

'Damn,' Harper said. 'You never agree that quick. I should have knocked you down another hundred.'

'Too late now, bruv,' Jonny said, with a huge grin. 'A deal's a deal, right?'

Harper put the Tupperware container on the front passenger seat, peeled the money off a wad of notes and handed it over. 'Thanks, Jony. Take care and watch out for the jealous husbands.'

'Those days are behind me now, bruv,' Jony said, as he started his engine. 'I'm strictly a one-girl guy now . . . well, one girl at a time.'

Harper watched him drive off, then got back into his own car. He slipped the Tupperware box under the seat and set off back down the motorway towards London. He pulled off at the first interchange, found a deserted lay-by at the side of the road and, after looking around and listening carefully, he peeled back the carpet in the passenger foot-well. He took a knife from his pocket and eased up the lid of a concealed compartment, so artfully hidden that only a very keen eye would have detected it. He put the pistol and the ammunition inside it, then replaced the carpet and drove back towards the motorway, heading south. While he didn't want his team carrying weapons in London, his personal safety was a different matter altogether.

23

Even with near-deserted roads in the dead hours of the night, Harper wasn't back in London until five in the morning, but he had the luxury of a lie-in until ten. He was woken by a call from Hansfree, who said he had something to show him. He arranged to meet him in a café close to the military club where McGovan was staying.

An hour later Harper sat down opposite Hansfree and nibbled a croissant as the technical wizard outlined his plan. 'I've stayed at the club a few times over the years,' said Hansfree, 'so I know the lay-out there reasonably well. I'm sure I'll be able to access his room easily enough because the security there is of the old-fashioned kind, that is to say virtually non-existent, and so are the locks. They still use physical keys rather than key cards, not that those are too much of an obstacle either, if you know what you're doing. So, I can install a camera in his room for you. I'll replace the LED stand-by light in his TV with a combined camera and microphone that will transmit through the club's communal aerial on the roof. That will give you coverage of any calls he makes or receives in his room as well as alerting you when he's getting ready to move, and will help to identify any visitors.'

'Sounds like a plan,' said Harper.

'I'm going to see about us using drones, too.'

'Seriously? Drones in London?'

'I've got access to some state-of-the-art kit,' said Hansfree. 'I wanted to check what was available before raising it with you.' He sipped his coffee. A woman at a neighbouring table stared at his claw, open-mouthed. Hansfree smiled at her and she looked away, embarrassed. 'The latest models have much longer operating times by building on solar power, and the camera resolution is improving every month. They have on-board high-resolution viewing devices and everything is gyroscopically controlled so we don't get any shiver or jumping. They can be launched from pretty much anywhere, and our radios can have automatic seeker devices installed, which the drones will find without guidance. If the subject leaves the London area, they can be carried by vehicle, launched from any piece of waste ground and monitored on any tablet. Everything they photograph is automatically recorded on-board and relayed back to the ops room for evidence purposes.'

'That's all very well in theory,' Harper said, 'but what about the cops? Won't a drone buzzing round over central London cause a few heart failures and trigger a full scale-terror alert?'

Hansfree shook his head. 'We're not talking missile-armed Reaper or Predator drones here. The ones I have access to are so tiny and quiet you wouldn't hear them above the birdsong in the countryside, let alone the traffic in a busy London street. And if anyone does happen to catch sight of one, they're likely to assume it's just some spoilt rich kid – God knows there's no shortage of those around here – playing with the latest toy.'

'What about radios?' asked Harper.

'Assuming money isn't a problem, I can supply you with the latest body-fit radios available, frequency hopping and automatically encoding, of course, and they work using redundant Home Office emergency services frequencies, which are off-limits to everybody else. They give literally countrywide coverage, just as you would expect from emergency services frequencies. None of this will stop you using your own codes, but belt and braces is best, I always think.'

'You needn't have any worries on that score,' Harper said. 'I've been told that money is no object on this one. I'll pay whatever's necessary for the kit we need.'

'Sounds good,' said Hansfree. 'I'll be right onto it.'

'How soon can you install the bug and get the rest of the kit together?'

'The equipment is no problem. I'll have it ready by tomorrow. Installing the bug depends on your subject's routine. It'll take just a few minutes to set it up. The problem is, we'll need more manpower. The two Barrys and Maggie are going to be full-time on watching Tango One and I'm going to need people to help me. Are you okay with me bringing in extra manpower?'

'Providing you trust them one thousand per cent, and providing they're not aware of the big picture, sure,' said Harper. 'Just let me know what you need in the way of money.'

'And I think I've got an ops room sorted,' said Hansfree. 'Not far from here.'

Harper finished his coffee and followed Hansfree outside.

Hansfree took him around the corner and along to a newsagent and off-licence. An elderly Sikh wearing a blue turban was standing behind the counter. 'Okay to go up, Mr Singh?' asked Hansfree.

Singh waved a hand at the stairs at the rear of the shop. 'It hasn't been cleaned in a while.'

'I'll take care of that,' said Hansfree.

Hansfree took Harper up the narrow flight of stairs, made even narrower by the stacks of beer cans crammed against the wall. 'Bit of a health-and-safety issue, but Mr Singh can be trusted, providing he gets paid enough,' said Hansfree. 'I've used this place before.'

There was a metal door at the top of the stairs and a large hasp but no padlock. Hansfree pushed the door open. The room was windowless, or if there had ever been a window, it was now bricked up. Hansfree flicked a switch and two fluorescent tubes flickered into life. There were more stacks of beer along one wall and cardboard boxes full of other stock, but the room was certainly large enough.

'Security won't be a problem because I'll get a camp bed brought in and be here twenty-four/seven, pretty much,' said Hansfree.

'And you're sure about Singh?'

'I've known him for years,' said Hansfree.

Harper nodded. 'Go for it,' he said. 'Tell the rest of the team we now have an ops room.'

Harper left Hansfree rearranging the stock and went back to Bayswater. He dropped into an internet café and left Charlie a short message in the Yahoo draft email file: *Up and running.*

24

Charlotte Button landed at Heathrow Airport using her own name and her genuine British passport. She'd flown business class overnight and had managed to get some half-decent sleep. She had breakfast airside and caught a late-morning flight to Glasgow. She had never been to the city when it hadn't been either raining or threatening rain and, true to form, the sky was grey and overcast as she walked out of the airport. She climbed into the back of a taxi and asked to be dropped at Queen Street railway station.

She had only just got out of the cab when her phone rang. The caller was withholding his number but she answered. 'You have a tail and not in a cat-like way,' said a southern American drawl.

Button cursed.

'Why, Charlotte, that's so unlike you,' said Yokely.

'You're sure?' she asked, and immediately regretted it. Richard Yokely was a professional and if he said she was being followed there was no doubt.

'You were clear at JFK and there was no one on the plane, but they picked you up at Heathrow. Airside.'

'Airside?' repeated Button. The fact that her followers

were able to move so easily through airport security suggested they were government-sanctioned.

'They went with you through Immigration and had three cars on your taxi. They're watching you now, Charlotte.'

'How many?'

'Four on foot that my people can see. Plus the three vehicles. This operation is seriously manpower-intensive. Money no object.'

'I'm glad you're watching over me, Richard.'

'I am, but I'm not sure there's anything I can do if they decide to take you.'

'I think they're just looking at me at the moment,' she said. 'If they were going to hurt or snatch me they'd have done it already.'

'Well, I do hope your third insurance policy isn't in Glasgow,' said Yokely.

'It isn't,' said Button. 'And now I know how desperate they are, I won't be going anywhere near it.'

'My offer is still open,' said Yokely. 'Let me know where it is and I'll collect it. I'd take good care of it.'

'I'm sure you would, Richard, but I need to handle this myself.' She ended the call, flagged down a passing cab and asked to be taken back to the airport.

25

Harper and the rest of the team fell quickly into operational mode. Early every morning they took up their positions around the club. Harper had purchased a second-hand Yamaha trail bike for cash and parked it in a bay around the corner from the entrance. They spent the day rotating their positions between the many coffee shops and snack bars in the area, while Hansfree monitored the images being transmitted from McGovan's room. Harper and his team used the ABC system, with A immediately behind the subject, B behind him on the same side of the street and C keeping pace with A, but on the opposite side of the street. Every time the subject approached a corner, C would move up almost level with him, so C could look down the side street and alert the other team members if the subject stopped, or made a U-turn back towards his close followers, or disappeared down an alley or into a shop. They rotated at irregular intervals, too, so the same person was never close behind the subject for long enough to be noticed by him, with B replacing A as lead, C and A swapping places.

McGovan was an easy target to follow, and on the few occasions he left the club, he didn't seem to employ anything in the way of counter-surveillance. Over two days he did nothing more than walk to local cafés and browse in second-hand bookshops. In the afternoons he would emerge from the club in shorts and a shirt and spend an hour jogging around Hyde Park.

Each morning at six the team would start the day with a briefing in the ops room. Not that there was much to be briefed about.

Maggie was running through the previous day's non-events when Harper's Thai phone rang. He took it out of his hip-pack. The number wasn't recognised but that was probably because he was overseas. He accepted the call. 'Lex, where the fuck are you?'

Harper recognised the East End accent immediately. Mickey Moore, East End boy made bad, an old-school villain who had made Pattaya his home along with his brother Mark and the rest of his crew of armed robbers. They funded their hedonistic Thai lifestyle by flying back to the UK on a regular basis to carry out major robberies, usually involving firearms and at least the threat of violence. 'Mickey, how's things? I'm out of the country at the moment, back in a week or so.' He walked out of the room to get some privacy on the stairs.

'Yeah, well, that might be the best place for you, mate,' said Moore. 'Now where the fuck are you?'

'Ducking and diving, mate. What's the problem?' He sat down and leaned against a case of cheap cider.

'You heard of a Russian called Lukin? Yuri Lukin?'

'No, should I?'

'He's Russian Mafia, Lex. Hard as nails. And he's pissed off at you, big time.'

'I don't know anyone called Lukin.'

'Apparently you shoved a bottle up his son's arse? Does that ring a bell?'

'Ah. That would have been me, yes.'

'Fuck me, Lex, you don't half pick them. You don't know who this Lukin is, then?'

'I'm guessing you're going to tell me.'

'Fucking former KGB, that's what. Soviet empire fell apart and it was every man for himself. Some went the economic route to make their fortunes, some went Darth Vader. I don't have to tell you which way Lukin went. Word is he grabbed a stack of KGB files and used it to extort and blackmail his way to the top of the Moscow crime tree.'

'So what the fuck's his son doing in Pattaya?'

'Grigory's got a thing for Thai birds and he persuaded his dad to let him set up a money-laundering operation here. They fly in money and wash it through bars and restaurants, all cash businesses. Millions a month, by all accounts. Grigory flies back and forth in a private jet full of cash. Except he's not flying anywhere at the moment. I mean, mate, a bottle up the arse, what the fuck was that about?'

'He did the same to a friend of mine. Damn near killed her. Sauce for the goose . . .'

'You always were the white knight, mate. But I've got to say, Lukin is one dragon you don't want to be fucking with.'

'Does he know who I am?'

'Your name? Yeah. A couple of Russian heavies were around at Ricky's bar, asking for you. And the word on the street is they're offering money to anyone who tells them where the fuck you are. Where the fuck are you, anyway?'

'Ha fucking ha. You looking for the reward money?'

'Yeah, because I'm a fucking grass. Seriously, you need to stay the hell out of Dodge until this blows over.'

'You think it will?'

'I can't see the father staying here for ever. He'll have to go back to Moscow eventually. But you're going to have to watch your back.'

'You got any suggestions, Mickey?'

'Like what?'

'Like how I can fix this?'

'You fancy going to war with the Russian Mafia?'

'Not unless I have to.'

'You fucked the guy's son with a bottle, Lex. He's not going to forgive and forget. Truth be told, you'd have been better off shooting the guy in the head. At least then there wouldn't have been any witnesses.'

'Yeah, well, no use crying over spilt milk. I'll buy you a beer when I get back.'

'Not in a Russian bar you won't. Be lucky, Lex.'

'Before you go, Mickey, have you heard anything about this heist in Manchester? The safe-deposit boxes.'

Moore chuckled. 'Fucking hell, that was a good one. The papers are saying twenty million or more, but who the fuck knows, right? Those bloody footballers are always trying to hide their money from the taxman. Serves them right.'

'What's the gossip?'

'Professional job, obviously,' said Moore. 'Same as Hatton Garden.'

'Different team, though, obviously.'

'You know how it works, Lex. Someone puts the plan together, someone else carries it out. I heard it was Poles behind the latest lot.'

'Poles, are you sure?'

'Mark's just back from London and he said he was talking to a guy in the Mayfair who said it was a Polish crew. A couple of them have been living it large in Marbella and were shooting their mouths off. You know how it is with some of them, they can't keep their fucking mouths shut.'

'Don't suppose you've got a name, have you?'

'Nah, it was just gossip from Mark. I'll ask him if he knows anything else, if you like.'

'Be handy, mate, thanks.'

Moore ended the call and Harper slid the phone into his hip-pack. He went back into the ops room. 'What do we think, guys?' he asked. 'Are we flogging a dead horse here?'

Hansfree shook his head. 'No, he's definitely up to something.'

'Specifically?'

'Day before yesterday, remember, when he turned into that street that led to the mosque? Full of Asians, it was. Okay, he didn't talk to anyone but it felt to me as if he was there for a reason. There was no brush contact, but he didn't make eye contact with anyone, and that in itself is a red flag. Especially for a soldier who's served out in Iraq. If anything, he'd be overdoing the eye contact. In fact, it made no sense to me that he went down the road he did.'

'Unless he wanted to be seen?' said Harper.

'That's how I read it.'

'And afterwards he just went back to the club, remember?'

said Maggie. 'Okay, he went the long way, as if he was out for a stroll, but it seemed to me that the whole point of the exercise had been the walk by the mosque.'

'Maybe he was trying to make any tail show out,' suggested Barry Big.

'Except he wasn't looking,' said Harper. 'And it didn't look to me as if anyone else was. Not that they would have seen us.' He grinned. 'Us being professional and all. Right, let's keep on him, then. If he has gone jihadist, I'm guessing he'll move sooner rather than later.' He explained that he had to leave London for a day or so. The team weren't thrilled at the idea of being a man short, but as Harper was paying the bills they kept any unhappiness to themselves.

26

Yuri Lukin had been waiting in the arrivals area for half an hour when Fedkin appeared, a small shoulder bag his only luggage. He was escorted by a uniformed immigration officer who saluted Lukin, then walked away. The officer had been paid to meet Fedkin off the plane and get him through Immigration, a procedure that on a bad day could take ninety minutes. Lukin hugged the man, then took him upstairs to a coffee shop.

'Our man is in France,' said Lukin, after they had bought coffee and sat down at a circular table. He spoke in Russian and kept his voice low. 'At least, he left Bangkok on a plane to Paris. His name is Lex Harper. Former soldier. The guy's got money – lots of money.' He took a photograph from his jacket pocket and slid it across the table. It had cost him five hundred dollars and had been taken when Harper had flown out of the country. All visitors were photographed entering and leaving Thailand and had to fill out a landing and leaving card. Lukin also had a copy of the card Harper had filled in when he left, including his name, date of birth and passport number. He gave it to Fedkin. 'I don't know if or when he's coming back,' said Lukin. 'We've searched his apartment in Pattaya and there's nothing personal there so he might have run away.'

'Running won't do him any good,' said Fedkin. 'I have good contacts in France. I'll find him.'

Lukin handed him an envelope. 'Here is money for your expenses. He also has a Thai mobile phone. He's only had it a few weeks – he appears to change his phone and Sim card on a regular basis. But if you can locate the phone, it might save you time.'

Fedkin nodded and pocketed the envelope.

Lukin smiled. 'I'll pay double your normal fee, plus any expenses incurred. But I'll double your fee again if you do something special for me.'

Fedkin grinned. 'What would that be?'

Lukin leaned closer to Fedkin. 'Before you kill him, I want you to shove a bottle up his arse, as far as it will go. And I want you to ask him how it feels to get a taste of his own medicine. Can you do that?'

'It will be a pleasure,' said Fedkin.

27

Harper knew that the cops and the intelligence agencies closely monitored all flights between London and Marbella as a matter of course, to the extent of running facial recognition on every passenger. He thought about flying to Belfast and driving to Dublin to fly from there, but a few minutes on the internet showed him that the quickest way was to catch the Eurostar and travel via Paris. He ended up flying in on Vueling, a low-cost Spanish airline that delivered him on time but with an aching back and sore knees. He wasn't a fan of Marbella – too much bling and Versace, too many wannabe gangsters and faded soap-opera stars, and so many undercover cops and grasses that any half-decent villain had to keep his mouth permanently shut. The tans might be real but most of the smiles were fake, as was the bonhomie. The vast majority of villains based on the Costa del Crime would have preferred to be in the UK. They pretended to like the sun, the sand and the sea but at the end of the day they were in exile, albeit self-imposed.

Harper had lived there for a few years but a spate of gangland assassinations and high-profile arrests had had him on the move and he'd settled on Thailand as a bolthole. He'd never looked back. The Thais were easier to deal with than the Spanish, the cops far more amenable to a brown envelope full of cash, and while there was an extradition treaty it was mainly for deporting paedophiles and rarely used for ordinary decent criminals.

Harper made one phone call from the airport, and Dave Brewer was already at the beachfront restaurant waiting for him, a bottle of Cristal champagne open and beading with sweat as it sat in the ice bucket.

'Fuck me, as I live and breathe, I never thought I'd see you back here,' said Brewer, standing up and giving Harper an enthusiastic bear hug.

'Flying visit,' said Harper. He sat down and looked at the multi-million-pound yachts and cruisers bobbing in the Mediterranean as Brewer poured the champagne. 'I never did get the attraction of boats,' he said. 'Too much moving about, crewed by strangers, what's the point?'

Brewer handed him the glass, then raised his own in salute. 'Good to see you, mate.'

'Good to be seen,' said Harper. The two men clinked glasses and drank.

'I've ordered lobsters,' said Brewer. 'The ones you get here are the best in Marbella.'

'They're fucking good in Thailand, too,' said Harper. 'You should come over some time.'

Brewer laughed. 'That's not going to happen,' he said. 'My missus has heard all the stories. There's no way in hell she'd let me go.'

'Bring her with you. Take her down to Phuket – great beaches and more golf courses than you can shake a club at.'

Brewer shook his head. 'Mate, if she came it'd be like

taking a dog into a butcher's and keeping it on a lead. Plus I'm too old to be led into temptation. Sixty this year.'

'Fuck me. Where did the years go?' Harper raised his glass in salute. 'Congratulations. When do you get your free bus pass?'

'Fuck off. I've still got the Roller.' He sipped his champagne and stretched out his legs. 'We did all right, didn't we?'

'So far, so good,' agreed Harper.

'You know what I mean. A lot of the guys we knocked around with fifteen years ago either ended up in jail or pissed it all away. You and me, we always had our heads screwed on. I'm pretty much legit now. Sally and I have got about fifty apartments along the coast now, with managers to handle the letting. All we do is count the cash.'

'So you're on the straight and narrow?'

'Have been for the last ten years, Lex. Haven't even dipped my toe in.'

'The temptation must be there, though?'

'I've too much to lose,' Brewer said. 'When you're twenty or thirty, the idea of a five-stretch or even a ten is no big deal. You do it and you pick up where you left off. But if I got sent down for a ten-stretch now, that'd be the end. I couldn't expect Sally to wait for me. The kids, well, I don't know what they'd do but I doubt they'd fly over every week for a prison visit. I wouldn't see the grandkids . . . Nah, Lex, it'd be game over. I'd top myself.' He grinned. 'But that ain't gonna happen because I'm now a respectable businessman and a leading light of the British Chamber of Commerce here.' He raised his glass and clinked it against Harper's again. They both drank.

Their lobsters arrived, each the size of a small puppy, along with industrial-sized claw crackers and various implements for removing all the meat. They tucked in, with relish.

'So what can I do you for, Lex?' said Brewer, as he dabbed at his chin with a napkin.

'Can't a guy just fly out to see a mate?'

'Don't try to kid a kidder,' said Brewer. 'We go back a long way, no question, but you calling me out of the blue and asking for lunch makes it more than a social call.' He put down the crackers and picked up his glass. 'Seriously, mate, I'm well happy to see you, and anything you need, just ask.'

'You're a star, mate. Thanks.' He sipped some Cristal and put down his glass. 'You know this robbery at the safe-deposit company in Manchester?'

Brewer nodded. 'Nice bit of work.'

'What's the gossip?'

Brewer's eyes narrowed. 'Why do you ask?'

Harper laughed. 'Don't worry, mate. I've not turned grass. Friend of mine had a box. There was stuff in it that's of no value to anyone else but means a lot to her.'

'Footballer's wife?' asked Brewer. 'I heard a lot of the City and Man U boys had boxes.'

'She's just a pal. I'd like to help her out.'

Brewer nodded. 'It was a professional job, no question. Similar to the Hatton Garden job.'

'Very similar,' said Harper.

'You spotted that? Same drill, same way of accessing the vault, not opening all the boxes?'

'But the Hatton Garden mob were pulled, right?'

'Weren't they just? While the cameras were there. Don't you hate that, the way the cops now work hand in hand with the press to make sure they get good coverage? They started with celebrities but now they're doing it with pretty much everyone. The filth have no shame.'

'None at all,' said Harper. 'The Hatton Garden mob, were they faces?'

'A couple of them were known, sure. We were bloody surprised to see them on the front page, I can tell you that much. I mean, none of them was in line for the Brain of Britain title.'

'So they were hired hands?'

'I guess so.'

'So if the Manchester job was a carbon copy, it could be the same brains behind it?'

'That's how I read it.'

Harper grinned. 'Any idea whose brains they might be?'

Brewer chuckled and waved a lobster claw in the air. 'Now that's the million-dollar question, isn't it?'

'Thirty million pounds, if you believe the papers. Military?'

'It had that feel, didn't it? Both of them. Both went off without a hitch, both took a hell of a lot of planning coupled with inside knowledge. My money would be on a mastermind who then brought in contractors.'

'And what about the latest job? Any gossip?'

'I heard it might be a Polish crew.'

'Where did you pick that up?'

'Guy I met in a bar the day before yesterday. Said a couple of Poles had flown in from London and were living it large. Cristal all round, and then they took half a dozen girls from one of the brothels in Puerto Banús.'

'They talked about the raid?'

'Talked about Manchester. And pissed themselves laughing when the story was on TV.'

'Don't suppose you know where I can find these Poles?'

Brewer shook his head. 'I got it second-hand. But he mentioned the brothel, if that's any help. The Pussycat.'

Harper laughed. 'Bloody hell, that's a name from the past. Still going?'

'On its last legs, I think. So is Porto Banús. Cheap drugs and cheap East European tourists, these days. All the decent gaffs shut down ages ago.'

'Fancy a run out?'

'To the Pussycat? You're having a laugh. Can you imagine what Sally would do to me if she found out I'd been to a brothel with you?'

'Fair point, mate. But back in the day you were a great wingman.'

'Those days are long gone, Lex,' laughed Brewer, refilling their glasses. 'But you go and knock yourself out.'

'Can you do me a favour?'

'Sure.'

'Lend me a motor. Just for the day. Anything will do.'

'Mate, you can borrow the Roller. Just be careful with it.'

28

Harper figured that late afternoon probably wasn't the best time to be visiting a brothel and his fears were confirmed when he walked into the Pussycat and found only four girls on duty. The woman who was in charge was probably in her fifties but had been under the plastic surgeon's knife so often it was difficult to know for sure. Her forehead was glass-smooth, her arched eyebrows gave her a look of perpetual surprise and her mouth was a duck-like pout. Her waist was unnaturally thin and her breasts were the size and shape of watermelons. When she had opened the door, her plumped-up lips curled back in what was supposed to be a smile. 'Come in, my love,' she had said, in a heavy accent. Not Russian but close. 'The early bird catches the worm.'

She had taken him into the main sitting area where three large sofas faced a floor-to-ceiling window that overlooked a large pool and barbecue area. The villa was on the outskirts of Puerto Banús, set behind a tall wall to keep the activities inside away from prying eyes. It had probably been seven or eight years since Harper had last visited but little had changed décor-wise. Terracotta tiled floors, white walls and low-backed sofas.

'You been here before, my darling?' purred the woman.

'A few years ago,' said Harper. 'What happened to Tracey?' She was the former top London escort who had set up the Pussycat in the late nineties, backed by a couple of East End gangsters. She had run a tight operation, everyone trusted her and she could smell a wrong 'un at fifty paces. The Pussycat had become the drinking den of choice for those gangsters who wanted to let their hair down away from their wives and kids. In its heyday, bowls of cocaine had been set out on the coffee-tables for anyone to use, compliments of the management, along with the best hashish ever to have come out of Morocco.

'She sold up two years ago,' said the woman. 'Married a Texan oilman of all things. She's as rich as God now, they say.'

'Good for Tracey,' he said, and extended his hand 'Jeremy,' he said. 'From London.' He decided to go the whole hog. 'Jeremy Willoughby-Brown.'

'Pleased to meet you, Jeremy,' she said, shaking his with a jewel-encrusted hand. Its discoloured patches of skin and raised veins betrayed her true age. 'I'm Sylvia. It's early yet but we do have these beautiful girls for you.' She waved at the four sitting on the sofas. Two were bottle-blondes, one was a brunette and the fourth a dyed redhead. They all smiled hopefully up at Harper, though they looked tired and a little worn.

'I can recommend Elsa,' said Sylvia, nodding at an anorexic blonde with skin the colour of porcelain. 'She's new. Well, relatively new.'

Elsa gave him a little wave. She was wearing a short black silk kimono and had painted her toenails to match the vibrant red of her fingernails. 'Actually, I was looking for someone in particular,' said Harper. 'I met a couple of Polish guys who said they'd had a great time a couple of days ago.'

'What were the names of the girls?'

Harper feigned embarrassment. 'To be honest, I don't think they asked for their names, just said they'd been to the Pussycat and had the best sex of their lives.'

'All our girls will give you the best sex of your life,' said Sylvia. She gestured at Elsa. 'There's nothing Elsa won't do. I'm told that being with her is like being in your own private porn movie. And if you take her with another girl, well, you'll be doubling your pleasure. Elsa loves the company of other women, don't you, Elsa?'

'I love it,' said Elsa, but the haunted look in her eyes suggested otherwise.

Sylvia gestured at the redhead. 'Natasha and Elsa work very well together. Wouldn't you like to be the filling in that sandwich, Jeremy?'

Natasha winked and licked her upper lip suggestively.

'I promised the guys I'd try their girls,' said Harper. 'Be rude not to.'

'Their names?'

'Ah, they were drinking buddies rather than pals,' said Harper. 'But you'll remember them. Polish. Quite loud. Big spenders.'

Sylvia spoke to Elsa in their own language. Latvian, maybe. Or Estonian. Elsa replied. Sylvia smiled at Harper. 'One of the girls is upstairs, sleeping. If you could wait, say, fifteen minutes?'

'Perfect,' said Harper, dropping down onto a sofa.

'Her name is Katrin. I'll tell her to get ready.'

As Sylvia went upstairs, Elsa curled up on the sofa next to Harper. Natasha asked him what he wanted to drink. He'd had half a bottle of Cristal with Brewer but figured a teetotal customer would raise suspicion so he asked for a beer. As she went off to get it, the other two began to play on their smartphones. Elsa ran a finger up and down his thigh. Harper realised that the nails were fake, stuck on top of the real ones.

'I can work with Katrin. It'll be fun.' She smiled at him but her eyes were flat. Harper had seen the look a thousand times in the bars of Pattaya. A lot of girls enjoyed working in the bars but a percentage had been forced into it, not at gunpoint but by family pressure. It was drummed into Thai children from birth that their primary duty was to support their parents, and if that duty involved selling their bodies, few had the courage to refuse.

'Thanks, but no thanks,' said Harper. He unzipped his hip-pack and pulled out a couple of hundred-euro notes. He slipped them to her. 'A tip,' he said.

'Are you sure?'

Harper laughed. 'I won it on the horses,' he said. 'Don't worry about it. Now tell me about Katrin.'

Elsa tucked the money into the top of her stockings. 'She's from Lithuania.'

'You too?'

She shook her head. 'I'm from Estonia, but we're friends. Her tits aren't real, but mine are.' She jiggled her impressive breasts to prove her point and Harper couldn't help but laugh.

The girl returned with Harper's beer and he sipped it, then chatted to her and Elsa until Sylvia came back with Katrin. Katrin's breasts were as fake as Sylvia's but she had a pretty face, long black hair and, though the dark patches under her eyes suggested she hadn't had much sleep, she didn't have the same haunted look as Elsa. She was wearing a white silk robe and, from the way it clung to her curves, nothing underneath it.

'You like?' asked Sylvia.

Harper stood up. 'I like a lot.'

Katrin shook her long, curly black hair and held out her hand. Harper took it and allowed her to lead him upstairs, along a corridor to a bedroom. There was a king-sized bed with red satin sheets but no duvet, and a mirrored ceiling. The windows were open and a soft breeze ruffled the lace curtains. There was a fridge by the bathroom door and Katrin opened it. 'Do you want a drink?'

Harper held up his beer. 'I'm good.'

'Do you mind if I have something?' she asked, pulling out a bottle of champagne.

Harper knew that if he said yes the cost would be added to his bill but he just smiled. 'Sure, why not?'

She popped the cork, filled the glass and sat on the bed. Her skin was tanned and, from what he could see, there were no tan lines. 'Sylvia tells me I partied with your friends.'

Harper nodded. 'Polish guys, a couple of days ago.'

'Tomasz?' she said. 'He was crazy. I got the feeling he hadn't had sex for a long time.' She threw back her head as she laughed, showing perfect white teeth.

Harper figured she was in her mid-twenties at most. 'That sounds about right. How long did he stay?'

'He didn't. He paid for us to go out. Me and Anna. And four other girls. Anna was for his friend. What was his name? Gabriel, like the angel?'

'Gabriel, yes,' said Harper. 'Good old Gabriel. So they gave you a good time?'

'They spent money like it was nothing and they were tipping like crazy. I told them our fee for the night and he gave me double that.'

'Did he give you his phone number?'

She shook her head. 'I gave him mine and he said he'd call me but he hasn't. He said he and Gabriel would come back last night and I waited but . . .' She shrugged. 'I suppose there are many places like the Pussycat.'

'Where was his villa?'

Her eyes narrowed. 'You said he was your friend.'

'He is, but he's on holiday and I'm not staying with him.'

She was still eyeing him suspiciously. 'Do you want to have fun or just talk?' She sipped her champagne.

Harper unzipped his hip-pack and took out a handful of hundred-euro notes. 'What's your normal fee?' he asked.

'During the day, two hundred euros for an hour.'

Harper placed two notes on the bed next to her. Then two more. Then another two. By the time he'd finished there was a thousand euros on the sheet. 'I don't do anal,' she said.

Harper grinned as he put the rest of his money back into his hip-pack. 'That's just for chatting to me,' he said.

'You don't want sex?'

'Not right now. I'm more of a night-time person.'

She scooped up the money and slid it into a drawer in the bedside table as if she was scared he would change his mind, then returned to sit next to him. She clinked her glass against his beer bottle. 'Thank you,' she said, and kissed him gently on the cheek.

'There is one thing you can do for me,' he said.

The suspicion was back in her eyes. 'What?'

'Just let me have Tomasz's address. I don't have his phone number and I want to say hi.'

'I don't have the address.'

'Ah. That's a pity.'

Her eyes narrowed. 'You're sure he's a friend?'

'Cross my heart and hope to die.' He crossed his chest solemnly.

She laughed. 'I don't have the address but I put the location on my phone. Sylvia makes us do that, just in case there's a problem when we do outcall.' As she leaned over and picked up her phone, her robe fell open and her breasts swung free. He couldn't help but admire them and she smiled when she caught his look. 'Are you sure you don't want to fool around? You've paid enough. I can ask Elsa to join us.'

'Just the address and I'll be a happy bunny,' said Harper.

She tapped on her iPhone and held it out, showing him the location of the villa. 'I can send it you, if you want?'

Harper took out his phone. 'I'll take a picture. That'll be fine,' he said. He photographed her screen, then stood up. 'Thanks. I'll tell Sylvia I came quickly but it was my own fault.'

She smiled up at him and let her robe fall open again. 'Are you sure I can't tempt you?'

Harper grinned, and looked at his watch. He really wanted to take a look at the villa, but Katrin had one hell of a body. 'You know what? You've talked me into it,' he said. He took off his shirt. 'Just be gentle with me.'

29

Fedkin found Stepan Kuznetsov sitting at a table outside a café in a side street not far from Notre Dame. There was a small steel-topped bar, where half a dozen men in overalls were drinking pastis, and a few tables where a crusty old woman begrudgingly served baguettes, Croque Monsieur and steak-*frites*. Tourists usually took one look inside and hurried away. Kuznetsov didn't smile or stand up to greet Fedkin – he had never been one for the social niceties. 'You're putting on weight,' he growled. 'And you look soft.'

'Let's do three rounds in the ring and we'll see who's fucking soft,' said Fedkin, pulling up a chair and sitting down.

Kuznetsov was always like a bear with a sore head – it was just his way. His name meant 'blacksmith', as common as 'Smith' was in the West, and he had the look of a man who worked with hot metal: big shoulders, massive forearms and scarred hands. He had been a relative high-flyer with the KGB when the Soviet Union had imploded and, like many, had moved on to work in the private sector, with as many files as he could take with him. He had married a Frenchwoman, he for the passport and she for the money he offered, but the business relationship had surprisingly evolved into a romantic one. They now had three children and lived in a large duplex apartment overlooking the Seine. Kuznetsov oversaw an investigations agency, which ran due diligence checks for French companies on their Russian counterparts. Russians were pouring money into France, as they were into the rest of Europe, but it wasn't always obvious what the source of the funds was, and while most French companies would happily deal with an oligarch who had a shady past, few would be prepared to go into business with a known Russian Mafia hoodlum. Kuznetsov, with his KGB background, was often able to fill in the blanks. He had a sideline, too, in running a black intelligence service, happy to help out any government who would pay his fee, as well as individuals like Fedkin.

Kuznetsov had an espresso and a large brandy-filled balloon glass in front of him. A cadaverous grey-haired waiter came out and wished Fedkin good day in a tone that suggested he couldn't have cared less what sort of day he was having. Fedkin ordered a *café américain* and a brandy to match Kuznetsov's. Kuznetsov had asked for the meeting so Fedkin sat back in his chair, intertwined his fingers over his stomach, and waited for him to speak.

'Your man is in Marbella,' said Kuznetsov. He held out a gloved hand, palm upwards. Fedkin reached into his coat, pulled out an envelope full of euros, and gave it to him. Kuznetsov slid it inside his jacket without checking the contents. 'He originally flew into Paris from Bangkok and checked into a suite at Le Meurice for one night. He was using an Irish passport in the name of Sean O'Donnell. Then he vanished. He didn't fly out of the country and there's no record of a Sean O'Donnell booking into another hotel. He could have taken the train or the ferry to the UK, of course.'

Fedkin nodded. He knew that Harper had been in England, but he had no intention of doing Kuznetsov's work for him. Lukin's Thai contacts were able to keep an eye on Harper's Thai mobile and he had used it in London. Fedkin didn't have a location yet but he had somebody working on it.

'Anyway, he came back to Paris because today he re-appeared at the airport as Sean O'Donnell and flew to Marbella on Vueling.'

'Vueling?'

'A low-cost Spanish airline.'

'And he's still there?'

'He hasn't flown back. But my Spanish contacts are patchy at best so I don't know what he's doing there.'

'No matter. I have people in Spain I can talk to. So, Marbella. What's in Marbella?'

'Sun, sea and sex,' laughed Kuznetsov.

'He lives in Thailand,' said Fedkin. 'He has all the sun, sea and sex he needs.'

'British gangsters,' said Kuznetsov. 'The English call that part of Spain the Costa del Crime.'

'That's what I was thinking,' said Fedkin. 'He's gone there to see someone. And the route he took suggests he wants to stay below the radar. He could have flown from London to Marbella but he chose to travel through Paris. And no record of him flying in, right?'

'Right.'

'Which means train or ferry. Which probably means he'll

travel back by the same route. You can keep a watch on the flight manifests into Paris?'

'Of course. It costs, but then everything does.'

Fedkin waved away the mention of money. 'You just let me know when he comes back. What about monitoring his phones in Spain?'

'I can ask around, but it's not something I've done before.'

Fedkin shrugged. 'I doubt he'll use his phones much anyway. And if he does he'll probably use a throwaway or a landline. He hasn't used his phone in France yet so I'm not holding my breath. The flight back is the best bet for catching him.'

Kuznetsov sipped his brandy. 'What did he do, this Englishman?'

'You know Yuri Lukin?'

'I know of him, of course. He's your client?'

'Harper shoved a bottle up the arse of Lukin's son.'

Kuznetsov tried to suppress a smirk but failed. 'A bottle?'

'A beer bottle.' He pointed a stubby finger at the man's face. 'But keep that to yourself, hear?'

30

The villa was a short drive from the coast in the area called Sierra Blanca, up a hill that gave it spectacular views of the Mediterranean, Gibraltar and Africa to the south, with the Marbella mountain range to the north behind it. It was a large plot – several acres at least – and it reminded Harper of Valentin Rostov's villa in Pattaya, a high wall topped with security wire around it and a barred gate covered by CCTV cameras. He didn't have a ladder or wire-cutters with him, and as the Poles wouldn't know him from Adam, he figured he might as well try ringing the bell and playing the lost tourist – though he made sure to park the Rolls-Royce where it couldn't be seen.

There was a brass bell push set into the concrete pillar to the left of the gate, and a grille. He pressed the bell several times but there was no response. He peered through the bars of the gate. A red Porsche was parked in front of the double garage and a black SUV closer to the house.

'Hello!' he shouted.

There was no reply. He shaded his eyes against the sun and stared at the villa for a while, then bent down and reached through the barred gate to grab a handful of gravel. He tossed a chipping towards the villa but it fell short. He tried again, harder this time, and the pebble clattered against the window. He waited a few seconds, then threw another. It, too, hit the glass. Still no reaction. Harper drew back his hand and threw the rest of the handful at the house and several tiny stones struck the window. No one came out to see what was going on. He looked around but the next villa was a hundred yards away and there was no sound of traffic on the hillside road. He grabbed the bars and climbed over the gate. He wiped his hands on his trousers and headed up the driveway to the front of the house, knowing he'd blown his chance of anyone believing he was a lost tourist.

He went through the motions of knocking a couple of times, but he already had a bad feeling about what he was going to find so he wasn't surprised when no one came to open the door. He reached out and turned the handle. The door was unlocked. It was a huge piece of carved wood but it opened easily. Harper wasn't sure what he became aware of first – the buzzing of flies or the stench of rotting flesh. Either way it told him all he needed to know about why no one had answered the door.

He found the first body sprawled across the bottom of a marble staircase. The man had been shot in the face, which was a mass of black flies. More flies buzzed around Harper as he stared down at the corpse. There were two more bullet holes in the chest, where flies were also feeding and laying their eggs, and a single spray of blood across the wall, which he thought had come from the first shot. That meant the gunman had gone for the head first and the shots to the body were overkill.

The 60-inch LED TV was showing a European football

match with an East European commentary. A dozen opened cans of lager stood on a glass coffee-table with a large ashtray overflowing with cigarette butts.

The second body was in the kitchen, face down in front of a massive stainless-steel refrigerator. There was blood spatter by the kitchen door and streaks on the tiled floor. Harper figured the man had been chased, shot in the back and the legs, and fallen down. The bullet to the back of the head had been the clincher. Harper was pretty sure two shooters had been involved. Maybe more.

They had made no effort to clean up after themselves and had left the bodies in plain sight, which probably meant they weren't local and in all likelihood had already left the country.

Harper padded upstairs. Two of the five bedrooms had been used. He found a Polish passport lying on a dressing table next to a wallet, which was full of credit cards, and two mobile phones. The passport and cards were all in the name of Gabriel Wawrzyniak. He left the wallet but put the phones and passport into his hip-pack. There was no cash in the wallet but Harper didn't think for one minute that robbery had been the motive. He opened a wardrobe and went through the man's clothing, all designer labels and brand new. He took a pair of socks from a drawer and slipped them over his hands, then wiped down the wallet and anything else he had touched.

There was no passport in the second bedroom but he found a boarding pass with the name Tomasz Twardsowski, matching the tag on a hard-shell suitcase that had been pushed under the bed. The suitcase was locked but a couple of hard stamps broke it open. Inside a padded envelope contained a thick wad of five-hundred-euro notes and an iPhone. He took off the socks and flicked through the notes. There were a hundred or so, which meant he was holding at least fifty thousand euros. 'Waste not, want not,' he muttered to himself, and slid the notes into his hip-pack, along with the iPhone. He took the envelope to the toilet, ripped it up and flushed away the pieces.

He put the socks back on and checked the rest of the room, then went downstairs and searched the ground floor quickly and efficiently. He found the CCTV monitors in a room off the kitchen. They were working but someone had taken a hammer to the computer and removed the hard drive. It was clearly a professional job.

31

Harper used a computer terminal at Marbella airport before flying back to Paris. He logged on to the Yahoo account and opened the draft folder. There was a single message from Charlotte Button, much longer than usual. He twisted the screen to the side to make sure it couldn't be overlooked and read through it slowly.

> *Lex, I need you to do something for me. I think I'm being followed and I need to check that the insurance policy I spoke about is still current. I can't go near it myself so I need you to visit the safe-deposit box and check that all's well. There is only the one copy left and I need you to make another and get it to me. Let me have a name that you have valid ID for and I'll have it put on the list of registered users. It's in Birmingham. You'll need a key so let me have an address where I can courier it to. Please be careful. I'm not sure who is following me but they are professionals. Let me know when you have the copy. I trust the other matter is proceeding apace. Keep me informed.*

Harper read it a second time, then deleted it and typed: *Will do. Sean O'Donnell.* He added the address of a mailbox centre not far away from the ops room and continued:

Good news bad news. I found two of the guys behind the Manchester heist in Marbella but someone had beaten me to it. Gabriel Wawrzyniak and Tomasz Twardsowki. Both shot execution-style which suggests to me that someone is making sure they don't appear on the front page of the Sun. *If this is your pal Jeremy's doing then he's upped the ante. Be careful. I will send you their phones. Might be useful. Let me have an address.*

He waited for a couple of minutes. A message appeared in the folder, with a mailbox address in Fulham. Then another message:

You need to be careful. I'm not sure how long the tail has been in place. We might have been compromised in Paris. Sorry.

Harper cursed under his breath. If there had been a tail on Button he wouldn't have spotted it because he wasn't looking. But the meeting had taken place in a hotel suite that he was sure was clean, so no one would have seen them together. But the fact that Button was worried enough to mention it meant he was worried, too. He deleted it and replied, *No problem.* He added a smiley face, logged off and went to catch his flight.

32

Fedkin had booked himself into the Sheraton Hotel in Terminal Two of Charles de Gaulle airport. His gut feeling was that Harper would fly back through the airport, but if he appeared in Paris it was only half an hour away. He lay on his bed, flicking through the channels on his television, but all seemed to be French and he barely spoke the language. He found a Russian news channel but it was only propaganda and, like most Russians, he preferred to take his news from overseas sources such as the BBC and CNN. His phone rang and he picked it up. It was Kuznetsov. 'Your man is in the air as we speak, flying back to Paris.'

'Same airline?'

'Yes.'

'What terminal do they use?' asked Fedkin, sitting up.

'Three.'

Fedkin swore. 'I'd been hoping for more notice, Stepan.'

'Yeah, well, as the French say, "When there's a lack of thrushes, one eats blackbirds."'

'What the fuck does that even mean?'

'The English say, "Beggars can't be choosers."'

'You have been here too long, my friend,' said Fedkin.

'Look, I need something else from you. Manpower. Can you get two heavies for me at the airport?'

'To do what?'

'Wet work. I might have to take him out before he leaves Charles de Gaulle. I'll be playing it by ear and that'll be a lot easier if I've got backup.'

'I'll see what I can do,' said Kuznetsov.

Fedkin ended the call, grabbed his coat and rushed out of the hotel.

33

Harper checked his phones as soon he was in the arrivals area at Charles de Gaulle. There was a text message from Hansfree – TALLY HO! – which he took as a good sign. And a short voicemail from Mickey Moore, which was less optimistic, just a gruff 'Call me, you bastard'.

Harper phoned Hansfree first. 'We've had two contacts,' said Hansfree. 'I think he's getting ready to move.'

'I'm all ears,' said Harper. 'Bring me up to speed.'

Hansfree ran through what had got him excited. The previous morning, with the team in position as usual, they had seen McGovan emerge from the club much earlier than he had done on any previous day. For the first time, he seemed to be walking purposefully, as if he had a definite destination in mind. He seemed to be carrying out anti-surveillance measures, checking in mid-stride and looking back at the people walking behind him, or stepping into a shop doorway to eyeball everyone walking past. However, the team were skilled and alert enough not to arouse his suspicions, and after a few more minutes of anti-surveillance drills, evidently reassured that he was not being followed, he had set off again, this time heading towards Hyde Park. There was a packet of cigarettes in his hand. As he'd walked through the park he'd bumped into a Muslim man wearing traditional dress. The cigarette packet McGovan was holding was jolted from his hand and it fell to the ground, but he kept walking, apparently not having noticed that he had dropped it. However, a moment later the Muslim man picked it up and slipped it into a pocket of his robe.

'We're calling him Yankee One,' said Hansfree. 'He's medium build, about five foot nine, black hair, straggly beard, wearing a fawn *dishdasha* and one of those little round hats Muslims wear.'

'A *kufi*?' Harper said.

'Erm, I guess so.'

'What happened then?'

'The aim now was to "house" the newcomer and, with luck, ID him and check his background,' said Hansfree.

The team had spent the next few hours following the Yankee across London. According to Hansfree, it was an easy follow at first because the man had little tradecraft and made few attempts to check if he was being tracked, to double back or alter his route. However, to their intense frustration, they lost their quarry in Brick Lane, east London, where the indigenous population and the hordes of tourists were so dense that it was next to impossible to follow anybody.

'Wait. You lost him?' said Harper.

'We've got pictures, we'll pick him up again,' said Hansfree. 'The thing is we now know for sure Tango One is up to something. And there's more.'

'Get on with it, mate. I've got a train to catch.'

The second incident had happened yesterday afternoon.

McGovan again left the military club, walking purposefully, but this time, he'd gone along Oxford Street and entered a branch of McDonald's. After ordering his food, he glanced around as if unsure where to sit, then sat at a table next to a Middle Eastern-looking man wearing a well-worn dark suit. Although he had apparently chosen the seat at random, Tango One then spent several minutes talking animatedly to the other man. The team had been unable to get close enough to eavesdrop without the risk of compromise, but from their body language and the way they spoke to each other, heads close together and glancing around frequently to make sure they were not overheard, it was clear that whatever they were discussing, it was not the quality of their burgers.

As with the first Yankee, when McGovan stood up and left a few minutes later, the surveillance team abandoned their pursuit of him and instead focused on Yankee Two. This time they didn't lose him. They followed him as he travelled by bus to north London, and eventually housed him in a smart semi-detached property in a street mostly populated by families of similar Middle Eastern origins.

'Thank God for that,' said Harper. 'Losing one is bad luck, but if you'd lost two . . .'

'Not only did we not lose him, we've got an ID for him as well,' said Hansfree. 'He has a criminal record as an Islamic agitator and has been convicted several times for public order offences.'

'Finally some good news,' said Harper.

'Here's the thing, though, Lex, that's puzzling me,' said Hansfree. 'We've been monitoring any calls in or out of Tango One's room, but there hasn't been a single one, not even a wrong number. Nor has he posted any letters and he's not been emailing or texting anyone either. So the question is: how did those two Yankees know when and where to meet him?'

'My guess would be that he's probably been using the communal telephone in the club. Any chance we can plant a bug on that?'

'It would be pretty difficult to do. It's in a prominent place near the desk, and even if we could bug it, that phone must be used by scores of people every day, and since we don't have any audio of Tango One speaking, we'd have no way of knowing on any particular call if we were hearing him arranging a meet with a terrorist suspect or just some squaddie who was home on leave and fixing a meeting with his mates for a few pints. But I've got my thinking cap on.'

Harper ended the call and used his Thai mobile to phone Mickey Moore in Pattaya. 'The shit thickens, mate,' said Moore.

'What's happened?'

'Word around town is that Lukin has put a million-dollar contract on your head. Or a million euros. Depends who you talk to.'

'Bollocks,' said Harper.

'You put his son in hospital. Worse than that, you shoved a bottle up his arse.'

'To be fair, it was only a Singha bottle, not a fucking magnum of Cristal.'

Moore laughed. 'You're a fucking madman, Lex. Seriously, the Russians have been saying there's a hitman from Moscow on your case. I don't have a name, just that he's a fucking nasty bastard who does a lot of wet work for the oligarchs.'

'How much do they know?'

'They know your name, which means they'll have your picture and passports you've used to enter the country. Plus any information you were stupid enough to write on any of your landing cards.'

'I'm usually pretty creative on that front, Mickey.'

'We all are. But seriously, Lex, watch your back. These Russian heavies are former KGB, a lot of them, and they've got access to all sorts of black intelligence networks.'

'I'll be fine, Mickey.' He ended the call, wishing he felt half as optimistic as he'd sounded.

34

Fedkin watched Harper put away his phone. He was standing next to the two men that Kuznetsov had sent him. They were both Algerians, olive-skinned and swarthy, one tall and lean, the other an inch or two shorter with slightly bowed legs. Both were wearing leather bomber jackets and cargo pants. The taller one was named Habib and the shorter one was Aziz, but Fedkin was fairly sure they weren't their real names.

He had met them in the arrivals area just fifteen minutes before Harper's plane landed, which meant that Fedkin was stuck with them. They weren't carrying guns but both men had flick-knives with them and professed to be experts. Fedkin had shown them a photograph of Harper, but had yet to decide what to do.

Lukin wanted the man dead, but carrying out a contract killing in a crowded French airport would be difficult at best. And Lukin had seemed serious about the manner in which he wanted the Englishman killed. Fedkin could always lie about the bottle, but he was a professional and would prefer to carry out the client's wishes to the letter, if at all possible.

The two Algerians kept glancing at Harper, and Fedkin

hissed. 'Eyes on me. We split up. When he moves, we move. Do you have passports?'

The two men nodded.

'French?'

More nods. That was something. At least they could follow him onto the Eurostar, if necessary. Fedkin was carrying two passports, his Russian one but he also had a Dutch passport. It was fake but it was a good one and it would pass muster on the Eurostar.

'He will probably go from here to the Eurostar terminal, then to London. The best place to get him will probably be at Gare du Nord, but if he travels on the Métro there will be an opportunity there. Until we know where he's going for sure, stick close.'

The two men grunted and walked away.

35

Harper spotted the three men while he was on the phone to Mickey Moore. Three was an unusual number at an airport. People travelled alone, in couples or families. Three men standing together was a red flag. There could be perfectly reasonable explanations, of course. Three company representatives travelling together. Three drivers having a chat while they waited for their clients. Three guys off on a stag do. But the three men on the far side of the terminal didn't look like they worked in an office, had nothing with them to suggest they were there for an airport pick-up, and lacked the happy faces of men who were heading off for a few days of debauchery. They were big men with hard faces, two Arab-looking and the other was either former special forces or ex-cop – 'former' because the gold watch on his wrist and the cashmere overcoat hinted at a pay packet way above what a government employee received. One of the Arab men was clearly an amateur because he kept openly staring at Harper.

Harper played it cool. He doubted they would try anything in the terminal – at least, not in the areas covered by CCTV. And plenty of armed cops from the Gendarmerie Nationale were strolling around with guns on their hips, and black-uniformed soldiers with automatic weapons and impenetrable sunglasses standing in pairs.

He wandered over to a bookshop, bought himself a map of Paris, then wandered over to a screen showing the latest arrivals. He wasn't in the least bit interested in knowing the geography of Paris or what flights were due in, but the behaviour of the three men convinced him that they were indeed on his tail. Losing them wouldn't be difficult – he could catch a taxi into Paris, then run anti-surveillance on the Métro before heading for the Eurostar terminal at Gare du Nord. The problem was the three men knew which terminal he had flown into, which suggested they had access to airline or government databases. It was possible that someone had tipped them off in Marbella, but doubtful. He hadn't put himself about and it had been a flying visit. It was more likely they had been accessing flight manifests, and if they were capable of that, there was every chance they'd be able to pick him up in London.

There wasn't much he could do in the main arrivals area, but there was no CCTV in the toilets. He headed for the men's room, looking at his watch as if he was on a deadline. He pushed through the door and glanced around. To the left, four stalls, all unoccupied. To the right, a line of urinals. Also on the right, two sinks and a hot-air hand dryer. The door opened so that anyone looking in would see the cubicles. Only when the door had closed behind them would they be able to see the sinks.

Harper took his holdall and pushed it underneath one of the sinks, then pressed his back against the wall and waited. After a couple of minutes the door opened and he tensed, but he heard the rattle of a wheeled case being pulled across the tiles and started to wash his hands. A middle-aged Asian came in and headed straight to the urinals as Harper continued to wash his hands. As the Asian finished, Harper moved to the dryer. The Asian zipped up and left, and Harper took his place by the wall again.

After a few minutes the door opened. This time it was two French businessmen in dark overcoats who went together to the urinals, talking animatedly. Harper went into a stall and shut the door, reappearing after they had left.

Assuming the men were following him – and he was ninety-nine per cent sure they were – then at some point one would have to come in and check on him. The more professional they were the longer they would wait, but eventually they would have no choice because there was an outside chance that there might be another way out, a window or an emergency exit. If the roles were reversed and Harper's team was doing the following, he would send someone in if the target hadn't reappeared within half an hour.

The men following him were less patient. Twelve minutes after Harper had entered the toilet, the door opened. One of the Algerians appeared and took a step inside, his eyes on the cubicles. There was a click as the blade of his flick-knife sprang into place, and Harper knew immediately that this was more than a check to see where he was. He moved quickly, stepping behind the man as the door began to swing shut, his fingers clasping the Algerian's right hand, his left hand pushing down on the man's neck. Harper grunted as he pulled the knife into the man's chest at the same time pressing his head down. The man sank down onto the knife and gasped, then struggled as Harper pushed the knife in deeper. The man sagged and Harper let go of his neck, put both arms around him, grasped the knife and shoved it up towards the heart. The man struggled and went still. Harper dragged him into the far cubicle, sat him on the toilet and locked the door. He worked quickly, snapping the blade back into its handle, slipping it into his pocket, then patting the man down for his ID. All he had was his wallet and Harper took that. The man was breathing, barely, and while there was little blood on his clothing, Harper knew there had been catastrophic internal damage and that death was only seconds away.

He shoved his left foot between the dying man's legs and levered himself over the top of the cubicle and onto the toilet next door, then quickly took his place behind the door.

It was several minutes before the main door opened again. A backpacker with a large rucksack and a Canadian maple leaf patch on the side came in. Harper went through the motions of washing and drying his hands while the Canadian used the urinal and left.

The next person in used the near cubicle and Harper went to the urinal and pretended to use it until the man had finished.

Three more men came and went and Harper was about to call it quits when the door opened slowly. 'Habib?' whispered a man. The door opened further. 'Habib?'

The man stepped inside, looking at the cubicles. The door began to close and he looked to his right but Harper was already moving. His right hand slashed against the man's throat, splintering the cartilage. He punched him in the solar plexus with his left, doubling the man over. He pulled the knife from his pocket, flicked out the blade and stabbed the man in the heart, twisting the knife between the ribs to do the maximum amount of damage. The man went down but Harper caught him by the scruff of the neck and dragged him into the cubicle next to the first Algerian's. From the man opening the door to Harper positioning him on the toilet had taken less than ten seconds.

Harper stood over the man, breathing heavily. Again, there was little blood. The man sighed and went still. Harper pulled his victim's wallet from his jacket pocket, and took a pearl-handled flick-knife from another. He pulled the first knife from the man's chest, wiped the handle and slid it to the back of the neighbouring cubicle. Then he took the man's own knife, flicked out the blade and stuck the handle into the dead man's right hand, letting it lie on his lap. The pair were almost certainly known to the police and, with any luck, they wouldn't put too much effort into investigating their deaths.

He climbed out of the cubicle, then checked himself in the mirror above the sinks to make sure there were no stray drops of blood on his clothing, bent down, picked up his holdall and headed out of the door. He took out his phone and pretended to study the screen but in reality his eyes scanned the arrivals area. The man in the expensive coat was standing by a pillar, his arms folded.

Harper smiled coldly and walked towards him. The man unfolded his arms as he realised Harper wasn't going to turn away, but he stayed where he was, staring at Harper, his jaw clenched. Harper kept walking, his eyes never leaving the other man's face. He raised his phone smoothly and took several photographs of him as he walked. He stopped when he was just three feet away, close enough to reach him with a kick or a punch but knowing that nothing was going to happen, not then. Harper smiled and winked. 'They're dead, mate. Lovers' tiff. You never can tell with Arabs, can you?'

The man said nothing but continued to stare at Harper. His eyes were brown but they were lifeless and he didn't blink.

'Cat got your tongue, has it?' said Harper, matching the man's stare. The man wasn't a cop, he was sure of that. Wasn't a cop now and never had been. Ex-military, certainly. And probably ex-special forces. Cops, especially those who had been in the job for a few years, tended to have eyes that suggested disappointment tinged with sadness. They were used to seeing the worst side of people, and more often than not the people they dealt with would lie to them. All a cop could do was follow the rules and get on with his job, for little thanks and not much money. After a while they came to realise that, no matter how hard they worked, the world would never become a better place and bad people would always lie.

Soldiers, past and present, were used to solving their problems physically, and that showed in their eyes too. There would always be a hint of aggression in their stare, a look that said, while they were happy to resolve an issue by talking, at the end of the day they weren't scared of fighting and would be happy enough to throw a punch or fire a gun. The eyes of the man Harper was staring at weren't disappointed or aggressive. They were cold and calculating. His posture had changed as Harper had walked up. Not aggressive, not defensive, just ready. Prepared. One foot had shifted back, just a fraction. The left shoulder was slightly ahead of the right now, giving him just a bit more weight to throw behind a right-handed punch. His chin was down, just enough to protect his throat.

'See, your silence tells me a lot,' said Harper. 'It tells me that if you did speak, I'd learn something about you, something you don't want me to know. That means you're not French because if you were you wouldn't give a fuck. Not English, either, or American. But foreign for sure, and you know that if I know where you're from I'll know who sent you. You're obviously not an Arab, like your pals in the toilet, so I'm going to stick my neck out and say that you're Russian.' He smiled as the man's eyes tightened fractionally and his lips pressed together. 'And your micro-expressions show me I'm right. You're Russian. And it's not personal because there's no hatred in your eyes. You're stone cold, which means you're a pro, which means someone is paying you. And the only Russian I've pissed off recently is Yuri Lukin.' The man's jaw tightened and Harper nodded. 'And what you did right there confirms it.' He held up his phone but the man didn't look at it. He kept staring at Harper impassively. 'I've got your picture and in no time at all I'll know as much about you as you know about me. But here's the difference between us. You're an employee. You're doing this because someone is paying you. But I'll tell you now, no matter what Lukin is paying you, be it a million dollars or a million euros, it's not enough. Because for me, it's not about money. I'll kill you to protect myself and, trust me, personal protection trumps money every time. And I will kill you, don't doubt that for one second. I'm going to kill Lukin, too. I have to. He's given me no choice. And once he's dead there'll be no one to pay your bill, will there?'

He smiled and gestured at the exit with his phone. 'I'm going to walk away now. You're good so you've probably already worked out that I'm going to London. And that at some point I'll be going back to Thailand.' Harper stepped towards the man so that their faces were only inches apart, but the Russian didn't flinch. 'So here's the thing. If I see you in London, I'll kill you. In fact, if I ever see you again, no matter where, I won't say anything, I won't ask you what you're doing, I'll just kill you. And if I ever find out you're in Thailand, and I will find out, trust me, then I'll kill you.' He stared at the man for several seconds, then smiled brightly. 'Right, I'm off. You have a great day. Be lucky.' He turned and walked away, knowing full well that the Russian was staring at his back but not caring. He had meant every word he had said.

36

Passport checks were little more than cursory on Eurostar and Harper's Sean O'Donnell Irish passport was merely glanced at. He had a business-class ticket so had a free meal on the train and even managed a catnap before arriving at the St Pancras terminal. From there he caught a taxi to Paddington and reached the mailbox centre in Praed Street at three o'clock in the afternoon. He showed his Sean O'Donnell passport to the shop assistant, a tall Eastern European brunette with pale blue eyes. She handed over the padded envelope that had arrived by courier from Charlotte Button. Harper paid her and left.

He waited until he was back in his hotel before opening the package. There was a small key and the business card of a Birmingham safe-deposit company with a nine-digit identification number on the back. He put the key and the card into his hip-pack, then spent half an hour wandering around Bayswater making sure he wasn't being followed before catching a black cab to the ops room.

Hansfree was ecstatic. McGovan had apparently moved up a gear and over the past three hours had met with two more Yankees. Hansfree had housed them both – they were low-level jihadi agitators with criminal records who were already known to the authorities.

'How's he doing the recruiting?' asked Harper. 'That's what I don't understand.'

'Maybe someone else is pointing them at him,' said Hansfree. 'They go to him and not vice versa. ISIS sleepers, maybe. Sent here over the past few years and waiting to be activated. By McGovan. Or maybe for McGovan.'

Harper agreed. 'Maybe he doesn't do the initiating. They're told to contact him and he gives them their instructions. Makes sense.'

'I'm worried by how poor he is at anti-surveillance,' said Hansfree. 'He should be better than this, a lot better.'

'Why worry?' Harper said. 'It just makes him easier to follow.'

'Exactly, but if he's that careless, it suggests that either he's not as good as we thought he was, or he isn't close to going operational. If he was, he'd be taking a lot more care. But however unprofessional and careless he appears to be, we still can't afford to relax for an instant. If he suddenly switches on and we're not on our game, the whole operation could be blown. We've already worked much too hard and invested too much time to let that happen.'

Hansfree was right. 'I get the feeling you have a suggestion,' Harper said.

Hansfree grinned. 'More people,' he said. 'More feet on the ground.'

'I'm reluctant to increase the size of the team.'

'Lex, we don't have any choice. We're way too stretched as it is.'

Harper sighed. Again, Hansfree was right. And to make matters worse, he was going to have to go to Birmingham the following day on Button's errand. 'I'm guessing you have a suggestion, name-wise.'

'I've got a few people I can call, Lex. All first rate, all reliable, all prepared to work on a daily rate of a grand a shift.'

'They'd have to be reliable. This is heavy shit we're getting into. Plus, you know what the end-game is going to be. The fewer people who know, the better.'

'To be honest, without more hands to the pump the end-game could blow up in our faces,' said Hansfree. 'We've got too many balls in the air and not enough jugglers.'

'Okay, bring in what you need,' said Harper. 'I'll make sure you get the cash.' He chuckled. 'I'm assuming they'll want cash. And on the subject of being overstretched, I've got to go up north tomorrow.'

'Not a great time, Lex. Seriously.'

'Nothing I can do,' said Harper. 'Favour for a friend.' He took a Sim card from his pocket and placed it on the table in front of Hansfree. 'There's a couple of photographs of a guy who was following me at Charles de Gaulle. I think he's Russian. See what you can find out, will you?'

'I'm on it,' said Hansfree.

37

Fedkin downed his brandy and waved at the waiter to bring him another. He was sitting at a café overlooking the Eiffel Tower, his collar turned up against the wind that was blowing from the Seine to his left. There was a coffee untouched in front of him, and a cigarette that he'd started but not finished.

The confrontation with Harper had hurt his professional pride, but he had to acknowledge that he had made mistakes. He shouldn't have used the men Kuznetsov had provided. As soon as he had seen them he should have sent them on their way. They had been amateurs, clearly, and it was Fedkin's own fault for sticking with them.

Kuznetsov wasn't happy about what had happened to them, but Fedkin got the impression that it was an inconvenience rather than a personal loss. He had called him to break the news and Kuznetsov had ranted about what a difficult position he was now in, but he had sounded to Fedkin as if he was acting and that behind the bluster the man was aware that he had sent boys to do a man's job.

The waiter returned with the fresh brandy, the fourth Fedkin had ordered since sitting at the table. He had a decision to make and it was one that was going to require a lot of thought. He lit a cigarette and blew smoke towards the iconic tower. Fedkin wasn't in the least bit scared by his confrontation with the Englishman. The man was a professional, clearly. The way he had dealt with the Algerians. The way he had stared Fedkin in the eyes as he'd spoken. The body language, the words he'd used, all had indicated that the man had meant exactly what he'd said. If he ever saw Fedkin again, he'd kill him. It hadn't been a threat, more a statement of intent. And Harper had been absolutely correct when he'd said that personal protection always outweighed financial considerations. When you killed for money you planned everything down to the last detail. You wanted the target neutralised but you needed to make sure you had an escape route and a fallback position. When you killed to protect yourself, you did what you had to do. The consequences were important, yes, but at the end of the day it was self-preservation that mattered.

The contract was worth a million euros. That was big money. The only targets that paid more were heads of state and government officials. Fedkin understood the lust for revenge and had been happy enough to take Lukin's money, half up front and half on completion of the contract. But Lukin had underestimated the man he wanted dead. Harper wasn't a simple tourist. He wasn't a simple anything. And Lukin had given Fedkin the impression that Harper was on the run, which clearly wasn't the case. Harper was on a mission that involved him travelling to Marbella, Paris and London. Lukin should have known who and what Harper was. And if he did know and hadn't told Fedkin, that was a serious omission, which could have proved fatal.

The big question was what Fedkin should do next. Harper

hadn't been able to do anything but talk at the airport, not with all the CCTV cameras and armed French cops around. If the confrontation had taken place in a dark alley, things might have been different. Or maybe not.

Harper had recognised Fedkin as a fellow professional and had treated him as such. Fedkin had options. There were almost always options in life, choices that had to be made. Fedkin could ignore everything Harper had said and continue to try to fulfil the contract. He knew where Harper was – London – and his contacts in the UK were as good as they were in France. It wouldn't take much time or money to track Harper down and try to kill him. Or he could wait until Harper was back in Thailand. But the Englishman would be ready for him and wouldn't be a soft target. And if Fedkin failed, his own life would almost certainly be forfeit.

He could choose to back out of the contract. He could tell Lukin the truth – that he had failed once and didn't want to try again. Or he could lie and say that he had simply failed to track the man down, that Harper was an expert at covering his tracks and that Lukin would be better to wait until the Englishman returned to Thailand. In either case Lukin would probably insist on having his money back but that would be no great loss as Fedkin had spent only a few thousand euros so far. The greater loss would be to Fedkin's reputation: he doubted that Lukin would keep the story to himself. Word would get around that Fedkin had failed and his professional reputation was paramount. Work would soon dry up if clients lost faith in his ability to follow through.

Harper had clearly meant what he had said about killing

Fedkin if he ever went near him. And he had been equally convincing when he said that he was going to kill Lukin. There had been no bravado, no bluster. It had been a straightforward statement of fact, no different from telling Fedkin what he planned to have for breakfast the next day. Lukin was well protected and he was no one's fool, but Fedkin didn't doubt for one moment that Harper would kill him, and soon. That being the case there would be no more money forthcoming from Lukin: the contract Fedkin had would end with Lukin's death. If – or, rather, when – Harper killed Lukin, Fedkin's current predicament would end because no one would know that he had failed, and no one would ask for the return of the two hundred and fifty thousand euros. His reputation, too, would be intact.

Fedkin nodded thoughtfully. That was the answer, then. All he had to do was nothing. Just wait. Harper would solve everything. The Englishman would kill Lukin, Fedkin's reputation would be unsullied, and he would get to keep the money. Fedkin finished his brandy and waved at the waiter for another. He smiled to himself, then took a long drag on his cigarette. Life was always so much easier when you dealt with professionals.

38

Charlotte Button was sitting at a coffee shop in JFK's Terminal Four. She looked at her watch and frowned. Her flight was closing in less than an hour and she still had to pass through security and Immigration, and even with her Virgin Upper Class ticket it was going to take her the best part of thirty minutes. She picked up her phone but there were no messages and no missed calls.

'Charlotte, so sorry,' said a voice to her left. It was Richard Yokely, smartly dressed as always but with a harried expression that was out of character. 'I was tied up in a meeting and then the traffic was a nightmare.'

'I'll have to go fairly soon,' she said.

'Nonsense. I'll walk you through Immigration. You can have the VIP treatment.'

'You can do that?'

He laughed. 'Of course I can. And what's the point of having friends in high places if they don't make your life easier from time to time?' He sat down at her table and gestured at her boarding pass. 'Good choice,' he said. 'Unlikely that jihadists would ever try to take down a Virgin plane.'

Button smiled. 'The joke in England was why would

anyone want to fly on a plane that won't go the whole way. Anyway, thanks for coming to see me off.' She looked around. 'Am I . . .?'

Yokely shook his head. 'No, you're good.'

'Your people are here now?'

'There are two within fifty feet of you, Charlotte. And don't even bother looking because they're the best in the business. It looks to me as if they leave you alone in the States. They just pick you up when you fly back.'

'So they're accessing airline manifests?'

'It isn't difficult, as you know. Government do it all the time and if you know the right palms to grease . . .' He shrugged. 'There will always be people who think they're not paid enough and that they deserve to earn a little on the side.'

'And have you been able to put names to the faces?'

Yokely smiled. 'Of course. I thought you'd never ask, my dear.' He took a thumbdrive from his pocket and gave it to her. 'Password protected. Your month of birth in capital letters plus today's date.'

Button put the thumbdrive in her pocket. 'You know it always causes trouble when Americans use dates,' she said. 'You mean American style, right? Month, day and year?'

'Of course.'

'You realise that America is the only country in the world to do dates like that? Everywhere else goes day, month, year.'

'Then everywhere else is doing it wrong.' He gestured at her pocket. 'Be sure you don't make a mistake, three strikes and you're out. The whole disk is wiped.'

'I'll be careful,' she said. 'And rather than keep me in suspense, can you tell me now who is on my case?'

'It's not government, which could be good news or bad,' said the American. 'We managed to identify four. Two are Israelis, both former Mossad but now in the private sector. The other two are Brits and work for a private security firm in south London. The Brits are just regular private detectives who do divorce and corporate investigations. The Israelis are more of a worry. But at this point they seem only to be interested in surveillance. There's no sense that they mean you any harm.'

'That's good to know.'

'Though, of course, that may well change if they think you don't have your insurance policies.'

'That's in hand, Richard.'

'Good to know,' he said. 'Now, how's the other matter progressing?'

She smiled thinly. 'Is that the real reason you were so keen to wave me off? Your congressman is getting impatient?'

'He's all for sending Delta Force over.'

Button laughed. 'Well, good luck with that.'

'I've explained to him that we can't use American special forces to kill British citizens on British soil. If it was out in the desert, it'd be a whole different ball game.'

'It's in hand, Richard. McGovan is under surveillance, and as soon as the opportunity presents itself, it will be done.'

'The sooner the better.'

'I hear you,' she said.

'And what about you?'

'I'm increasing my insurance. And then I'm going to talk to an old friend. See if she'll tell me what's going on.'

'If you need my help, just whistle.' He grinned. 'You know how to whistle, don't you?'

Button laughed. 'That was a great movie. I've never seen myself as Lauren Bacall but there's definitely something of the Humphrey Bogart in you.'

Yokely beamed, clearly taking it as a compliment. 'Here's looking at you, kid,' he said, and faked a salute. 'Now, come on, let's go get you patted down and on your way.'

39

Harper drove up to Birmingham early the next morning, taking a circuitous route that saw him in Reading, then Swindon and Gloucester. He took his time and avoided the motorways, doubling back and taking turns sometimes at random. Within an hour he was sure there was no one on his tail, but he still kept off the motorway. He stopped for breakfast at a small café outside Cheltenham, then cut across to Stratford-upon-Avon and spent half an hour driving around the tourist spots before heading up to Birmingham. He finally parked his car in a multi-storey in the city centre, took a small leather briefcase out of the boot, then walked around the major shopping areas, including the Bull Ring, Corporation Street and the Piccadilly and Burlington arcades. During his walk around the shops he paid cash for a MacBook laptop and a nylon carrying case. Eventually he was satisfied that he was tail-free and walked to the building that housed the safe-deposit company. He showed the O'Donnell passport and the business card with the ID number on it, then signed two forms and followed a young man in a pinstripe suit down a flight of stairs to the basement area. There was a large steel door covered by two CCTV cameras and the young man tapped in a four-digit code, then pulled the door open. It was several inches thick but Harper knew that was only for show: if anyone was going to force their way into the vault they'd simply drill through the concrete around the door.

'Ever been broken into?' asked Harper, as he followed the man into the vault.

'Never,' he said. 'State-of-the-art security in here. Infrared and motion detectors, and a laser couldn't get through that door.'

Harper smiled at the mention of lasers. There was no need for anything as hi-tech as a laser: an industrial drill would do the job. The one that had broken into the Hatton Garden Safe Deposit Company had cost just three and a half grand and had done the job in under two hours.

The assistant had a clipboard with a key attached and he used it to open one of the two locks in the flap of a box at about waist height. Harper used his own key to release the second, then the assistant lifted the flap and slid out the long metal box. He carried it out of the vault, closed the door, then took Harper along a corridor to another room, which contained just a metal table. He put the box on the table and pointed at a button to the right of the door. 'When you're ready just press that and I'll come and take the box back.'

'Brilliant, thanks,' said Harper. As the man left, Harper looked around the room. There was no sign of CCTV, which made sense because the whole point of safe-deposit boxes was that the owners wanted the contents kept away from prying eyes. He opened the box and looked inside. There was a stack of fifty-pound notes, a couple of inches thick, a small velvet bag tied with a piece of golden rope that he knew without touching contained sovereigns, half a dozen envelopes, a battered Filofax and a grey thumb-drive. Harper didn't even think about opening the letters or the Filofax. He took the thumbdrive out of the box and placed it on the metal table. He opened his laptop case and took out the MacBook. It booted up within seconds and he quickly configured it before he plugged in the thumbdrive and copied the file onto the computer's hard disk. He switched off the computer, put it back into his briefcase and the thumbdrive into the safe-deposit box, then pressed the button to summon the assistant. Half an hour later he was on the motorway, heading south to London.

He left the computer locked in the boot of his car while he went to the internet café and opened the draft message folder. He typed a new message: *All sorted.* He went to the counter and bought himself a coffee. By the time he had got back to the terminal the message he had written had gone and there was one from Button in its place: *You're an angel.*

He sat down, sipped his coffee, and typed a new message: *What do you want me to do with my copy?*

She replied a few minutes later: *Just keep it safe. You're my safety net.*

Are you OK?

I've been better.

Anything you need, just ask. Harper sat back and sipped his coffee again.

You're sweet. Stay in touch.

As Harper watched, one by one the messages were deleted.

40

Hansfree was alone in the ops room late that night when Harper turned up with a couple of coffees. 'Did you get the extra manpower?' he asked, as he flopped down on a folding camping chair.

'Half a dozen. Three are working with Maggie and three with Barry Whisper. I've got two more coming in later.'

Harper took an envelope from his jacket pocket and tossed it onto the table where Hansfree was working. 'There's thirty thousand euros to be going on with,' he said. It was part of the money he'd found in the villa in Marbella. 'I'll get more as and when you need it.' He sensed that Hansfree was unhappy about something. Just a feeling, but they'd known each other for so long that he could read the signs. 'Something happen while I was away?' he asked.

'I'm not sure. Maybe nothing.'

'And maybe something. Come on, spill the beans.'

'It was about midday. Maggie's team were following Tango One along a street just off the Edgware Road. One of the new guys, Reggie, was in the A position closest to the subject, with a woman called Nancy behind him. Maggie was working as C on the opposite side of the street, while Barry Big was mobile in a vehicle not far away, cruising, ready to take up the follow if the subject hailed a taxi or got into a car. There had been nothing to indicate anything out of the ordinary, with Tango One strolling along, apparently without a care in the world. There were enough other people in the street for the team to remain inconspicuous as they followed him. Anyway, everyone is as happy as Larry when Reggie calls it off. Break, break, break.'

'What had happened?'

'Well, Reggie says he'd seen a guy, a dark-haired man in a blue suit, olive skin scarred with pockmarks, old smallpox scars maybe. He says the man's expression didn't change as he approached, but he says that when the guy got closer to Tango One he winked.'

'Winked? He called it off because of a fucking wink?'

'Reggie's a pro, Lex. He's not a kid. He's in his seventies and spent thirty years as a follower with Five. He does a bit now and again to keep his eye in but, trust me, he's not the sort to panic.'

'He's sure it was a wink? Not just a dodgy eye or an insect or something?'

'Reggie says he saw a wink so he was doing the right thing by breaking it off. They came back here for a debrief. No one else spotted anything but Reggie was closest. He did the right thing.'

'So what's your assessment?'

'If Reggie was right, and I've no reason to doubt him, then maybe Tango One was laying a trail. The big question is how many watchers he had stationed along his route and whether any of them had been observing us long enough to be able to identify that we were following him.'

'That's guesswork,' said Harper. 'And if Reggie's as good

as you say he is, surely he'd have spotted any other watchers beforehand.'

'I think you're right,' said Hansfree.

'So, well done, Reggie, and full steam ahead,' said Harper. 'Everyone needs to be on full alert, obviously. I don't have to stress how vital it is that we all bring our A-game to work tomorrow. But the good news is that if he was laying a trail to see if there was any surveillance on him, it suggests that he may be making last-minute checks before going operational.' He raised his coffee cup in salute. 'We're entering the end-game, mate, and that's always my favourite part.'

41

Patsy Ellis unlocked the front door, placed her briefcase next to the hall table and went through to the kitchen. Her husband, Roger, was bending down to peer through the glass panel in the oven door. 'Dinner'll be ready in half an hour,' he said, without looking around.

'Where are the boys?'

He stood up and gave her a peck on the cheek. 'In with Charlie. Why didn't you tell me she was coming? I mean, there's enough to go round but some notice might have been nice.'

Ellis had to fight not to show surprise. She smiled as her mind raced. 'I'm sorry, honey, it completely slipped my mind,' she said. 'Where are they?'

'Sitting room. She volunteered to help them with their homework.'

Ellis went along the corridor to the sitting room. Charlotte Button was sitting on the sofa with the two boys, nine-year-old Jamie and eleven-year-old Harry. They both had exercise books on their laps. Button was wearing a blue Chanel suit and what looked like Chanel heels, very similar to how Ellis was dressed. 'Charlie, what a lovely surprise,' she said.

Button looked up and smiled. She brushed a stray lock of hair behind her ear. 'I'm not as good at algebra as I thought,' she said.

Harry sighed theatrically. 'I keep telling you, Auntie Charlie, it's calculus, not algebra.'

'Potato, tomato,' said Button, ruffling his hair. 'I can't believe how they've grown.' There was a bottle of wine in an ice bucket on the side table next to her and a flush to her cheeks that suggested she'd already drunk a fair bit of it.

'Well, it's been a while seen you've seen them,' said Ellis. 'Boys, can you take your books upstairs while I talk to Auntie Charlie? Supper will be ready soon.'

The boys grabbed their books and clattered out of the room. Ellis narrowed her eyes. 'Seriously, Charlie. My home?'

'I'm under a bit of pressure at the moment,' said Button, quietly. 'I needed somewhere safe.'

'And you figured nothing bad could happen with my husband and sons under the roof?'

'Is that so bad? Can't an old friend pop around for a surprise visit?'

'I'd rather you'd called first.'

Button smiled brightly. 'But then it wouldn't have been a surprise, would it?' She took the bottle out of the ice bucket and held it up. 'I brought a gift. Roger said I should open it.'

Ellis smiled at the bottle. It was a Chardonnay, and a good one. It was her favourite brand, and she was sure that was no coincidence. It was also half empty.

Button poured some into a glass and held it out to Ellis. 'Cheers, then.'

Ellis took the glass and they toasted each other. 'What am I going to do with you, Charlie?' She sighed.

'Sit down, drink some wine and relive old times,' said Button. 'That's what friends do.' She sat down on the sofa and crossed her legs.

Ellis sank into an armchair and sipped her wine. 'How can I help you, darling?' she asked. 'I'm assuming you do want my help.' Ellis worked for the Joint Intelligence Organisation, the agency responsible for intelligence assessment and forward planning. It offered advice and support to the Joint Intelligence Committee, which oversaw the work of MI5, MI6 and GCHQ. No one knew more about the workings of the British intelligence agencies than Patsy Ellis. Prior to joining the JIO she had worked for MI5 and had been something of a mentor to Button.

Button took a long drink of wine. 'When we talked last, you suggested I loaded a file onto a website, which could be revealed in the event of my death.'

'Your insurance policy? I was talking hypothetically.'

'And I agreed. But to be honest, Patsy, that thought hadn't occurred to me. I put my faith in good old-fashioned hardware. Thumbdrives, three of them.'

'As I said at the time, it's the obvious thing to do.'

'Right. And two of those thumbdrives have been stolen.'

Ellis raised her eyebrows. 'Ah, that's unfortunate.'

'Please tell me it's nothing to do with you, Patsy.'

'Of course it's not. Perish the thought. Where were they? Not under the mattress, obviously.'

Button smiled. 'Safe-deposit boxes. Hatton Garden and Manchester. Both broken into by professionals.'

'Professionals who were arrested fairly promptly in the

case of Hatton Garden. Charlie, I can assure you, this is none of my doing.'

'You can see why I'd be worried, though. Two of my three insurance policies have now gone. And I really shouldn't be telling you that.'

'I don't know what else I can say to convince you that I'm not your enemy, Charlie. What happened happened. You got caught, you resigned and that's the end of it. I was just brought in so that you'd be dealing with a friendly face.'

'What about Willoughby-Brown?'

'Jeremy got what he wanted. Your job. I doubt he'd be still pursuing you.'

'Well, someone is. And they're good. Both the Hatton Garden robbery and the Manchester one were planned like military operations. And when they thought I was heading for the third, I was followed. By pros.'

'That's . . . interesting.'

'Isn't it? Whoever is on my tail they're good. Government standard. And they're able to go airside.'

'I won't ask you how you know that.'

'How sweet. I need you to check with Five and Six that they're not behind this.'

'I'm sure they aren't, but I'll check.'

Button leaned towards Ellis. 'And I need more. I need to know who it is, Patsy. Otherwise I might start to think that attack is the best form of defence. I have now put another copy out there and it's not in a box. If I continue to feel under pressure I might reach the conclusion that the best option for my safety is to go and have a chat with the editor of the *Guardian*.'

'Oh, I do hope not, Charlie. And, please, if ever you do

decide to talk to a journalist, please make it the *Telegraph*. The *Guardian*'s an awful rag, these days.' She held up her hand. 'I'm joking. I don't want you to go to any newspaper. And I know you don't either. We have the same views on journalists. Most of them, anyway.'

'There are still some serious journalists around who care about something other than how fat the latest pop star is getting,' said Button. 'The point I'm making is that, once the information is in the public domain, there's no point in anyone trying to keep me quiet.'

'That's certainly true. But once the cat is out of the bag, heads would have to roll. And you'd be first in line. You killed people, Charlie.'

'Terrorists.'

'For personal reasons. That's good old-fashioned murder, whichever way you look at it.'

'I'd happily take my chances with a jury of my peers,' said Button. She sipped her wine. 'A grieving widow pushed over the edge when she witnessed her husband killed in front of her? With the right jury I'd get probation, but even with the wrong jury I'd get ten years, out in five. You think I'm scared of five years in a British prison? I'd appreciate the rest, frankly. And it'd give me a chance to catch up on my reading.'

'Well, yes. You could see it that way. But you're forgetting that you'd be up against the whole weight of the Establishment, looking for a scapegoat to hang out to dry, if you'll forgive the mixed metaphors. With the right judge, the right prosecuting counsel, and a carefully vetted jury you might well find yourself facing a life sentence. And is there anything involving the Americans in that file, Charlie? That's the question you need to be asking yourself. Because if the Americans take an interest and they press for extradition, well, you could be spending eternity in a metal box under the ground in some Midwestern state where same-sex marriage is illegal but wedding your cousin is okay.'

Button shrugged. 'So the best thing all round is for the file to stay out of the public domain. And for that to happen, you have to make sure I stay safe and well.'

'I've already told you, darling, this is nothing to do with Five. Or Six.'

'Not officially, no. But there could be someone within the organisation who is pursuing their own agenda.' She smiled at the look that flashed across Ellis's face. 'Please, no snappy comment about pots and kettles.'

'You do see the irony, though?'

'Yes, I do.' She reached for her bag, opened it and took out a padded envelope. She passed it to Ellis, who peered inside.

'Why, thank you, Charlie, but really I have all the phones I need.'

Button smiled thinly. 'Two of the men involved in the Manchester safe-deposit heist were killed in Marbella. Executed. Gabriel Wawrzyniak and Tomasz Twardsowski. These are their phones.'

Ellis frowned. 'That's news to me.'

'Their bodies haven't been found yet. Not officially, anyway.'

'And they were involved in the robbery?'

'They have form for similar break-ins in Poland and Germany. It's the first time they've worked in the UK.' She smiled. 'And the last, obviously.'

'And the Spanish police aren't aware of this because?'

'Because they're the Spanish police,' said Button. 'They generally have trouble finding their backsides with both hands.'

'And who executed them, do you know?'

'Presumably whoever hired them. I'm guessing it's the same person who hired the guys who did the Hatton Garden job. He didn't want the Poles being picked up so . . . You can see why I'm a little nervous.'

Ellis patted the padded envelope. 'So you want me to find out who they spoke to, where they went?'

'All the information will be on their phones and Sim cards. I could probably get it done myself but it'll be quicker and easier through you. Plus you'll get to see for yourself.'

'And then what?'

'Well, I suppose that depends on who's behind this. You can either deal with it, or you can bounce it back to me. Either way it'll be taken care of.'

There were half a dozen surveillance photographs in the envelope. Ellis slid them out and looked at them. There was writing on the back: the names of the subjects and details of where the photographs had been taken. 'Those are four of the watchers who have been on my case in the UK,' said Button. 'They pick me up at the airport and stick to me like glue.' She saw the unease that flashed across Ellis's face. 'Don't worry, they didn't follow me here. They're good but they're not perfcct. Two work for a British security company, two are former Mossad.'

'Are they now? That's interesting.'

'I don't think it's the Israeli government. I think whoever wants me tailed hired an Israeli company, that's all. I'm guessing they then took on extra manpower in the UK. I think whoever is having me followed also ordered the robberies and the murder of the Polish crew.'

Ellis nodded thoughtfully. 'Okay, let me see what I can do. Are you okay, darling?'

Button flashed her a tight smile. 'I've been better.'

'Stay for dinner. Roger's cooking.'

'Are you sure?'

'That Roger's cooking? Absolutely. He's doing his *hachis parmentier*. Just don't call it shepherd's pie – he'll never forgive you.'

Button chuckled. 'About me staying, I mean. Are you sure you want me here?'

Ellis raised her glass. 'Charlie, we're friends. No matter what's happened, that's never going to change.'

42

Harper was standing in his usual spot close to the military club when he heard Hansfree's voice in his earpiece. 'Lex, I've just heard Tango One on his mobile, via the in-room camera,' he said. 'He was contacting a vehicle retail site in Staffordshire and asking about the availability of second-hand Land Rovers. I've just done a quick internet search and found out that the company specialises in the sale of ex-military vehicles.'

'So it sounds like they're going for a military target, then.'

'Could be,' Hansfree said. 'Though, of course, there are plenty of civilian targets that would be easier to access using military vehicles.'

Harper thought for a few moments, then took a calculated gamble. 'Give us the details of the site, Hansfree,' he said, into the mic at his shoulder. 'Barry Big, take one of the leased vehicles to the site, I'll follow you on the bike. Maggie and Barry Whisper, remain in position, keep staking out Tango One and track him if and when he leaves. We could be on the move, everyone on full alert.'

'Roger that,' said Maggie, in his ear. 'About bloody time.'

Later that afternoon McGovan came out of the club wearing a long coat and a woollen beanie hat. Maggie May and Barry Whisper trailed him along Euston Road to Euston station, where they saw him meet the man they had named Yankee Four. He was mixed race, clean shaven, other than a small, neat moustache, and, like McGovan, was wearing a long coat. The two men went into the station and bought tickets. Maggie was behind them and overheard their destination: Lichfield in Staffordshire. She bought tickets for herself and Barry Whisper and they boarded the same train, managing to get seats at the far end of the same carriage. Throughout the two-hour journey they remained in radio contact with Harper and by the time the train arrived at Lichfield, he and Barry Big were already in position outside the station, Harper on his bike and Barry Big in one of their rental cars.

The two targets left the train and jumped into a cab, Harper on his bike in close pursuit, and the rest of the team three-up in Barry Big's car.

The taxi drove out of town for a few miles and eventually pulled up at a long-disused and abandoned airfield, now an expanse of cracked, weed-strewn concrete, dotted with heaps of fly-tipped rubble and other rubbish. A large area, surrounded by a much newer-looking steel-mesh and barbed-wire fence, enclosed the disused control tower and crew room, and the assorted old hangars, administrative buildings and bunkers, which were now housing the offices, repair shops and stores of a company specialising in the sale of ex-military vehicles. Hundreds of ex-army Land Rovers and Bedford trucks, still in their original military camouflage, were parked in rows on the concrete hard-standing around the buildings.

The two men were soon deep in conversation with a

salesman, who was showing them two ex-army Snatch Land Rovers. Harper, meanwhile, was wandering around the site, pretending to be interested in buying a vehicle, but often close enough to the group to catch snatches of their conversation and overhear what was being discussed. Eventually the two men came to an agreement with the salesman and they retired to the office to fill in the paperwork.

Harper went over to the car. The passenger side window wound down. 'Have you got any trackers with you?' he asked Barry Big.

'I never leave home without them.' He nodded at the glove compartment. Barry Whisper opened it and took out two compact devices.

'Hansfree's finest,' said Barry Big. 'They'll stick to anything metallic and once they're in place they kick off automatically. He can pick them up on any iPad.'

Harper nodded at Barry Whisper. 'Do the honours, mate, and fix those to the Land Rovers they were looking at. I've got a feeling they're going to be buying them.'

'Roger that,' said Barry Whisper. He climbed out and headed over to the vehicles. Harper went to a Bedford truck parked outside and climbed into the cab so that he could look into the office. He glimpsed McGovan handing a wad of cash to the salesman. 'Have we missed a brush contact somewhere along the way today?' he murmured, into his shoulder mic. 'Or has Tango One been packing a fortune in cash ever since we started surveillance on him? Where did that cash come from?'

Shortly afterwards the two men set off, each driving one of the ex-army Snatch Land Rovers.

Harper's team followed them back to London, Harper

taking the lead on his bike and the rest following in the car. It was after dark before the long drive back to London ended with the targets circling the capital on the eastbound M25, then turning off just south of the river. To the south-east of the junction the unearthly glare of light from the Bluewater shopping centre lit the night sky, but the two vehicles turned in the other direction, driving upstream from the Dartford River Crossing for a few miles, parallel to the south bank of the Thames, then turning off again into a light industrial estate, stopping outside one of thirty or forty units on the site, most of which looked to have seen better days.

The sprawling estate was dominated by a crumbling concrete structure, like a tower, part of a factory that must once have stood there and which the developers had not yet got round to demolishing. The units were occupied by the usual post-industrial mixture of service companies, printers, plumbing supplies, waste-product recyclers and direct-sales companies, leavened with a mixture of vacant and derelict sites, festooned with optimistic 'To Let' and 'Development Opportunity' signs. At first glance, the unit the targets had rented was no different from the others, but it stood out from its neighbours in one way: it was surrounded by a pristine new high-security fence.

Harper parked his motorbike, clambered part of the way up the concrete tower and, using a small pair of high-powered binoculars, he watched as McGovan unlocked the gates of the compound and the two men parked the Land Rovers in two lean-to garages, which formed part of the unit. The main building was a single-storey warehouse with a main entrance at the front but no windows that Harper could see. Before leaving the compound, McGovan tested the doors of the buildings, then walked around the site, checking the fence. Two twenty-foot shipping containers – one blue, the other blood red – had been parked at the far end and he examined them carefully, testing the padlocks on the doors. He waited until Yankee Four was safely outside the fence, before releasing a ferocious rough-coated German Shepherd, which had been locked up in a small shed at the side of the main building. 'Where the fuck did the dog come from?' said Maggie.

The two men left the site, locking the gate. They walked up the road together to the far end of the estate, then parted company, McGovan turning left towards Erith, while Yankee Four walked in the opposite direction, heading east.

Harper stood down the team, though Hansfree remained at his post in the ops room, monitoring the electronic equipment and the feed from McGovan's room at the military club. Before climbing down from the tower, Harper fixed a small surveillance camera to the rough concrete surface, using strips of gaffer tape to hold it in place, and adjusting it so that it was pointing at the jihadists' compound. When Hansfree's voice in his earpiece confirmed that he was receiving and monitoring the signal back in the ops room. Harper climbed down and walked towards the compound.

At that time in the evening, the other units on the site were quiet, locked up for the night, and, after making sure that the targets really had left the area and were not doubling back on their tracks, Harper walked around the perimeter of their unit, peering in through the chain-link fence. All the time he was doing so, he was being tracked by the dog, which kept pace with him all the way round. The Alsatian made no noise but its eyes never left Harper, and once or twice when it decided that he was too close, it flung itself at the fence, regardless of its own safety, baring its teeth. Even with a chain-link fence between them, Harper took an involuntary step back, startled by the savagery of the animal.

Using his binoculars, he looked closely into every part of the unit. Finally, when he was satisfied that he had seen everything there was to see on the site, he walked back to where he had left his bike and rode back into London at high speed.

43

Harper hurried up the stairs to the ops room, where Hansfree was sitting in darkness, staring at his computer screen, his face lit only by the cold metallic glow from the display. 'Give that a rest a moment,' he said. 'I need your help to access the site where the targets have stashed their vehicles and equipment.' Hansfree had his equipment cases stacked at the far end of the room, and after a few minutes' rummaging through them, he had what he needed: a battery-driven electric drill, a set of drill bits, and a fibre-optic endoscope, a super-thin, flexible extending device that enabled the user to penetrate sealed or inaccessible spaces. With the device came a couple of attachments that fitted onto the end of the optic cable: a small camera and an even smaller light.

The pair travelled in Hansfree's van, out through the hinterland of new builds, drab suburbs and fading industries that lined the south bank of the Thames.

On the way, Hansfree briefed Harper on what he'd discovered about the man he'd photographed in Paris. 'Dmitry Fedkin, assassin for hire,' said Hansfree. 'He operates mainly in Russia. Former Spetsnaz, as all the best Russian assassins are. As you know, Spetsnaz has become a catch-all for any sort of special-operations group, from the cops to bog-standard military. But Fedkin is the real thing, Alpha Group. It was created by KGB boss Yuri Andropov after the 1972 Munich Olympics massacre. The Germans fucked up big-time and the Russians wanted to make sure the same thing couldn't happen to them. They're on a par with the SAS or Delta Force. They were used as storm troopers, cracking the whip right across the former Soviet Union. After it fell apart, Alpha Group was downgraded and moved from pillar to post before being swallowed up by the Federal Security Service. Fedkin joined in 1996 and left five years ago to go private. Works for a company based in Moscow. Most of the clients are Russian Mafia or oligarchs, though these days those terms are pretty much interchangeable.' Hansfree looked across at Harper, frowning. 'Was he just following you, Lex? This guy isn't about surveillance, as a rule.'

'He didn't try anything, but he had a couple of henchmen who had a go.'

Hansfree nodded. 'Well, if this guy's on your case, you've got problems.'

'I spoke to him professional to professional,' said Harper. 'I think I'm good.'

It took them just over two hours to reach the industrial area where the targets had stored their vehicles and equipment. Hansfree parked well away from the unit and the two men studied the live pictures from the surveillance camera being relayed to his laptop before they got out of the van. All appeared quiet at the site, but they still made a covert approach, slipping between the patches of shadow in the lee of the other buildings on the site and pausing frequently for minutes at a time to look and listen before moving forward again. As they reached the compound, the German Shepherd spotted them and stood stock still as it stared at them, ears pricked.

'I can see what you mean about the dog,' Hansfree said. 'It's got a head like a bleeding alligator. Have you seen the state of those teeth? That's the most evil-looking guard dog I've ever seen.'

'It's not a guard dog,' Harper said. 'It's an attack dog. If they'd wanted a dog to work as a guard, they would have used one that barked whenever anyone walked within yards of the compound. This one is much too quiet for that, which makes it even more dangerous. Given the chance, it'll attack and kill if it can. The question is, where the hell did it come from? Muslims won't have anything to do with dogs – they reckon they're unclean. McGovan obviously has others helping him put this together.'

Harper walked parallel to the fence for a few yards, then turned back, all the time watching the dog intently. It kept its gaze just as firmly fixed on him and when he moved towards the fence and placed a hand against it, his fingers projecting through the steel mesh as if about to scale it, the dog launched itself at him in a heartbeat, its jaws closing with a snap on the point where Harper's fingers had been, its body crashing into the mesh with an impact that set the fence rattling for several yards in both directions. Harper had only just been in time as he snatched his hand away. The fact that it had attacked in total silence, without emitting so much as a growl, had been even more frightening.

Hansfree's face had gone even whiter than its usual pallor. 'Bloody hell,' he said. 'That's not a dog, it's a Terminator.'

'It's good, all right,' Harper said. 'I've got a mate who

makes a decent living training attack dogs. Normally the first stage in training a dog is to boss it. In effect you become the pack leader, and once you've dominated it, you can make it do what you want it to do. But with attack dogs it's just the opposite. You have to brutalise it, but if you want a dog to be a killer, of humans as well as other dogs, you have to defer to it constantly and retreat before it whenever it moves towards you. That tells the dog it's the leader of the pack, even when humans are around, which makes it much more aggressive and fearless.'

'That's all very interesting,' Hansfree said, 'but it doesn't tell me how you propose to deal with it.'

'I'm not quite sure myself yet,' Harper said. 'But it's going to have to die, there's no question of that. I can't see there's any way of us getting inside with the bastard thing alive. But we're going to have to make it look like natural causes or an accident, because if there are any unexplained wounds on it McGovan will know we're on to him. But I've got a plan. We'll just need a few bits and pieces before we start.' He led Hansfree back to where they'd left his van.

'Where to?' Hansfree said, as he started the engine.

'A corner shop will do.' Harper glanced at his watch. 'If you can find one that's still open, that is.'

They drove for a couple of miles before Hansfree spotted an open corner shop and pulled up outside. Harper went in and bought a can of some luridly coloured soft drink that only kids would have contemplated drinking and a packet of Haribo sweets. When he came back outside, he poured the drink into the gutter, crumpled the empty can and slipped it into his pocket. He ripped open the sweets and tipped them into the rubbish bin outside the shop, but once again he kept the crumpled packet and put it into his pocket with the can.

'What was that all about?' Hansfree said, but Harper merely winked and tapped the side of his nose with his finger.

'Now we need to find a charity shop or maybe some recycling bins would do.'

'There won't be any charity shops open, Lex – it's the middle of the night.'

'I know. It shouldn't make that much difference with what I'm looking for.'

Hansfree shot him another quizzical look, but Harper said nothing. They drove along a run-down high street where even the few shops that had not been boarded up or left empty had long since closed for the night. They passed several closed charity shops in a succession of rust-belt north Kent towns before they found what Harper was looking for. In the doorway of an Oxfam shop there was a stack of cardboard boxes and three or four carrier bags but, having rummaged through them, Harper returned to the van, shaking his head. 'No good,' he said. 'We'll have to try again.'

'If I knew what we were looking for, it might help,' Hansfree said.

'Children's shoes.'

Hansfree thought for a moment, then broke into a grin. 'Now I get it,' he said.

Having exhausted the local supply of charity shops, they drove to a large supermarket on the outskirts of a town. There was a row of recycling bins at the side of the access road, including two for clothes and shoes. Both were full to overflowing and several carrier bags had been left on the ground around them. This time Harper's search was rewarded and he returned to the van holding a carrier bag containing two pairs of children's trainers. 'We've hit the jackpot,' he said, with a smile.

They drove back to the industrial site, and as they walked towards the compound, Harper paused long enough to snap a thin branch from a spindly tree planted in a feeble attempt at landscaping the site. He carried it with him as they moved on towards the compound. The area was still silent and deserted but the dog was no less alert and watchful.

Harper ignored it and, keeping his feet clear of the muddy puddles in front of the compound's gates, he took the trainers out of the carrier bag and placed them on the ground, positioning them in as natural a way as he could, then putting his own foot on top of each one in turn. He pressed them down into the mud so that when he lifted them up again a pair of child-size footprints had been imprinted in the mud. He repeated the process a couple of dozen times altogether, until it appeared that a small group of children had paused by the gates, then moved towards the fence and stood there for some time. To reinforce that impression, he took the crushed can from his pocket and tossed it onto the ground, then crumpled the empty Haribo bag into a ball and placed it at the foot of the fence next to the gate, hooking it onto a loose strand of wire so it couldn't blow away. He poked the thin branch through the bars of the gate. The dog pounced on it at once, biting it savagely and, as Harper tried to pull it back, it broke off the end with a vicious jerk of its head.

Harper withdrew what was left of the branch and examined it carefully. The broken end was now scored with the dog's tooth marks. He nodded to himself and dropped the stick on the ground next to the gate. 'Right,' he said. 'Job done. Let's get to work.' He left Hansfree taunting the dog by rattling the fence while he quietly moved to the opposite side of the compound. The dog was puzzled and didn't know which target to pursue first, repeatedly switching its gaze from one man to the other, but Hansfree kept goading it and forced it to focus on him by repeatedly moving towards the fence and rattling it. Every time he touched the fence, the dog hurled itself at the other side of it with such force that it left a few tufts of its fur caught on the wire. It became even more confused when Hansfree put his prosthetic hands through the gate and tried to entice the dog to bite them. It needed no encouragement but found its jaws closing on steel fingers rather than flesh-and-blood ones. While the dog's full attention was focused on Hansfree, Harper seized the moment to climb up and jump over the fence at the back of the compound.

As he hit the ground, he immediately crouched in a boxer's stance, bracing himself for the onslaught from the dog. It had heard the thud as his feet hit the ground and immediately stopped biting at Hansfree's prosthetic hands. It spun around and raced across the yard towards Harper. A few feet from him, it launched itself into the air, its hackles raised, yellow teeth bared and jaws gaping, ready to tear out Harper's throat.

As the dog approached, Harper forced himself to suppress any fear and kept a cold, savage focus on the animal that was hurtling towards him. At the last possible moment before it struck him, so close that he could feel the dog's foul breath on his face, Harper grabbed both of its front legs in his hands. Just as the dog's jaws filled his vision, he put all his strength into one vicious jerk, first forcing the dog's legs inwards and then yanking them apart. He heard a distinct crack as the animal's sternum and ribcage collapsed and the jagged ends of the bones were driven deep into its heart. It was already dead as its momentum sent it crashing into Harper. He fell onto his back, with the dog pressing down on his chest.

Harper exhaled in a long, juddering breath, then pushed the beast to one side and got to his feet. It took several seconds of deep, controlled breathing before he had recovered enough to carry on. He stared down at the animal, examining the fur on its chest for any external sign of what had killed it. It looked far less fearsome in death and seemed diminished in size, more like a discarded and dilapidated fur coat than the savage and powerful creature it had been just moments before. Harper hoisted it onto his shoulders and walked over to the fence, close to where he had left the footprints. He hefted the dog up and poked its front two legs through the fence, making it look as if it had hurled itself there and become entangled.

'I get it,' said Hansfree. 'Kids tease the dog, dog goes crazy, dog dies. Think they'll buy that?'

'I don't see why not,' said Harper.

'I didn't think you were going to kill it with your bare hands,' said Hansfree. 'Where did you learn that trick?'

'In the Paras,' said Harper. 'But that's the first time I've done it for real. They're vulnerable once they leap. They lose all traction and they can't see what's underneath them.

Then it's just a matter of timing. Now let's get a move on. It's already almost two o'clock and we've still got a lot of work to do.'

Hansfree went to the gate and passed the drill and the fibre-optic endoscope through to Harper, who took them back to the unit while Hansfree kept watch. He walked around to the back of the first of the two sea-containers, and drilled a narrow-diameter hole through the steel wall near the top so that it was well above anyone's eyeline. He fed the endoscope with the light attachment through the hole and put his eye to the scope. The container was partly filled with uniforms – British Army by the look of them – in plastic bags. Next to them was a stack of wooden boxes. Harper moved the endoscope to get a better look. He caught his breath as he saw that the boxes were marked PE-4A. PE-4 was the British equivalent of the widely available plastic explosive C-4, a mixture of explosive with a plastic binder and a plasticiser to make it as malleable as Plasticine, so that it could be formed into any shape desired. An explosion could only be initiated by the combination of intense heat and a shock wave produced by a detonator. All manufacturers of C-4 and its variants, including PE-4A, routinely added to the mix a chemical tag or marker, a constituent unique to that particular batch of explosive, so that forensic teams could trace the batch's origins if it was later used in a terrorist attack or any other unauthorised way.

Harper knew that plastic explosives were not hard to find on the international black market in arms, providing you had the necessary funds, but they were almost always from corrupt sources in Russia and the former Soviet republics. However, the PE-4A labelling showed that this batch was of British origin, which was a worry.

There were other items inside the shipping container, but even with the endoscope it wasn't possible for Harper to identify all of them. Harper withdrew it, removed the light from the end and swapped it for a miniaturised camera. He then fed the endoscope back through the hole in the container wall and took a number of photographs for later analysis.

The contents of the second container were equally alarming. It held a variety of weapons, including a number of British SA-80 rifles and a tripod-mounted AT-4 Spigot anti-tank missile, a piece of ex-Soviet equipment that, despite its age, still packed a very formidable punch. The SA-80s were the L85 IW version, with IW standing for 'individual weapon'. It was the standard issue rifle for the British armed forces.

'With what they've got in the other container,' Hansfree said, 'that is some very heavy-duty kit.'

'Right,' Harper said. 'And you don't need to put something like this together just to carry out some penny-ante operation. They must be planning something big and we need to discover what it is pronto – before we find out the hard way when the bombs go off.'

Hansfree recorded everything they had seen and made a note of the serial numbers stencilled on the outside of the containers, so that their origins and the route by which they had come to the site could be traced and their onward movement tracked, if the jihadists later transferred them to a different site.

While Hansfree was doing that, Harper did a quick walk-around of the main warehouse unit. There was only one way in, which was locked and shuttered. He spent several more minutes carefully erasing every trace of his presence, including scooping up a little mud from a puddle and rubbing it over the drill holes he had made in the container walls, obscuring the thin line of bright metal that had been just visible around the edge of each hole. He slipped off his jacket and dragged it along the ground, using it like a brush to erase his footprints and the marks where the dog had dug its paws into the ground as it launched itself towards him, then took a final, careful look around, searching for any other incriminating traces he might have missed. He climbed back over the fence and walked away, with Hansfree, at a steady pace, without any visible sign of haste but putting distance between himself and the compound as quickly as he could.

44

As soon as he got back to central London, Hansfree dropped Harper close to an all-night internet café in a side street on the fringes of Soho, a few blocks north of Leicester Square. As usual, Harper seated himself at the furthest terminal from the cash desk, then left a message for Charlotte Button using the usual drafts folder technique. He kept it short and sweet: *We need to talk. Are you in London?*

He ordered a coffee and sipped it as he waited for a response. After half an hour he gave up and went back to his room in Bayswater. In the early hours of the morning his phone beeped and he rolled over to look at the screen. It was a text message: *You've got mail.* He cursed, got out of bed, dressed, and headed out. He managed to find a black cab and had the driver drop him in Soho. The area was still busy, with more than its fair share of gay couples walking home arm in arm, and Harper received a number of admiring glances, which he managed to ignore, on the way to the internet café.

Button's message was in the draft folder: *I'm in London but am pretty sure I'm being followed most of the time. I can lose them if necessary but if I slip up and they see you then we will have all sorts of problems. Call me on this number on the hour from six a.m. onwards.* He scribbled it down on a piece of paper, rearranging the last four digits, then deleted the file.

He put a new message in the drafts folder, *Six it is*, and signed off. He looked at his watch. It was four o'clock, which meant he had two hours to kill. He bought another coffee and passed the time on the internet, reading up on the weapons and explosives he'd seen in the containers and studying Google Maps of the area.

At five he caught a black cab to Bayswater, which, like Soho, was one of the areas of the city that never seemed to sleep. He spent forty-five minutes running all the anti-surveillance techniques he knew, made easier by the fact that the streets were much quieter now than they were during the daytime, then walked to Paddington station. At precisely six o'clock he called the number from a public phone on the station concourse and Button answered on the third ring. 'I'm so sorry about the cloak-and-dagger,' she said.

'Who's after you?' he asked.

'Israelis, I think. An Israeli company anyway. Though it looks as if they've subcontracted it to a UK security firm.'

'So not the government?'

'I don't know. They could be doing it at arm's length. Same as they did with the Pool. And whoever it is has access to airline manifests. I'm working on it but I can't risk putting you and your team in the firing line, so I'm going to have to steer clear of you until it's resolved.'

'I appreciate that,' said Harper. 'But there's a lot you need to know.'

'I'm listening.'

'Your man is getting ready to move. No question. He has a team in place, some Asian, some white, and he has two shipping containers filled with gear, including British Army uniforms, SA-80 rifles, anti-tank missiles and a hell of a lot of plastic explosives.'

'Explosives?'

'PE-4A, which can only have been sourced – I'm assuming stolen – from within the UK.'

'And where is this equipment?'

'An industrial estate near Gravesend, not far from the Dartford River Crossing. This is big. Huge. He's got arms and explosives and jihadists ready to go, and with the best will in the world all I have is a team of surveillance people. If you're serious about wanting to stop your man, then all you need to do is make one phone call. There's all the evidence you need to send him away for a long time.'

'It's not about sending him away,' said Button. 'The contract is for a cancellation.'

'Cancellation' was Button-speak for a killing. Someone was paying to have Caleb McGovan killed. Harper didn't know who would be paying the bill, but he could think of lots of reasons why someone would prefer a home-grown jihadist to be in the ground rather than on trial. But at the end of the day it wasn't his place to question the contract: he was just a hired hand.

'That's not a problem,' said Harper. 'I know where he is and where he usually goes, I can do it from the back of a motorcycle anytime I want. But what about the jihadists? What about his plan? Isn't that a concern?'

'Not to the person who wants the cancellation,' said Button. 'I can't go into details but it's a very personal matter and seeing McGovan behind bars really won't cut it. He wants a cancellation, end of story.'

'And that's fair enough,' said Harper. 'McGovan has clearly crossed over to the dark side, and he's exactly the sort of target you would have been sent after by HM Government in the good old days. I'm not saying he doesn't merit cancellation, just pointing out there's a lot in play here. He's got home-grown jihadists working with him, and it looks as if someone else is pulling the strings. Someone behind the scenes is putting this together because McGovan himself isn't doing enough. The industrial unit near Gravesend, for instance. He can't have arranged that. The shipping containers. The money that's paying for it all. Yes, I can cancel McGovan but all the rest will still be in place.'

Button didn't say anything and, for a moment, Harper thought that he'd lost the connection. 'Are you still there?'

'I'm here. Just considering my options.'

'Look, we know McGovan is bad. No question. Give me the go-ahead for the cancellation, then make a phone call to the authorities.'

'Except that if you cancel McGovan tomorrow, the rest will presumably scatter. You're not going to keep a street-shooting quiet, are you? The cops will be called in, he'll be identified and, yes, we'll get the containers but we'll lose the jihadists and the mastermind who's behind it.'

'Maybe. But if we continue to let them run and the shit hits the fan – what then? If you were privy to what was going to happen and didn't do anything, we'll all be accomplices before the fact. People could die. A lot of people.'

'I hear what you're saying. Let me take advice and get back to you. In the meantime, keep a close eye on things. And keep me in the loop.'

'I've got to be honest, that's bloody difficult to do with all this Secret Squirrel stuff.'

'I don't think I've got any choice,' said Button. 'If the people after me are government-sponsored they'll be able to eavesdrop on any mobile I use.'

'So you're sticking to landlines or the draft folder? That's a pain. A real pain. How about this? Get a throwaway mobile but don't use it. Send me the number. If there's an emergency I'll call you, you can ditch it immediately afterwards and get another. It'll be expensive but I guess you can afford it.'

'I'll do that now,' she promised, and ended the call.

45

Harper went straight from Paddington to the ops room to brief the team. It was just Hansfree, the two Barrys and Maggie, as Hansfree was keeping his new hires at a distance, briefing them separately by radio and phone. His man Reggie had spent the night in a van outside the club and was due to be relieved by Nancy. Harper briefed them on what he had found in the containers and Hansfree used one of his laptops to show them the video Harper had taken through the endoscope.

'That explosive is a worry,' said Barry Whisper, stating the obvious.

'It's all a worry,' said Maggie. 'Especially the uniforms. What the hell are they planning?'

'Hopefully we'll find out soon enough,' said Harper. 'We're heading out there as soon as we've got fixed up with some four-by-fours. Barry Big, can you get on that now?'

'No problem,' he said, pulling out his phone. 'Any preferences?'

'Just something that can outperform the Land Rovers the bad guys have,' said Harper. 'Hansfree, what's the story with the camera I installed?'

Hansfree tapped on his keyboard and showed them the feed from the camera that Harper had fitted to the concrete tower overlooking the target unit. It wasn't a great picture and unfortunately didn't give anything like a clear view of the containers. 'That's a pity,' said Harper. He patted Hansfree's shoulder. 'How good are the drones you were talking about?'

'As good as anything the authorities have,' said Hansfree. 'But what about piloting them? Have you got experience with drones?'

'Enough,' said Harper. 'I was on special ops with the Paras in Afghanistan and I got to fly them then. I doubt they've changed much.'

'If anything, they're easier now,' said Hansfree. 'The new models have self-stabilising sensors and GPS hover capability.'

'Then hook me up and I'll get back there,' said Harper. 'The rest of you guys can follow me down once you've got the four-by-fours sorted.'

46

Harper had no trouble launching the drone Hansfree had given him, and it took him just a few minutes to relearn the skills he had picked up in the Paras, adjusting the throttle to increase and decrease the speed, and altering the pitch, roll and yaw of the four rotors to send the drone rising, falling or moving across the sky. It was illegal to fly a drone above five hundred feet in Britain without official permission, but the legality of his actions was the least of Harper's concerns and he sent the drone soaring higher until it was no more than a speck in the sky, and the sound of its motor was lost in the traffic noise from the main road on the far side of the industrial site. He had been controlling it manually but now he set the controls to 'Loiter', causing the drone to hold to a specific GPS setting, and maintain its position stationary over the industrial unit. He called Hansfree and within five minutes Hansfree reported that he was picking up the video feed from the drone's camera.

Harper had a laptop with him and Hansfree talked him through connecting it to the video feed. Within a few minutes he was able to view the astonishingly clear pictures from above. He brought the drone down and stored it in the boot of his BMW.

The rest of the team arrived a couple of hours later, Barry Big in a Range Rover, Barry Whisper and Maggie in a Jeep Cherokee. They parked half a mile away from the industrial unit. They didn't have long to wait. At ten o'clock Harper's earpiece crackled into life. 'Tango One is in motion,' Hansfree said. 'He's heading east.'

'Vehicle?'

'He was picked up by Yankee Four in a white Honda. We're on it.'

A succession of messages let Harper and the rest of the team keep track of McGovan's progress across London and out along the south bank of the Thames. When they were ten minutes away, Harper launched the drone and called his team to full alert as their subject entered the industrial area and drove to the site.

Two other men were with McGovan: Yankee Four was driving and an unidentified Asian male was sitting in the back. Harper watched on his laptop as McGovan and the jihadists got out of the vehicle. McGovan unlocked the main gate and the two men pulled it back. As the car drove through, McGovan spotted the dead dog.

Harper watched him examine the corpse. He straightened, looked around, then peered through the fence. The quality of the video was good enough for Harper to see what McGovan was peering at – the drinks can, sweets packet and kids' footprints.

McGovan waved for Yankee Four to park the car, then jogged out of the gate and around to where the footprints were. Harper saw him pick up the stick bearing the tooth marks of the dog, then peer at the clumps of the dog's fur still clinging to the fence. McGovan squatted on his haunches to study the footprints in the mud, then went back through the gate and took another look at the dead animal. He examined the dog minutely, then began a painstaking search of the area, paying particular attention to the locks on the sea-containers. Eventually he seemed satisfied and beckoned to one of the Asians. Together they pulled the dog off the fence, carried it, now rigid with rigor mortis, and dumped it in a nearby rubbish skip.

Harper heaved a huge sigh of relief. 'He's bought into it,' he said, into his shoulder mic. 'We're in business. Stand by, stand by.'

Slowly, over the course of several more hours, more men turned up at the industrial estate. Three arrived in another white Honda, all Asian. Two white men, who didn't look long out of their teens, arrived in a van. Two of the Asians began working on the Land Rovers but the rest either went inside the containers or into the industrial unit. There was no way of monitoring their activities because even the sophisticated spy drone couldn't see through steel.

'Are you getting all these new arrivals?' Harper asked Hansfree.

'I am,' said Hansfree over the radio. 'They're all new faces. Someone is overseeing this, for sure. Tango One hasn't seen them before.'

At midday a delivery van also dropped off a number of cardboard containers at the site. By narrowing the focus of the telescopic camera on the drone and zooming it in to the maximum, Harper managed to read off the numbers, and within a few minutes, Hansfree had identified the boxes as army patrol rations.

In the afternoon the jihadists began transferring most

of the stores and equipment from the containers to the Land Rovers. The task took several hours, and when they had finished they all disappeared inside one of the containers, reappearing with armfuls of uniforms that they carried inside the warehouse. Maggie left her vehicle and came to sit in Harper's BMW to watch the feed from the drone as she snacked on a cheese sandwich and a can of Red Bull.

Some thirty minutes later, eight of the men came out. Four were Asian, three were white and one was the mixed-race man they had called Yankee Four. They were all dressed in British Army issue military camouflage gear with webbing and backpacks to match. They lined up and McGovan inspected them.

'They're getting ready to move,' Harper said into his radio. 'On your toes, everyone. Hansfree, I count eight. There are ten jihadists, right?'

'Affirmative,' said Hansfree. 'The other two must still be inside the warehouse.'

Harper brought the drone back down, flying it well away from the area before descending. He stored it in the boot of the BMW, along with the controller.

'I no longer have eyeball,' said Harper.

'I have,' said Barry Big. 'Tango One is carrying out a final inspection of the Land Rovers. Now they're getting on board. Four in each vehicle.'

'What about Tango One?' asked Harper.

'Tango One is getting into a blue VW Jetta.'

'That means they're leaving two men behind. Okay, Barry Big and Barry Whisper, you follow the convoy. Hansfree, you need to keep a team in surveillance here.'

'Understood,' said Hansfree. 'Reggie and Nancy are already in place and I have another team of four en route.'

'And the trackers are still functioning?'

'I'm looking at them as we speak.'

'Game on, then,' said Harper. He looked across at Maggie. 'You might as well stay with me,' he said.

'I could do with my bag,' she said.

Harper drove her to her SUV. She nipped out, grabbed her bag, climbed back in and they headed off in pursuit of McGovan and his convoy.

47

A few minutes later, the targets were driving counter-clockwise on the M25 and soon afterwards they turned onto the A1, heading north. It was an easy follow for Harper and his team: the men were travelling in typical military-convoy style, driving with fully lit headlamps, sticking religiously to every speed limit. After four hours they stopped at a service station to refuel the vehicles. They also filled several onboard jerry-cans. Harper could see that McGovan was very careful to ensure that only the non-Asian jihadists left the vehicles while the refuelling was taking place.

To Harper's surprise, just north of Leeds the convoy split into two, with McGovan's VW peeling off west from the A1.

Maggie told Barry Big and Barry Whisper to keep after the Land Rovers while Harper followed McGovan.

McGovan drove past Harrogate, then off the main road onto a narrow lane. On the skyline ahead of them, Harper could see the tops of the radomes of the American listening station on Menwith Hill. It was a still, chilly day, and the ground mist clinging to the moorland around the base gave the white radomes dotting the site an even more unearthly air than usual, as if they were alien craft hovering just above the ground.

Harper dropped back even further behind the VW as he saw it slow, then pull onto the grass verge. He watched as McGovan climbed out and began observing the listening station through a pair of binoculars. Menwith Hill was supposedly an RAF establishment – the sign by the gates proclaimed as much – but 90 per cent of the operatives manning the computers in the hardened concrete bunkers beneath those radomes were US personnel, and Menwith Hill could scarcely have been more American if it had been flown across the Atlantic and dropped in the middle of Kansas.

Warning notices hung from the fence every few metres and CCTV cameras on every stanchion kept watch for intruders.

'He doesn't seem worried about the CCTV,' said Maggie.

'He's standing in a blind spot,' said Harper. 'Plus the security is a hangover from the days when there was a peace camp next to the site and the guards were on perpetual full alert. But the women protesters were evicted years ago and the peace camp bulldozed so I think everyone is a bit more relaxed these days.' McGovan stayed at the site for no more than a couple of minutes, then made a U-turn and drove back the way he had come.

As soon as he saw the Jetta begin to turn, Harper drove down the lane and up a muddy farm track to a point where a copse of trees shielded him from view. He waited until the VW had passed the end of the track, then pulled out and continued to follow it as McGovan returned to the northbound A1. Driving quickly, he soon caught up with the Land Rovers that had been maintaining the same stately pace as they headed north.

As the day wore on, they continued driving still further north and crossed the county border into Northumberland. They passed to the west of Newcastle and, turning off the A1, drove deep into the Cheviots to within a few miles of the Scottish border. Harper had been in no doubt for some time about where they were heading and it was confirmed as, not long after dark, the convoy turned onto the road leading to the Otterburn Ranges, the vast training area used by the British Army.

They passed through Otterburn village, but instead of approaching the main entrance to the sprawling 60,000-acre site, with the squat guardhouse behind high steel gates topped with razor wire, they carried on along the edge of the ranges, skirting them to the east. They passed occasional conifer plantations, barely visible as belts of deeper black against the dark moorland.

They drove on even further into the wilderness, along minor roads that were now completely deserted but for the Land Rovers and the four-by-fours of the surveillance team trailing them. To avoid being detected, Harper and his team had switched off their lights and were driving using passive night goggles, which made the road show up as an eerie yellow-orange ribbon of brighter light in the surrounding moorland. The eyes of rabbits and other animals watching in the darkness shone out like torch beams.

They followed the convoy for several more miles until they turned off down a track towards the main firing range and drove into a valley, a narrow stretch of wooded, gently rising low ground between two parallel ridges. It was flanked on three sides by higher ground and visible only from directly below. The valley had a screen of fir trees close to the road, with a barrier to prevent civilian traffic entering the range's danger area, and McGovan left one of the Land Rovers there, behind the barrier but still in clear sight of any passing traffic. He also posted a sentry in full military gear, holding a rifle.

While Barry Big and Barry Whisper drove off to find an observation point on the far side of the valley, Harper found a track where he could leave the BMW out of sight. He and Maggie got out of the car and moved silently through the woods to a point where, still using their night-vision goggles, they could observe the targets. 'What the hell are they up to?' Maggie whispered, as they watched McGovan posting his sentry at the barrier. 'They're just asking to be challenged, out in the open like that.'

'They're hiding in plain sight, and the chance of anyone challenging them there is pretty remote,' said Harper. 'To any casual observer, even a passing military patrol, it'll look like another small military deployment and there are always plenty of those going on here. Once you've got yourself onto the ranges, and it's not hard because security is pretty lax, all you have to do is mount a guard, look like you know what you're doing, stay out of the red-flagged areas when the guns are firing and no one will bother you, especially here.'

'Why here in particular?' she said.

'Because it's so vast. There's a firing range down the middle so long and wide that it's the only place in Britain where the army can test fire its AS-90 self-propelled artillery pieces and the M-270 Multiple Launch Rocket Systems.

They have a maximum range of forty miles, and even with a reduced propellant charge to shorten their range, they have to be tested here because none of the other army ranges is big enough for them to be fired without the risk of wiping out a few civilian motorists or hikers enjoying a day out just beyond the ranges. There are four hundred square miles of rough moorland out there on those ranges plus some other very weird stuff. There are long-abandoned replicas of Belfast streets and Londonderry apartment blocks, where the troops used to practise before deploying to Northern Ireland, and much more recent replicas of Iraqi streets, and villages in Afghanistan as well. I kid you not, if there were some mulberry trees, a few kites flying in the sky overhead and the mountains of the Hindu Kush in the distance, you'd swear you were actually in Afghanistan.'

'You still haven't answered my question. Why are they here?'

'I'm pretty sure that the listening station on Menwith Hill is a target. That's what McGovan was looking at earlier. But I'm guessing he's here to do some training with them. It looks to me like this is the first time he's met his team and he needs to know how they'll react under pressure.'

'So we watch and wait?'

'I'm afraid so. Make yourself as comfortable as you can, though I appreciate that's not going to be easy.'

48

Once his team had settled down for the night, Harper phoned Hansfree for a private conversation. During active operations Hansfree rarely slept and Harper pictured the man sitting hunched over his computers, fuelled by Red Bull and coffee.

'Two more have arrived at the unit,' said Hansfree. 'Both white. It happened after dark so we don't have any usable pictures. And I've managed to track the serial numbers of the containers. Interesting route. In reverse we have Felixstowe, Rotterdam and Karachi. They had previously been used by the Ministry of Defence to ship stores to Camp Bastion in Afghanistan, and then, supposedly empty, they were shipped back to the UK. So the only question remaining is how the hell the weapons came to be in the hands of McGovan's mates in ISIS.'

'Who knows?' Harper said. 'The Spigot is probably old Russian Army stock left behind after the Soviet pull-out from Afghanistan in 1989. But the odds are that the SA-80s, the plastic explosives and the rest of the kit, were either stolen or captured in Afghanistan, though it's also possible that they were made in Peshawar, in north-west Pakistan. I passed through there a while ago. There are about three million people in the city and it seemed like half of them were involved in the arms trade. They claimed they could copy and make any weapon in the world. I heard one arms trader boasting that he could even make a copy of a Stinger missile. It sounded like bullshit to me but, having seen what else they can produce, I wouldn't have wanted to bet too much money on it.'

'One other thing,' Hansfree said. 'Did you see the metal stuff in the first container you looked at?'

Harper frowned. 'What metal stuff?'

'I've got some stills.' His claws tapped on the keyboard and a shot of some metal brackets filled the screen. 'They look like shelving or something?'

Harper grinned. 'Nah, they're for making shaped charges. You use them to gain explosive entry to a building by blowing out the doors or windows, or blasting holes in the walls. You pack the brackets with plastic explosive to make the charge, then set them off with electric detonators. It's a bit of an art. The SAS are masters at it but we did it in the Paras. When you use them, you have to tamp the charge with sandbags or something similar to make sure the explosion goes the way you want it to go or it can dissipate into the line of least resistance. They're the dog's bollocks when it comes to getting you into a heavily defended building. I've made one or two shaped charges in the past myself and I'm sure McGovan will have done too. The question is, what the hell is he planning to do with shaped charges?'

'What do you want me to do with the extra surveillance bodies?' asked Hansfree. 'Do you need anyone else up there?'

'Keep them on the industrial unit,' said Harper, and

ended the call. He got out of his car for some fresh air while he decided what to do about Charlie Button. He needed to tell her what was going on but standard operating procedure was for him to initiate contact through the draft email folder and he was miles away from the nearest internet café. He could access the folder through the laptop in the car, but if she was being tracked by any of the government agencies there was a chance they would follow any electronic trail to him. Using proxies wouldn't help if GCHQ was on her case, and if they traced his laptop they were perfectly capable of accessing all the files on his hard drive.

He paced up and down for a while, looking up at the blanket of stars overhead. There was little light pollution or cloud cover so he felt as if he could see to the end of the universe. The more he stared at a section of the night sky, the more stars became visible.

'Penny for them?' said a voice behind him, and Harper jumped. It was Barry Whisper, who was as quiet when he moved as when he spoke.

'Bloody hell, Barry, don't creep up on me like that,' he said. 'And why have you left your post?'

'The bad guys have bedded down for the night. Just a couple of sentries, and I guess they'll rotate them. They're here to train, right?'

'Looks like it.'

'For how long?'

'Fucked if I know, Barry. Why?'

'Because we've no water, no toilet facilities, no food. We're going to be in a pretty poor state tomorrow, and even worse the next day.'

'What are you suggesting?'

He shrugged. 'Like I said, they're bedded down for the night. I could take a run out to the main road, see if I can find an all-night place. Stock up on food and water, plastic bags to shit in, all the basics.'

Harper nodded. 'Good call.'

'You want something?'

Harper grinned. 'Anything with caffeine in it.'

'I hear you.' Barry Whisper slipped away into the darkness as quietly as he had arrived. Harper unzipped his hip-pack and took out a Samsung smartphone. He hadn't used it, or the Sim card it contained. He switched it on, launched the browser and went to the draft file. There was a message from Charlotte Button, with a list of six telephone numbers, presumably throwaway mobiles she had purchased. He took out another phone, switched it on and tapped the numbers into a memo, rearranging the final digits as a security measure.

He paced up and down, considering his options. He really didn't like calling Button mobile to mobile, even when they were both using throwaways. It wasn't just the danger of being overheard – GCHQ was able to listen out for specific voices and home in on them – it was the fact that GPS technology now meant that a phone's location could be pinpointed to within a few feet, with or without an active Sim card. It also meant a direct traceable link between Button and Harper, which wasn't good for either of them. But he had to talk to her, and soon, and the nearest internet café was probably fifty miles away, certainly not open at that time of night.

He cursed under his breath and tapped out the first of the numbers she had given him. It rang out for more than a minute before she answered. From the sound of it she was inside. Music was playing, something classical. 'It's me,' he said. Neither would be using names.

'Problem?'

'They've moved from the industrial estate,' said Harper. 'They're up near the Scottish border on the Otterburn ranges. Looks like they're going to do some training. They're planning some serious mischief, and the longer you let it run, the more the risk someone is going to get hurt.'

'How many are there?'

'There's Tango One and eight other males, some Asian, some white. There are another four back at the industrial unit in Gravesend. We've only identified three. If it was me, I'd pass this on to the SAS and get them in, slot the lot of them.'

'Unfortunately the SAS don't do that any more,' said Button. 'That's why they created the Pool.'

'I can't take on nine men armed with automatic weapons and explosives,' said Harper. 'Not when one of them is former SAS.'

'I don't need you to cancel them all,' said Button. 'Just Tango One.'

'So that's a go on Tango One, is it?'

'It is. Whenever you're ready.'

'The problem with that is he's now on an army training ground surrounded by heavily armed jihadists. It isn't a case of being able to swing by on a motorcycle and put one in the back of his head, like it was in London.'

'Can you get to him?'

'At the moment, no. At least, not without considerable risk to myself and my team. We've got one handgun between us.'

'So what are your options?'

Harper sighed. 'Watch and wait. At least while they're on the range they're only a danger to themselves. Tango One had a good look at the Menwith Hill listening station on the way up so I think he's considering that as a target. Once they're on the move we'll have a better idea of what they're up to and I might be able to get closer.'

'Do that, then.'

'My advice to you would be to get the professionals in. If this blows up and they find out that you knew it about it, you could be in deep shit.'

'While I appreciate your concern, I'm in deep shit anyway at the moment. And my problem is that I don't know who I can trust and who I can't.'

'I hope you're not including me in the can't-be-trusted list.'

'You know that's not what I meant. If there is government involvement, something like this could be the last nail in my coffin.'

'Or it could be your salvation. You ride in and save the day. They might give you a medal.'

'They might. Or they might look at what happens to Tango One and start asking questions. I just want this to go away. At the moment I feel like I'm under a microscope and it's making me very nervous.'

'How is your situation?'

'It's being looked at by a couple of friends, here and in the US. Once I know who's on my case I'll know how to deal with it.'

'You're sure I can't do more to help?'

'Just take care of Tango One. And keep me in the loop. That'll be more than enough.'

'What about intel on the guys Tango One has hooked up with? Do you want that?'

'It can wait until you're back in London,' she said.

Harper ended the call and took the phone apart. He slid out the Sim card, broke it in half, pulled out the battery and threw it away, then stamped on the phone until it was beyond repair. He scraped a hole in the soil and buried it. As he straightened up he saw that Maggie had got out of the car and was watching him, clearly bemused. 'Bad news?' she said.

49

Harper and his team took it in turns to doze or catnap for a couple of hours during the night. At just after three thirty Barry Whisper returned with several carrier bags of provisions. The only place he'd been able to find open was a shop attached to an all-night filling station so he had packs of sandwiches, other snacks, bottles of water, cans of coffee and Red Bull. On the hygiene front he'd bought some toothpaste, toothbrushes, disposable razors and cans of shaving foam, plus several packs of wet wipes. He had persuaded the cashier to let him have a dozen small plastic bags, though he hadn't explained what he'd be using them for.

Well before first light the next morning, they were in position and ready to monitor the activities of the targets in the valley. Harper launched the drone and had it in a hover high overhead so he could watch what they were doing on his laptop.

Tutored by McGovan, five of the jihadists were taught to strip and assemble their SA-80s, and while that was going on, a further three-man team did 'dry' practice training with the Spigot anti-tank missile, assembling it, stripping it down, reassembling it, and practising range-finding, loading, reloading, and sighting – everything, short of actually firing it.

After their basic training in weapon-handling, the jihadists moved on to fire and movement drills using live ammunition, with some of the group providing covering fire while the rest were advancing towards a notional target. Known in the military as 'pepper-potting', it was the basis of all infantry manoeuvres, but the surveillance team concluded that it was as foreign to McGovan's raw jihadi recruits as Ancient Greek. However, while they were raw and untutored, they weren't lacking in bravery. Even with live fire whistling a few inches over their heads, Harper didn't see a single one flinch, or hesitate for a second in rising from cover when McGovan gave the order to move.

Screened by the terrain of the valley and the belts of forestry that surrounded it, the jihadists' training continued without any interruption from outsiders. The noise of their activities, even the rattle and crack of live firing from semi-automatics, was lost in the heavy crump of artillery and mortar rounds, and the barrages of small-arms fire from the main ranges on the other side of the hill, where various army groups and new recruits were being put through their paces.

The jihadists' training went on until just before last light, when McGovan ended the practice drills. He formed his jihadists into a circle around him and spoke to them for almost half an hour. The surveillance team could not pick up what was being said but it was obvious from the jihadists' body language – the way they sat motionless, not speaking but listening intently – that he was delivering the final briefing before their long-planned attack. When he had finished speaking, the jihadists embraced each other, then packed up all their weapons and equipment and began loading them back on to the Land Rovers. Harper concentrated on identifying which vehicle held the Spigot anti-tank missile – he was sure it would be the crucial piece of the jigsaw.

By now Harper was reasonably sure that the jihadists intended to attack the listening station on Menwith Hill, using the Spigot missile from long distance, followed by a short-range attack, probably using suicide bombers and shaped charges to gain entry, but he wouldn't know for sure until they were on the move.

50

Harper was woken just after dawn by a warning from Barry Big in his earpiece. 'Look lively, Lex, the Tangos are getting ready to leave.'

Harper was sleeping in the back of the BMW and he sat up, rubbing his face. 'What's happening?'

'They're loading up the Land Rovers. Looks like they're leaving the range.'

Maggie was awake. She had been napping in the front passenger seat and pulled it into the upright position.

'Barry Whisper, you hear this?' asked Harper.

'Roger that,' said Barry Whisper. 'I'm ready to go.'

'Okay, Barry Big take point, Barry Whisper car two. Maggie and I'll bring up the rear. Hansfree, do you still have the trackers?'

'Both are running just fine,' said Hansfree.

'Let's give them plenty of space, then,' said Harper. Maggie shifted over to the driving seat. Harper grabbed a bottle of water as he got out of the car. He rinsed his mouth, spat, then got into the front passenger seat. 'Where are they, Barry Whisper?'

'Heading for Otterburn village, probably towards the A1.'

Maggie put the car in gear and they headed off in pursuit.

Barry Big and Barry Whisper took it in turns to give updates on the progress of the three-vehicle convoy as it headed south. The Land Rovers followed the strict discipline of a military convoy, driving with headlights on and observing all the speed limits. McGovan's VW led the way but his headlights were off.

As they got closer to the intersection with the A59, Barry Big closed the gap with the convoy. He kept up a running commentary over the final mile: they would be taking the westbound route if they were heading back to Menwith Hill.

'The Land Rovers are turning off,' said Barry Big, as the convoy reached the intersection. 'But Tango One is not indicating and is not changing direction. Repeat, Tango One is leaving the convoy, continuing south along the A1.'

Harper's mind raced. It could be that McGovan was in a rush to get to the target first or that he was heading somewhere completely different. If that was the case there was a risk they would lose him because, unlike the Land Rovers, there was no tracking device on his car. 'Okay, I'll go with Tango One, you stay with the Land Rovers.' He motioned for Maggie to pick up the pace and she stamped on the accelerator.

'To do what exactly?' asked Barry Big.

'Just stick with them,' said Harper.

'Roger that, but they're armed to the teeth and all I've got is my wit and charm.'

'I'll send reinforcements. Just keep eyeballing them,' said Harper. 'Barry Whisper, you stay behind Barry Big. Hansfree, you're still tracking them?'

'Affirmative,' said Hansfree.

'Keep me posted. Maggie and I'll be with Tango One.'

As Maggie accelerated, Harper unzipped his hip-pack, took out the phone he'd used to store Button's numbers and tapped one out. It rang out for a minute and she didn't answer. He redialled and this time she picked up the call. 'The RAF station at Menwith Hill is going to be attacked,' he said.

'When?'

'The jihadists are heading there with all the gear. But Tango One is still driving south and I'm going with him.'

'What do you think's happening?'

'I'd say they're definitely getting ready to attack Menwith Hill but that might be a diversion. Get everyone's attention focused up here while they do something bigger down south.'

'What about Tango One? Are you still on schedule for the cancellation?'

'If I get him on his own, yes. That's more likely now that the main group has split off. But as I said, at the moment I've no idea where he's going. You need to take care of Menwith Hill otherwise it's going to be a bloodbath.'

'The professionals are on their way,' said Button. 'What about you?'

'I'm following Tango One. He's on his own so he's less of a threat now. But I've no idea what he's up to. You need to get Menwith Hill sorted.'

'I heard you the first time. I'll deal with it. You just concentrate on McGovan.'

She ended the call. Harper peered through the windscreen. There was still no sign of the VW Jetta and he was about to tell Maggie to put her foot down even further when she gestured with her chin. 'There he is. Just in front of that coach.' She eased back on the accelerator.

'Nice job,' he said. 'All right, everybody, we have eyes on Tango One, heading south.'

51

McGovan kept his VW at a steady 70 m.p.h. and Maggie had no trouble following him as he headed down the A1. He joined the M1 outside Leeds, and Harper had assumed that McGovan was driving back to London so he was caught by surprise when the car took the M62, heading west to Manchester.

'What's he up to?' he wondered. 'Manchester hasn't been on our radar.' He called up Hansfree and asked him for a sit rep on the Land Rovers.

'They're not moving,' said Hansfree. 'They're about a mile away from the listening station.'

'Barry Big, Barry Whisper, either of you have eyeball?'

'Roger that,' said Barry Big, in Harper's earpiece. 'They're unloading their gear. They're not going anywhere.'

'Keep well clear. The SAS are heading their way,' said Harper.

'Lex, four more Yankees have arrived at the unit,' said Hansfree. 'All Asians.'

'Four more? How many's that now?'

'That makes eight. The latest arrivals came in two cars so there are four vehicles there now.'

'Can you see what they're doing?'

'Negative on that. They're all inside the unit. To be honest, if it was me I'd be calling three nines by now. They're clearly up to something and there's enough ordinance in there to put them away for a long time.'

'Just maintain surveillance,' said Harper. 'Let's see what Tango One is up to.'

McGovan drove into the city. Maggie had to get closer to make sure they didn't lose him but McGovan didn't seem to be checking his mirrors or doing anything in the way of anti-surveillance.

Harper's mobile rang. It was Button. 'Where are you?' she asked.

'Manchester.'

'Manchester? What's happening in Manchester?'

'That's where McGovan is.'

'He's on his own?'

'Yes. And if I get the chance I'll take care of it.'

'And everybody else?'

'One of my team is with me. The rest are split between the industrial unit in Gravesend and the jihadists up at Menwith Hill.'

'That's why I'm calling,' said Button. 'The SAS are heading to Menwith Hill now. You need to make sure your people are clear by the time they get there.'

'Will do.'

'And keep me posted on McGovan.'

'Understood,' said Harper. He ended the call and switched to the radio. 'Barry Whisper, Barry Big, you need to pull out now. Back to Gravesend.'

'They're all out of the vehicles, Lex,' said Barry Big. 'I think it's going to kick off.'

'That's why you need to get the hell away,' said Harper. 'The heavy mob are moving in.' Ahead of them, McGovan's VW was slowing and indicating a left turn into a multi-storey car park. 'I've got to go,' said Harper.

McGovan stopped at a ticket machine, took a ticket, and after the barrier had gone up he drove through. Maggie followed him.

McGovan parked on the third floor. Maggie drove past and reversed into a parking space. McGovan got out of his VW and headed for the lift.

'Do I stay or come with you?' asked Maggie.

Harper had to make a split-second decision with almost no intel to go on. All he had was his gut feeling. 'Come with,' he said, grabbing his backpack. He climbed out, lifted the carpet, retrieved his gun from the hidden compartment and shoved it into his backpack. They hurried down the stairs and got to the ground floor just as McGovan stepped out of the lift. They followed him outside. McGovan was walking purposefully with no anti-surveillance techniques. Maggie slipped her arm through his. 'Cover,' she whispered.

Harper laughed. They walked faster, closing the gap. Harper realised they were heading for Manchester Piccadilly station. 'Hansfree, looks like he's catching a train,' he whispered into his radio mic.

'Where are you?'

'Manchester Piccadilly.'

'The trains run every twenty minutes to London Euston. Journey time just over two hours,' said Hansfree. 'But there are trains leaving for Liverpool, Hull, Norwich, Blackpool – he could be going anywhere.'

The pavements were relatively crowded so they were

able to stick fairly close to McGovan as he headed inside the station. He joined the queue for the ticket office. Harper let a couple of people join the line, then took his place. Maggie put a phone to her ear and faked a phone call, standing close to the ticket windows.

When it was McGovan's turn to buy a ticket they were lucky – the window was only a few feet from where Maggie was standing and she was able to overhear his destination. She nodded at Harper and went to one the automatic machines, still pretending to talk on her phone. Harper waited until McGovan had paid for his ticket before leaving the queue and joining her at the machine. 'London,' she said, feeding notes into it.

'We're London-bound, Hansfree,' Harper said into his mic. 'Get someone to meet me and Maggie, and set up surveillance there. A bike would be good.'

'No problem,' said Hansfree.

Maggie pulled the tickets from the dispenser. Harper looked around. McGovan was buying a baguette and coffee. Harper looked up at the departures board. The next train to London was due to leave in six minutes.

52

It took the twin-rotored Chinook less than an hour to travel from Hereford to Menwith Hill. The helicopter flew the last twenty miles at treetop level and came in to land some ten miles from the RAF station. The rear ramp came down and eight SAS troopers drove out on two-man silenced four-wheel all-terrain vehicles. The four passengers were facing to the rear, their carbines at the ready. They were all dressed in camouflage gear, including Kevlar helmets. The troop leader had a GPS on his handlebars and headed off cross-country. The three others followed him in an arrow formation, like geese heading home for the winter.

They got to within a mile of their target, then left their vehicles parked in a small copse that bordered a field of bright yellow rape. They hurried up a slope and lay down at the crest of a hill overlooking the Menwith Hill listening station.

Two of the troopers had high-powered binoculars and soon located the eight jihadists, who were preparing their attack. Two of the men were assembling the Spigot on its tripod, which suggested the attack was imminent.

'We need to move,' said the oldest member of the squad,

a ten-year veteran called Gary Jones, who went by the
nickname Shagger, in reference to his Welsh ancestry rather
than a description of his sexual prowess. He looked over
at the squad's medic, a former paratrooper who had been
in the Regiment for just a couple of years. 'What do you
think, Dusty? Five minutes?'

'It's rough terrain,' said Dusty. 'Seven, maybe.'

'You're not in the Bird Shit now, chum. I say five.'

Bird Shit was the common nickname for the Parachute
Regiment. It came from the observation that only two things
fell from the sky – paratroopers and bird shit.

'I suppose the vehicles are out of the question?' said the
medic.

'They'll hear us coming,' said Shagger. 'Even with the
exhausts silenced.'

'We could keep to the other side of that ridge. That'll
disperse most of the noise.' He pointed off to the right.

Shagger nodded. 'You'll do anything to avoid a walk,
won't you?'

'Fuck it, you take the vehicles and I'll run,' said Dusty.
'But we could get a nice crossfire situation going. They
wouldn't know what'd hit them.'

Shagger knew that he was right. 'Go,' he said. 'Take
Jethro and Sumo with you.'

The four troopers hurried back down the slope and
retrieved their vehicles. They started them up and cut across
the fields.

Shagger looked through his binoculars again. The jihad-
ists were having trouble assembling the Spigot but they
were making progress and he couldn't wait too long.

'That's a Fagot, right?' asked the trooper on his left. He

was a Geordie called Beanie because of his likeness to the actor Sean Bean. 'Saw a few in Afghanistan.'

The anti-tank missile had the NATO reporting name AT-4 Spigot but the Russians called it the 9K111 Fagot, which meant 'bassoon'. It had been developed as a weapon that three men could carry and use to destroy a tank, but it would make a decent dent in the listening station. The launcher and tripod were carried by one man in a backpack, and the other two carried two launch tubes. So far as Shagger could see, the men down below had a full complement of four missiles.

'How the fuck did they get one of those?' asked Bean. 'That's a big boy's toy, that is.'

The missiles were fired with the gunner lying prone and a good team could fire one every twenty seconds. Considering the trouble they were having assembling the equipment, Shagger doubted the men he was watching would get anywhere near that.

The missiles were easily big enough to take out a tank. It left the launch tube at 80 metres a second, then a solid-fuel motor kicked in more than doubling its speed. It was a fly-by-wire weapon, which meant that the gunner had to keep aiming until the missile reached its target, up to two thousand metres away. It wasn't a weapon for amateurs.

Shagger put away his binoculars. 'Lock and load, and let's get this started,' he said. 'The enemy down there are in uniform and carrying weapons, so this is a military engagement, pure and simple. We're looking to take out the opposition, not collect prisoners.' The men nodded, all eager for the off.

They crested the ridge and headed down the slopes, their carbines at the ready.

They moved at a slow run, crouched down, spread out across the hill. It took them the best part of two minutes to reach the bottom, and then they were moving across a field. Ahead was a ditch and they went through the muddy water without breaking stride.

Ahead the Spigot team finished assembling the weapon. One of the men stood up and looked at his watch, then towards the listening station in the distance. Another was lying down, preparing to take the shot. The third was arranging the missile tubes.

Shagger increased the pace. The man who had looked at his watch shouted something and the jihadists with rifles began to move towards the listening station. It was a mile away and they weren't SAS fit, which meant it would take them at least ten minutes to cover the ground, probably longer. Shagger figured they wouldn't fire the missile until the men were closer to the installation.

'In position now,' said a voice in his earpiece. Dusty.

'Wait until we have contact,' said Shagger. The closer they got to the targets the better, though they were already within range.

The jihadists were about halfway there and the man standing by the Spigot was shading his hand against the sun as he watched his colleagues' progress. Then, slowly, he began to turn, scanning the area. Shagger knew he had two choices: to drop and hope the man wouldn't see them or to start firing. They were well within range and the closer the jihadists got to the listening station the greater the risk they would start shooting.

'Contact!' he shouted, stopped and raised his carbine to his shoulder. He fired a short controlled burst at the man standing by the Spigot and was rewarded by the sight of his chest exploding in a mass of red. The rest of his team opened fire at the Spigot gunner and his assistant. More than a dozen rounds thwacked into them and they went still.

The sound of gunfire stopped the armed jihadists in their tracks. They turned, saw the troopers and began firing but their shots went wide. The troopers dropped to lower their profiles and began to return fire. As they did, a hail of bullets ripped into the jihadists from the ridge to the side as the second SAS team opened fire.

Two days' practice on a firing range counted for nothing against highly trained SAS troopers who between them had more than a hundred years of special-forces experience including firefights in Iraq and Afghanistan. The jihadists were screaming, '*Allahu Akbar!*' as they fired, as if somehow that would help their aim. It didn't, and one by one their guns fell silent as the troopers picked them off. It was over in less than thirty seconds.

53

Harper and Maggie followed McGovan down the platform, arm in arm. They slowed as McGovan got into a carriage midway down the train. 'What do you think? Sit together or split up?' asked Maggie.

Harper knew that usually two sets of eyes were better than one and it would have made more sense to follow him separately, but the train was only going to make one stop and that was at London Euston. And a couple travelling together always looked less like a tail. 'You grab us a seat in the next carriage, I'll wait until the train pulls out.'

She climbed on while Harper took out a mobile phone. He used a new Sim card to call the third number on the list that Charlotte Button had given him. He quickly brought her up to speed. 'Can you carry out the contract?' she asked.

'I'm about to get on a train. Give me a break.'

'What about when he gets to London?'

'I'm working on it. What happened at Menwith Hill?'

'Let's just say it was a very satisfactory conclusion.'

'So we won you some Brownie points at least?'

Button chuckled. 'It would seem so, yes.'

'We might be able to add to that,' he said. He explained about the growing number of jihadists who were gathering at the industrial unit.

'What do you think's happening?'

'I'm not sure. But they have a hell of a lot of explosives there. What happened at Menwith Hill was a diversion, to get attention focused up north. I think that's why he's heading south.'

'Your people are on top of it?'

'Well, yes. In terms of surveillance. But they're not armed.'

'I've already explained that I don't want McGovan arrested. He has to be cancelled.'

'I hear that. But he's on a train. Too many witnesses.'

'Then wait until he's in London. As soon as he's cancelled, I'll send in the cavalry.'

'You're playing with fire. So long as you know.'

'It has to be done this way.'

The train was about to leave. Harper ended the call and climbed aboard, watching through the window to make sure McGovan didn't jump off at the last second. He didn't. Harper found Maggie sitting in a window seat and dropped down next to her. 'All good,' he said. 'Hansfree will have someone at Euston so we can relax. Catch some sleep if you want.' He held up his backpack. 'I'm going to pop into the bathroom and have a quick shave.'

'Maybe spray a bit of deodorant around, too.'

'Bit ripe?'

She grinned. 'Just a bit. And when you're done, pop along to the buffet car and get me some breakfast, will you?'

He saluted her. 'Yes, your ladyship.'

'Thank you so much,' she said, closing her eyes and settling back in her seat.

54

Harper and Maggie took out their earpieces while they were on the train. He used his mobile phone to keep in contact with Hansfree, making regular calls well away from the carriage where McGovan was sitting. An hour before the train was due to get in, one of the jihadists had left the industrial unit in Gravesend in a grey Volvo. Two of Hansfree's men had followed, one in a car and one on a bike. Fifteen minutes before the train arrived, Hansfree confirmed that the car had gone to Euston station.

When the train arrived, McGovan was one of the first off. Harper and Maggie followed him along the platform and onto the station concourse. Hansfree told them that a watcher called Will would be waiting for them. 'Black, bald, glasses and wearing a suit,' was the description he had given, and they spotted him at once, leaning against a shop window and studying a copy of the *Evening Standard*. Harper and Maggie closed the gap with McGovan in case their quarry headed for the Underground but there was no need to worry because he was walking slowly and looking around. An Asian man in a denim jacket and jeans nodded at him and they embraced. Laughing at nothing, Harper and Maggie walked past the two men, then waited at the exit to see what they would do.

Will had clocked McGovan and was circling, pretending to make a call on his mobile. McGovan and the man headed for another exit and Harper and Maggie followed.

'Hansfree, Tango One is heading out with an Asian in a blue denim jacket and jeans.'

'That's the driver of the grey Volvo,' said Hansfree. 'I've a bike outside watching it. We're good to go.'

'Roger that,' said Harper. 'Will, where's your car?'

'East exit,' said Will, in Harper's ear.

'Get the car ready. Hansfree, who do you have outside?'

'His name's Sammy. On a courier motorbike. He's good. He'll go ahead of the Volvo, though I think it's pretty obvious where they're headed.'

'Tell him Tango One is on the move with your man.'

'I'm on it,' said Hansfree.

Will led Harper and Maggie outside to his car. They climbed in, Harper in the front passenger seat and Maggie behind him. 'Sammy has eyeball,' said Hansfree in Harper's ear. 'They're getting into the car now. It's a grey Volvo.'

Will started the engine. He had a sat-nav on the dashboard and it booted up within seconds.

'He's on the A501, heading east,' said Hansfree.

'Probably going back to Gravesend,' said Will, pulling away from the kerb.

'Probably, but let's not go counting chickens,' said Harper.

55

McGovan did go straight to the industrial site where Hansfree had a team of five keeping the unit under surveillance and one had a drone in the air. With Hansfree's motorbike tail keeping ahead of the Volvo, Will was able to stay well back. Having a tail ahead of a target was by far the best way of running surveillance. People rarely concerned themselves with what was happening ahead of them. The biker could keep an eye on the target in his mirrors, and if the target did turn off it wouldn't take him long to double back and catch up.

Hansfree relayed through the radio that McGovan had arrived at the industrial unit. He was inside with the other seven jihadists plus the one who had driven him from the station. 'Hansfree, I'd like to have a look at the drone feed,' said Harper.

Hansfree gave him the location of the watcher who was piloting the drone and Will drove him over. The drone operator was a small man in his sixties, sitting in the front seat of a van with the name of a tropical-fish company on the side. Harper climbed in and sat next to him while Maggie squatted in the back and looked over his shoulder. A laptop open on the dashboard gave them an overhead view of the industrial unit, the two containers and the land around it.

'What's been happening?' asked Harper.

'Not much,' said the man. 'They come, they park, they go inside.'

'What about the gear in the containers?'

'They carried most of the stuff inside this morning.'

Harper sat back and spoke to Hansfree on the radio. 'Do we have registration numbers on the vehicles?'

'All of them,' said Hansfree. 'They were all sold to private buyers within the last two weeks. All taxed and insured and seem legit, but I have my suspicions.'

'Because?'

'Because they're all showing owners in Birmingham with names like Khan and Patel.'

'Do me a favour and text me each car's details. Just the registration number, model and colour. Don't bother about the owners.'

'Will do,' said Hansfree.

'I've a question for you,' Harper said, to the man operating the drone. 'If we had to, could you follow a car with one of those?'

'I'd like to say yes but, hand on heart, they're not fast enough plus you'd be playing catch-up trying to keep it in range. They're great for static surveillance or getting into difficult-to-reach places, but you need the military stuff to follow a moving vehicle.'

'That's what I thought,' said Harper. He climbed out of the van and called up the next number on Button's list of throwaway mobiles. 'Tango One is back in Gravesend,' he said. 'He's got eight jihadists with him and we haven't managed to identify most of them. He hasn't met them before, that's for sure, or we would have seen them.'

'What's he up to?' asked Button.

'Fucked if I know. They're all inside. But they're up to something, obviously. They're not here for a prayer meeting.'

'How close are you to cancelling Tango One?'

'A lot depends on his next move. If they pile into two cars and head out mob-handed, I won't be able to get near him. But if they move out separately, maybe. The problem is, what do we do then? They've got explosives, remember.'

'You're thinking suicide bombers?'

'I don't know. Like I said, they're inside. But we're not that far from central London.'

The man in the van wound down his window and shouted across at Harper, 'They're on the move.'

'I'll call you back,' said Harper, and jogged to the van. As he climbed into the passenger seat, his phone beeped to let him know he had received a text message. He looked at the laptop. One of the cars was driving away from the industrial unit. A blue Mondeo. 'Hansfree, do we have a tail for the vehicle?' Harper said into his mic.

'Affirmative,' said Hansfree.

'How many on board the Mondeo?'

'Two,' said Hansfree.

'Is it Tango One?'

'Negative.'

'Let me know if anyone else moves out. And keep me updated on that vehicle.'

'I'm on it.'

Harper looked at the drone operator. 'What did you see?'

'Two men came out. Asians. They got into the car and left.'

'Anything unusual? Were they carrying anything?'

The man shook his head. 'One thing. The passenger was wearing a coat and he wasn't wearing one before.'

Harper cursed.

'Is that significant?' asked the man, frowning.

'It is when they've got all that explosive,' said Harper. 'It could be they've spent the day building suicide vests and Tango One is now sending them on their way.'

He got out of the van and checked the text Hansfree had sent him before forwarding it to Button's mobile. He gave her two minutes to review the message, then phoned her. 'Did you get that?'

'I got it.'

'The two that have left are in the blue Mondeo. We have a tail and I can update you with texts. But you need to take care of it. The tail isn't armed. The passenger is wearing a coat that he wasn't wearing before so the suicide-bomber option is looking more likely. I think he's setting them up as suicide-bombers. Menwith Hill was a distraction to get everyone's attention focused up north. Meanwhile the real attack will be on London.'

'But are you sure?'

'Let's see what happens next. As things stand there's a car driving into London with two Asians on board, one wearing a long coat he didn't have on before. There are eight of them and four vehicles. Do the maths.'

'What do you suggest?'

'I've got a surveillance guy tailing the Mondeo but you need to get them picked up. Armed cops, SAS, whoever's available. I'm guessing they won't be primed but I wouldn't put money on it. If I were you, I'd get the Mondeo pulled over and you'll have a better idea of what's going on. But if it was really up to me I'd just shoot them in the head, to be on the safe side.'

'And there's just the one vehicle so far?'

'Just the blue Mondeo. If that changes, I'll let you know.'

Button ended the call and Harper went back to the van. He climbed in and stared at the laptop.

'Anything wrong?' asked Maggie, from the back of the van.

'We'll know in the next few minutes,' said Harper.

56

'Are you okay, brother?' the driver asked his companion. The driver's name was Omar but he didn't know the passenger's. The first time they had met was when they had arrived at the industrial unit and McGovan had insisted they did not identify themselves. Omar was the driver, and the man in the passenger seat was the *shahid*. The martyr. Under his coat he wore a canvas vest and in the vest were several pounds of explosives. He sat with his hands in his lap, staring straight ahead with unseeing eyes.

Now he nodded. 'I'm okay,' he said.

'It's a great thing you are doing,' said Omar.

'We are not to talk. We were told not to talk.'

'I know, brother. But I just wanted you to know. Respect.'

Omar looked at the sat-nav. They were north of the river, between Dagenham and Barking, just over twelve miles from their destination. Downing Street, home of the prime minister. They wouldn't be able to get close to the man, or to the house: McGovan had made that clear. The road was one of the most secure in the country, as secure as the area around the American Embassy, which would be the second target. The *shahid* was to get as close to the target as possible. There were always tourists standing at the black steel gates that blocked off the road, along with armed police from the Diplomatic Protection Group. It didn't matter who died, what mattered was that ISIS was seen to be able to strike at the heart of government.

Omar looked back at the road. He frowned. There was a black SUV ahead, just a few car lengths, that he hadn't noticed before. He braked, and as he did so he looked in his rear-view mirror. There was a second black SUV behind him.

'Watch out!' shouted the *shahid*.

Omar looked ahead again. The SUV in front was slowing sharply. Omar stamped on the brake and swore.

The *shahid* wasn't wearing his seat belt because he didn't want any pressure on the vest, and as the car braked he was slammed against the window. He fell back into his seat as the vehicle stopped. 'What the fuck, man?' he shouted. He put a hand to his head and felt blood.

Men in black overalls were piling out of the SUV. Men with guns. 'It's the fucking cops!' screamed Omar. His eyes flashed to the rear-view mirror. More armed police. 'Fuck, fuck, fuck!'

'What do we do?' asked the *shahid*.

The cops were screaming now. 'Armed police! Raise your hands! Armed police!'

'I don't know,' said Omar.

'Do I go now? Do I do it now?'

'ARMED POLICE! PUT YOUR HANDS IN THE AIR!'

'I don't know,' said Omar, again.

'I think I should. If they get closer, they'll kill us anyway, and if they kill us they win.'

Two armed cops were standing at the front of the car, their carbines at their shoulders. Both were screaming, 'Put your hands up! Put your fucking hands up now!'

'I don't know, brother. I just don't know.'

The *shahid* fumbled for the trigger. His fingers caught hold of it and he held it up. '*Allahu Akbar!*' he shouted.

He looked across at Omar and their eyes met. Omar took the *shahid*'s left hand and smiled. Together they shouted, '*Allahu Akbar!*'

The *shahid* closed his eyes and pressed the trigger.

Nothing happened.

'The switch!' screamed Omar. 'The fucking on-off switch!'

The windshield exploded and Omar saw the *shahid*'s head fold in on itself and blood sprayed across the back seat. Then he felt a punch in the face and everything went black.

57

'One of them isn't Asian,' said Harper, as he looked at the laptop screen. Two men were walking from the industrial unit towards a white Honda.

The man operating the drone nodded. 'Yeah, he went in a few hours ago. That's his car.'

The Asian was wearing a long coat. He got into the front passenger seat while the other man sat behind the steering wheel.

Harper's phone rang. It was Button. 'You were right,' she said. 'Suicide-bombers. We got them on the A13.'

'Anyone hurt?'

'No collateral damage, as they say, just the two in the car. They were shot before they could detonate.'

'There's another vehicle leaving now,' said Harper. 'The white Honda. You've got the details.'

'I'll get it targeted. How many left?'

'There are three cars still parked there. Four jihadists inside, plus McGovan. If they keep operating in pairs, we have two more. But that's supposition. They could just as easily leave alone.'

'Call me as and when they leave.'

'You could take them all out here. There'd be less risk of civilians getting hurt.'

'Just do as you're told. It's going to work out just fine.' Button ended the call.

The white Honda drove through the gates and headed towards London. 'Hansfree, make sure you have a tail on the white Honda,' Harper said into the radio.

Hansfree chuckled. 'No need to teach this grandmother to suck eggs,' he said.

58

McGovan examined the suicide vest and nodded his approval. 'You're good to go,' he said. The vest was a standard design that required next to no skill to assemble. Anyone could do it, even a child, and the design had remained the same since the concept had been developed by the Tamil Tigers in the 1980s. There were four plates of PE-4A plastic explosive sitting in four pockets evenly spaced around the vest, with a detonator in each plate, all wired to the control unit in a pocket at the back of the vest. Two wires ran from the control unit to a metal trigger. An on-off switch on the front of the belt ensured that the vest could not be detonated prematurely.

McGovan patted the shoulder of the man wearing the vest. His name was Zayn. Born in Bradford, he was a Pakistani Muslim who had spent three months fighting with ISIS in Syria before returning home, flying from Turkey to Canada and from there to the UK. 'You'll make us proud,' said McGovan. Zayn nodded but his eyes were dull and lifeless as if his spirit had already left his body.

Another of the jihadists helped fit the fragmentation jacket over the explosive vest. The explosives created the shock wave but it was the shrapnel from the jacket that would do the damage, dozens of pockets filled with nuts, bolts, nails and ball bearings. When the PE-4A was detonated, the lethal shrapnel would radiate outwards, killing or maiming anyone within fifty feet.

The jihadist muttered an Islamic prayer as he fitted the jacket, then stood back to admire his handiwork. '*Allahu Akbar*,' he said.

'*Allahu Akbar*,' muttered Zayn.

McGovan and the jihadist helped Zayn put on a raincoat. It was several sizes too big so that it would go over the vest and jacket. The jihadist buttoned up the coat, muttering another prayer, as McGovan fed the wires of the trigger down the sleeve. 'Don't forget. Only make the vest live when you're within sight of the target.'

Zayn nodded again, but didn't say anything.

'Repeat that back to me,' said McGovan, putting his hands on the man's shoulders and looking into his blank eyes.

'Only make the vest live when I'm within sight of the target.'

'Good man,' said McGovan. He beckoned Zayn's driver. He was one of the non-Asians in the group, a twenty-five-year-old Glaswegian, who had converted to Islam in Scotland, then spent a year in Syria as a foreign fighter. An ISIS talent-spotter had realised the man's potential and persuaded him that he could best serve Islam back in the UK. His name was Bruce, but McGovan didn't know if that was his family name or his first name. He didn't know and he didn't care. Names didn't matter. All that mattered was that the men did their jobs. Bruce was to drive Zayn as close to Waterloo station as he could get. Zayn was to walk into the middle of the station to detonate. 'Off you go, lads,' said McGovan. '*Allahu Akbar.*'

The two men smiled thinly. '*Allahu Akbar,*' they chorused, then headed outside.

59

Harper watched on the drone feed as the two men walked from the industrial unit towards a blue Hyundai. One was Asian, wearing a long coat. The other was white, in his twenties, in jeans and a leather jacket.

'I have a tail up and running and a bike on the way back from the A13,' said Hansfree in Harper's ear.

The two men got into the Hyundai. A few seconds later it drove away and was soon out of range of the drone's camera.

Barry Whisper drove up and parked behind the van. Harper climbed out, waved at him, then took out his mobile and called Button. 'The third team has just set out. A blue Hyundai. We have a tail on it. I'll call in the location once we know where they're headed.'

Harper ended the call and got into Barry Whisper's car. 'How's it going?' Barry Whisper asked.

'Two-man suicide-bombers. We're dealing with them as they leave. The third has just headed and so we think there's one team left. I've a job for you, Barry, if you're up for it.'

'I'm up for it,' he said immediately.

'At least let me tell you what it is.'

Barry Whisper shrugged. 'We go back a long way, Lex. If you want something doing, I'll do it.'

Harper grasped the man's shoulder and squeezed. 'You're a star, but this is different from the normal jobs. I've got to slot this guy McGovan and I've got to do it myself. I think the best way is from the back of a bike and even I'm not good enough to drive and shoot at the same time.'

'No problem,' said Barry Whisper. 'I'll drive. What about the bike?'

'We can get it off Hansfree's guy. In fact, talk to Hansfree now, then head over with the car and come back on the bike.'

60

'There it is, dead ahead, white Honda,' said Glenn Marsden. He was at the wheel of the black BMW X5, favourite vehicle of the Metropolitan Police's armed-response unit. Sitting next to him in the front passenger seat, Jon Cooper was the most experienced of the three-man unit.

Cooper checked the registration number on the screen in front of him. 'That's it,' he said. 'Guns out, Paul.' He picked up his radio mic. 'Trojan Six Three Four, we have the target vehicle in sight.'

Paul Evans, the youngest member of the team, was sitting behind Cooper. He pulled down the seat next to him revealing the three SIG Sauer 516 assault rifles. The SIG 516s the unit used came with a telescoping stock and a thirty-round magazine. Evans slid the guns out and handed one to Cooper.

'Right, just so you know, if this is the same situation as the other Trojans had, the passenger has a suicide vest on and the driver is clear,' said Cooper. 'There's an on-off switch that has to be in the on position before the trigger is pressed so, providing we act quickly enough, we can stop the detonation.' Marsden and Evans grunted.

'Trojan Six Two One, we're right behind you. How do you want to play this?' It was Stan Mitchell, senior officer in the second armed-response vehicle that had been assigned to the situation.

Evans twisted around in his seat. A second black BMW X5 was three cars behind. 'I see them,' he said.

'We'll pull ahead and stop the Honda,' said Cooper. 'It has to be fast but we need to issue clear warnings. Any attempt to detonate and Operation Kratos applies.'

'Understood,' said Mitchell.

The Met had laid down the Operation Kratos tactics in 2002 specifically to deal with suicide-bombers, and although the term had been officially dropped in 2008, the tactics still applied: if a suicide-bomber was in danger of detonating, he or she was to be shot in the head until the threat was neutralised.

Cooper nodded at Marsden. 'Let's do it, Glenn.'

Marsden accelerated, pulling smoothly in front of the white Honda. He braked, slowly at first, but then increasing the pressure on the pedal. The driver of the white Honda pounded his horn but Marsden continued to slow. Cooper and Evans flicked the safeties off as the car stopped and piled out of the offside.

They ran to the Honda, shouting, 'Armed police!' Cooper to the passenger side, Evans covering the driver. Trojan Six Two One had pulled up behind the Honda. Traffic continued to drive past but slowly as motorists craned their necks to see what was going on.

'Armed police, hands up!' shouted Marsden. The driver kept his hands on the wheel, his mouth wide open.

'Put your hands in the air, now!' screamed Cooper.

Marsden was climbing out of the X5, his gun in his right hand. The men in the second X5 were getting out too, guns at the ready.

The passenger opened his mouth to shout and his right arm moved. Cooper fired twice. The windshield shattered and the man's head exploded.

Evans kept his weapon aimed at the driver. 'Stay exactly where you are!' he shouted.

The driver blinked, frowned, then looked at the body next to him. He glanced back at Evans, then lunged towards the body. Evans pulled the trigger. The shot took off the top of the driver's head. He fired again, twice, a professional double-tap with both shots hitting the face, dead centre.

Traffic had slowed to a crawl now and in almost every car a mobile phone was pointing at the Honda and the two dead bodies inside.

'Let's move these vehicles on and set up a roadblock,' Cooper shouted to Mitchell. 'This is now a crime scene.' He waved at Marsden. 'Glenn, move these vultures on. Anyone not out of here in double-quick time is to be charged with using their phone while driving.'

61

Harper watched as the final two jihadists walked out of the industrial unit and got into a white van with the name of a courier company on the side. 'They're taking the van,' said Harper into his mic. 'You've got a tail ready?'

'Barry Big's in place,' said Hansfree, over the radio.

'Roger that,' said Barry Big. 'Raring to go.'

'I've a bike ready, too,' said Hansfree.

'Just keep updating me. Once we know which route they're on, the cops can take over.'

'How do we stand so far?' asked Hansfree.

'Two neutralised, one on the way,' said Harper.

'Any collateral damage?'

'So far so good,' said Harper. 'Looks to me as if Tango One is now alone in the unit. So I need you to pull off all surveillance. Only those following the vehicles are to stay in play, everyone else is now off the clock.'

'You're sure?' asked Hansfree.

'I'm sure,' said Harper. 'I'll take care of Tango One. Barry Whisper will help. Everyone else can stand down, job well done.'

'Roger that,' said Hansfree. 'You just be careful. I'd hate

anything to happen to you before my money goes into the bank.'

'Good to know you have my best interests at heart,' said Harper. He patted the drone operator on the shoulder. 'We're done, mate, thanks. Pack up and head on home.'

Harper climbed out of the van and went over to the BMW. Maggie was in the driving seat, drinking from a bottle of water. He leaned down and winked at her. 'All done, the authorities will take care of it now.'

'What about Tango One?'

'I'll deal with him.'

'I'll give you a hand.'

'Nah, I'm good,' he said. 'You can stand down.' He nodded at the BMW. 'You can keep the car, sell it for whatever you can get or give it away. It's untraceable.'

'I'm happy to stay, Lex, you know that.'

'I know. But it's not necessary. I'll call you.'

She blew him a kiss. 'Make sure you do.'

As Maggie drove off, the drone came in for a perfect landing close to the van. The operator climbed out, put it into the back, waved to Harper and disappeared down the road after Maggie.

Harper went over to Barry Whisper. He took out his gun, checked it, then put it back in his underarm holster. Barry Whisper was already wearing a black full-face helmet and he handed a white one to Harper. 'Let's get this done,' said Harper, climbing onto the pillion.

62

The police took down the occupants of the blue Hyundai about three miles from central London, south of the river. There were two occupants: a Caucasian was driving, an Asian sitting in the front passenger seat. Three armed-response vehicles were involved, working together to slow down the Hyundai at a quiet section of road.

As soon as it had stopped, six armed officers surrounded the car, their SIG Sauer 516 assault rifles aimed at the occupants. They knew now that there was no doubt about the threat. Two cars had already been dealt with and both had contained suicide-bombers.

'Armed police, raise your hands!' shouted a sergeant, who had his carbine trained at the passenger's face. All the intel suggested that only the passenger was carrying explosives but both men were a threat because either could operate the trigger.

The two passengers looked at each other, their mouths open and their eyes wide. It wasn't unusual for suspects to freeze when they were confronted by armed police. It was a natural human reaction, and a result of brain chemistry rather than conscious thought. The amygdala – a small region of the brain near the top of the spine – kicks out a neurotransmitter called glutamate in response to any sign of danger. It activates the freeze response first because evolution has taught that freezing is the best way to avoid a predator. But within less than a second that same neuro-transmitter reaches the hypothalamus where it triggers the flight or fight response. That is when the heart rate jumps and adrenalin courses through the body. At that point a conscious decision has to be made – fight or run. But until that decision is taken the body stays in freeze mode. That was where the two men were as they stared out at the armed police. They couldn't run because they were in a car surrounded by policemen with guns. They couldn't fight because they had no weapons. So they froze.

'ARMED POLICE, HANDS IN THE AIR NOW!'

The passenger moved his right hand. Just his right hand, not the left. The sergeant took that to mean he was about to reach for the trigger and fired. The side window shattered into a thousand cubes and the sergeant fired again. The second bullet slammed into the side of the man's head and exited the other side before blowing off the top of the driver's skull. The driver slumped forward and, as he did so, two of the other officers opened fire. The windshield shattered and both men's heads blew apart. Blood, brain matter and pieces of skull sprayed across the interior. More than a dozen shots were fired, then everything went quiet.

The sergeant's eyes were stinging from the cordite in the air. He knew that, strictly speaking, neither man had made a threatening gesture, but he didn't care. If the vest had gone off everyone would have died. So far as he was concerned, two dead terrorists and no collateral damage was a perfect result.

63

Harper had his gun in his hand as Barry Whisper revved the engine. They were at the entrance to the industrial unit. The gate was open but, with no windows in the unit and the door closed, there was no way of telling what McGovan was doing inside. Time was ticking away and he didn't want to wait for ever. He tapped Barry Whisper's shoulder. 'Drive in, drive around the unit and let me off at the side. Then head back to the entrance and attract his attention. But be careful, mate – he's got some serious weaponry in there.'

Barry Whisper revved the engine again, and drove through the entrance. He accelerated hard, then turned to the left to drive by the lean-to garages. He slammed on the brakes and Harper was off the bike before it had stopped. Barry Whisper accelerated and disappeared around the back of the unit.

Harper kept close to the building as he went around to the front. He reached the corner as the bike appeared at the other side, heading for the exit.

Harper heard the door open and ducked back. McGovan was holding an L85 with a thirty-round magazine in place, and as Barry Whisper reached the exit, McGovan swung the rifle up to his shoulder. Harper knew he had to react quickly – the Heckler & Koch assault weapon had an effective range of close to 400 metres and, as ex-SAS, McGovan would be a marksman more than capable of killing Barry Whisper, even on a motorbike.

McGovan was totally focused on Barry Whisper so didn't see Harper step out and raise the Smith & Wesson until the last second, just as he was pulling the trigger. McGovan had started to turn as Harper fired and the slug slammed into his left shoulder. The impact spun him around and the rifle clattered to the ground. McGovan bent down to pick it up but Harper fired again and McGovan's right hand practically exploded. He staggered back and disappeared inside the unit.

Harper ran after him and pushed through the door. There was a small office to the left but the rest of the building was open plan, empty except for a few trestle tables piled with weapons and provisions. There was a tailor's dummy with a canvas vest on it, but no explosives. McGovan was staggering as he ran, blood dripping from his wounded shoulder and hand.

He was running towards a table on which there was another rifle. Harper shot him in the leg and McGovan pitched sideways and fell to the floor. He rolled over, then slowly pushed himself up so that he was sitting against the wall. He watched impassively as Harper walked over to stand in front of him.

'They got them all,' said Harper. 'They killed the guys you left at Menwith Hill. They didn't get anywhere near the listening station. And those suicide-bombers? All dead, mate. Not one of them even got to press their trigger. All shot in the head. Bang, bang, bang, bang. It was all for nothing. Everything you did. A total waste of fucking time.'

McGovan's shirt was now soaked with blood from the shoulder wound. His right hand was shattered and useless. What was left of it was lying in his lap. Two fingers were missing. There was blood all over his trousers.

'Get me a field dressing, will you?' asked McGovan. 'There's one on the table over there.'

'Fuck you,' said Harper. He pushed up the visor of the full-face helmet.

McGovan tilted his head on one side as he looked at Harper. 'You were in the Regiment, right? Or are you still in?'

'Never was, never will be,' said Harper. 'I was a Para, and happy with that. I couldn't be doing with all the crap you have to go through to get in.'

'But you were a soldier.' McGovan winced, and gritted his teeth. He took a long, slow breath before speaking. 'You've won. I accept that. But now I'm a casualty. I'm bleeding to death here.'

Harper shrugged. 'I'm not a medic. That's not what I do.'

'Just take me in. Let me have my day in court,' said McGovan. 'I'll tell the world why I did what I did. They need to understand.'

Harper shook his head. 'That's not going to happen. No one gives a fuck why you did what you did. You did it for a fictitious god that you believe doesn't want you to eat bacon or drink beer, a god that says women should cover their faces and not drive cars. You're fucking deluded, mate.' He tapped the side of his helmet with the barrel of the gun. 'You're a few rounds short of a magazine, not right in the head, get it? I dunno what made you become a Muslim nutter, but that's what you are. That's all anyone will remember.' He levelled the gun at McGovan's face. 'No one gives a shit who you are or why you did what you did.'

'At least I kill for something I believe in,' said McGovan, his eyes blazing with hatred. 'You kill so that your masters can continue to persecute Muslim innocents all around the world for no other reason than they want their oil.'

Harper smiled. 'You've got it all wrong, mate. I don't kill for politics or religion or because I'm ordered to. Someone's paying me to kill you, pure and simple. You killed a Yank in the sandpit. A Yank with a very important father. He wants you dead and I'm the guy who's going to make that happen. I don't care what you've done or why you're doing it. All I care is that the money goes into the bank. You're a job, mate. That's all you are. Now *Allahu Akbar* and fuck off.' He pulled the trigger and McGovan's face imploded. Blood began to pool around what was left of the man's head as Harper pumped two more slugs into his chest.

He turned and walked outside. Barry Whisper had driven back to the unit and was waiting beside the door on the bike, the engine running. Harper climbed onto the pillion and patted him on the shoulder. 'Home, James, and don't spare the horses,' he said. As the motorbike sped towards London, Harper took a phone from his hip-pack and sent Button a final text.

64

The driver of the white van checked in his wing mirror, indicated and pulled out to overtake the truck ahead of him.

'You don't have to drive so fast, bruv, there's no rush,' said the passenger.

'He's crawling along,' said the driver. 'We haven't got all day.'

'There's no rush,' repeated the passenger.

The driver eased back on the accelerator. 'Okay, whatever.'

The passenger looked across at the driver. 'What's your name, bruv?'

The driver shook his head. 'He said we weren't to know each other's names. Security.'

'Fuck that. I'll be in Heaven in less than an hour, who gives a fuck? I'm a *shahid*, mate. A martyr. Don't see why I shouldn't know the name of the brother who's driving me to Paradise.'

The driver smiled. 'Mohammed Tariq. But everyone calls me Mo.'

'*As-salamu alaykum*, Mo. I'm Ali. You went to Syria?'

'Fuck, yeah. It was something.'

'You kill anyone?'

Mo grinned. 'Fuck, yeah. They had us shoot some prisoners the first day we were there. A test, like. I wasn't sure I could do it but, fuck, yeah.' He beat a rapid tattoo on the steering wheel with his hands. 'And you?'

Ali shook his head. 'I was on patrols, mainly. Then they started giving me extra tuition. About the Koran and stuff. Said there were better ways of serving Allah than firing an AK-47. That everyone has to play to their strengths.'

'And you're okay about what you're doing?'

'Sure,' said Ali. He held up the trigger. 'This will achieve more than any bullet,' he said.

'The Houses of Parliament,' said Mo. 'You'll be like Guy fucking Fawkes.'

Ali smiled. 'He failed. I won't.'

Mo was to drop Ali on the Embankment and Ali was to walk the rest of the way. No one expected him to get inside the building, but he'd be close and the area was always packed with tourists. His aim was to approach one of the security checkpoints and take out as many police officers as possible. There would be plenty of tourists using video cameras so what happened would be seen around the world.

A black SUV moved in front of the van and Ali groaned. 'What's he playing at?'

'Relax, bruv,' said Mo. 'Enjoy the drive. Enjoy the moment. What we're doing today will resonate for eternity. Like the warriors who carried out Nine/Eleven.'

The SUV slowed sharply and Mo had to stamp on the brake to avoid a collision.

To Ali, it was as if everything was happening in slow motion. He saw armed police officers dressed in black pile out of the car in front of them. He heard shouts behind him. He heard Mo cursing. Ali smiled. He felt as if he had all the time in the world as he raised his right hand and started to squeeze the trigger.

'*Allahu Akbar,*' he whispered. He was disappointed that he wouldn't be taking out his designated target, but this way was fine. His fingers tightened on the trigger but then the windscreen shattered, something thudded into his face and everything went black.

65

Patsy Ellis removed her headset. She looked up at the massive monitor that took up almost the whole of the far wall in the operations room they had commandeered at Thames House. There were only four people in it – Ellis, Charlotte Button and two young men in shirtsleeves, who had spent the whole two hours staring at the screens in front of them without making a sound other than to acknowledge Ellis's instructions. The only interruption had been when a young man in a suit had delivered a round of teas and coffees and plastic-wrapped sandwiches, none of which had been opened.

Four locations showed on the map: the places where the suicide-bombing teams had been intercepted by the armed-response vehicles. 'All done,' said Ellis. 'No casualties. Not on our side, anyway.'

'That's a relief,' said Button. Her phone beeped to let her know she had received a message. It was Harper: JOB DONE. And a smiley face.

The two men took off their headsets, picked up their jackets from the backs of their chairs, and Ellis thanked them by name as they left.

'It would have been less stressful if you'd brought us in earlier,' said Ellis.

'But, still, all's well that ends well.'

'Charlie, if we'd missed one, it could have ended very differently.'

'But it didn't. You and the police saved the day. MI5 and the Metropolitan Police working hand in hand took out four suicide-bombers with no collateral damage. Applause all round.'

'And the man who planned it? Can you let me into that little secret? I'm sure that's what that message was, right?'

Button took the back out of the phone, removed the Sim card, and broke it in half.

Ellis smiled. 'It would have been so much funnier if you'd swallowed it,' she said.

'The mastermind was a former SAS man, Caleb McGovan. He converted to Islam at some point and offered his services to ISIS. He appears to have sold them on the idea of a joint operation – the attack on Menwith Hill and the multiple suicide-bombers.'

'And where is this Caleb McGovan now, pray tell?'

'An industrial unit outside Gravesend.'

'Dead or alive?'

'He didn't make it, I'm afraid.'

'Why do I get the feeling you're not telling me everything, Charlie?'

'It was a very complicated situation. I had a lot of ducks to line up.'

'You could have told me what was happening much

earlier. This has all been very much on the fly, and that's never the best way of working, as you know.'

'Hand on heart, Patsy, I didn't get the full picture until very recently.'

Ellis sipped her tea. 'And who killed Caleb McGovan?'

'Probably best we put it down to friendly fire and leave it at that. There'll be surveillance footage of McGovan setting up the suicide-bombers so I don't think anyone will be shedding any tears for him. If the SAS or the police want to take the credit for it, I don't think anyone will be complaining.'

'And who was all this for, Charlie? Who were you working for?'

'Does it matter? We took out an ISIS cell, thwarting what would have been a series of very damaging attacks. The security services and the police come out of it smelling like roses.'

'When you put it like that, of course I sound like I'm looking a gift horse in the mouth. It would just be nice to know who's been pulling your strings.'

Button flashed Ellis a tight smile. 'Client confidentiality, I'm afraid.'

'Of course. And as you said, Charlie, all's well that ends well.'

'And the quid pro quo? Can you tell me now who's been making my life a misery?'

Ellis grinned. 'Actually, I can,' she said. 'And after what's happened today, the chance that you'll ever have any problems with Five or Six in the future is slim to none.'

66

Harper's team split up and went their separate ways. There was no group hug, no drinks down at the pub, they just left. Their fees would be paid into their offshore bank accounts and they wouldn't speak again until the next time they were needed. The only member of the team left in the ops room when Harper arrived was Hansfree, who was sipping a coffee, his feet on the table. He looked exhausted, which was hardly surprising since he'd functioned with almost no sleep over the past four days. 'All's well that ends well,' said Hansfree.

'It was a close-run thing,' said Harper. 'The guys you brought in did a bang-up job. Tell them I'll put them through for a bonus. You, too. After what we did today, we should all get fucking knighthoods.'

'I won't be holding my breath on that score,' said Hansfree. 'The money'll do just fine.' He swung his legs off the table and reached for a black thumbdrive with his right claw. He held it out to Harper. 'Everything you need is on there,' he said. 'IDs on the jihadists we identified, surveillance pictures of them all.'

Harper took it and slipped it into his hip-pack. He planned to put the documents in the drafts folder for Button to use as she wanted. 'There's something else I need you to do for me before you pack up,' he said. He unfolded a piece of paper and gave it to Hansfree. 'Can you rig up something like that for me?'

It took Hansfree only seconds to work out what it was. 'A detonating circuit?'

'Yeah, using a Sim card. It needs to be totally fail-safe.'

Hansfree grinned. 'My stuff always is, Lex. You know that.'

'How much do I owe you?'

Hansfree held up the sheet of paper. 'For this? On the house. Just make sure the rest of my fee goes into my bank account.'

'It's already there.' Harper jerked a thumb at the stack of boxes and cases. 'Do you need a hand with your gear?'

'Reggie and a few of my guys are coming over, so I'm all sorted. How soon do you want this circuit?'

'As soon as,' said Harper. 'I need to get back to Thailand.'

'Couple of hours should do it,' said Hansfree, reaching for a circuit board and a soldering iron.

'Perfect,' said Harper. 'I've got something else to pick up, so I'll catch you later.'

He went downstairs, getting a friendly wave from Mr Singh as he headed out. He caught a black cab to Chinatown and wandered around the restaurants, appearing to look at roast ducks hanging from their necks in the windows but actually checking reflections for tails.

The shop he was looking for was above a dim-sum restaurant. It had its own door on which there was a small brass sign with a dozen or so Chinese characters and below it, in English, DR LI, CHINESE MEDICINE AND

ACUPUNCTURE. Harper pushed open the door and went up a narrow flight of stairs that turned to the right and led to a beaded curtain that he pushed through.

Dr Li's shop was lined with wooden cabinets containing glass-fronted drawers of dried herbs, plants and leaves. On one of the walls posters of the human body showed what looked like acupuncture or pressure points marked in Chinese characters, and four framed degree certificates, which Harper had never examined too closely. He didn't care what, if any, professional qualifications Dr Li had. All he cared about was that he produced results. The man himself came out of a side room where he had an examination table, polishing his spectacles. He was short and plump with a totally bald head and pixie-like ears. He peered at Harper with screwed-up eyes, put his glasses on and smiled. 'Mr Lex, long time no see. What can I do for you?'

Dr Li had lived in London for the best part of forty years but he still spoke like an extra in a kung fu movie.

'Something a little special, Dr Li.'

'Anything for you, Mr Lex, always a pleasure.'

By the time Harper got back to the ops room, Hansfree had finished the circuit. It wasn't much bigger than a mobile phone, with a slot for a Sim card and a socket for a nine-volt battery. There didn't seem to be an on-off switch but there were two wires that could be connected when necessary to make the circuit live.

'You didn't say anything about a timer, right?' said Hansfree.

'Yeah, phone only, and it'll be line of sight because I don't want there to be any mistakes.'

'That'll fit the bill, then,' said Hansfree. 'You'll need to put in a Sim card and a battery, then run the red wires to the detonator. The circuit is inert until you connect the black wires together. At that point a call to the Sim card activates the circuit and Bob's your uncle.'

Harper wanted to shake hands but he always felt awkward touching Hansfree's prosthetic claw so he punched him gently on the shoulder. 'You're a star,' he said.

'A five-year-old could put that together,' said Hansfree. 'Next time give me something difficult.' He saluted with his right claw. 'It's been a pleasure, Lex. As always. Keep me in mind for your next job.'

'You're always top of my list, you know that,' said Harper. He headed downstairs, dropped off a wad of banknotes with Mr Singh by way of thanks, and caught a black cab to Bayswater. When he got back to his room, he transferred the contents of the bottle Dr Li had sold him to a small white plastic bottle that had once contained eye-drops, easily small enough to pass through airport security. The circuit board Hansfree had built went into a side pocket of his holdall, along with three of his mobile phones. He doubted that the circuit would show up as suspicious on any scan but even if they did examine it there was no battery in it and it didn't contravene any airport security regulations. He was good to go.

67

Harper was lying on his bed, staring up at the ceiling, when there was a soft knock on his door. He reached for the gun under his pillow, then smiled to himself as he realised that, generally, killers didn't knock. He swung his feet off the bed, opened the door and relaxed when he saw Charlotte Button. 'I wanted to catch you before you went,' she said. She was wearing a dark blue suit and carrying a Chanel bag with a gilt chain. She had tied her hair back and had on almost no makeup. She looked tired and Harper had a sudden urge to hug her, which he resisted because, at the end of the day, she was his boss and he was the hired hand.

'I'm flying back this evening,' he said, 'but I'm glad you dropped by.' He picked up the thumbdrive Hansfree had given him. 'There are surveillance pictures of the bad guys. Might be helpful.'

She took it from him and thanked him.

'So are you back in HM Government's good books?' he asked. 'You saved a lot of people today.'

'You mean you did. You did a great job.'

'It was a close-run thing,' said Harper, sitting down on the bed and waving her to the one chair in the room, next to the plywood dressing table. She looked at its dusty seat and grimaced, but sat down anyway. 'But all's good, yeah? Your client got what he wanted, and the authorities took out a jihadist cell. But I guess that's not why you're here, right?'

She nodded and forced a smile. 'I know who's been giving me grief,' she said. 'His name's Malik Sharif but he uses Malcolm. Malcolm Sharif. One of the richest Pakistanis living in the UK. He's been on the *Sunday Times* Rich List since 2012. And, ironically, we helped him get there.'

'We as in the government?'

'The Pool, specifically. Sharif is very close to a member of the cabinet. That member of the cabinet pushed through Sharif's citizenship papers. And it turns out that, as part of a quid pro quo, Sharif passed them some very damaging intel on another Pakistani businessman based in Birmingham. The intel showed that the businessman was a direct threat to our national security and it was decided to use the Pool to eliminate the threat without an embarrassing trial.'

'Embarrassing why?'

'Because the same minister who got Sharif his papers also fast-tracked the businessman's citizenship application. If that had become public knowledge, it could have brought the government down. Can you imagine what a field day the press would have had – "British Minister Gets Citizenship For Al-Qaeda Mastermind"? The Americans wouldn't have been best pleased, either. So, as I said, the job was given to the Pool. All well and good, except it now turns out that the businessman was totally innocent. Sharif faked the intel. He wanted the businessman out of the picture so that he could take over his companies, and that was what happened. Shame on me for not checking more closely, but the order came from the top and I was told it had to be done.'

'I hope it wasn't one of my contracts.'

Button shook her head. 'It wasn't.' She looked around the room. 'I don't suppose there's a minibar, is there?'

'With a nice cold Pinot Grigio in it?' He laughed. 'Charlie, this place is sixty quid a night, cash, no questions asked. I don't think they even change the sheets. So Sharif arranged for the safe-deposit boxes to be raided?'

'I'm assuming so. That's conjecture. But what isn't conjecture is that he's having me followed. He's been doing it through an Israeli security company. Former Mossad. It's all been one step removed but there's no doubt it's him. Somehow he'd got to hear about my insurance policies and was worried that if anything happened to me his dirty little secret would get out. He has a lot of enemies back in Pakistan so if he was stripped of his citizenship and sent packing, he'd lose everything. Including his life, probably. He obviously figured that he'd be safer if I wasn't around. He paid the Israelis to track down my insurance policies, remove them and presumably me, too.'

Harper nodded. 'Now what? I'm assuming a stern talking-to isn't going to get this sorted.'

Button tried to smile but Harper could see how worried she was. 'Can you do it for me, Alex? Can you cancel Malik Sharif before you go back to Thailand? For your usual rate, of course.'

Harper grinned. 'Charlie, honey, this one's on me. It'll be a pleasure.'

68

Malik Sharif lived in a mansion in St John's Wood, not far from the one owned by the former Beatle, Paul McCartney. Sharif's mansion was twice the size of McCartney's, standing alone in a large garden with a double garage at the side. Harper was parked outside the house when Sharif arrived home at just after six in the back of a chauffeur-driven Rolls-Royce. He let himself into the house and there didn't appear to be anyone around to greet him. Harper was able to get to the rear garden and watched the house as darkness fell. A woman was in the kitchen, too portly and plain to be Mrs Sharif. He watched her cook a meal, then disappear into the house. Security was non-existent, pretty much, with no CCTV, no bodyguards and an alarm system that seemed unused.

Harper was wearing dark clothing – black jeans, and a bomber jacket over a black pullover – and had a small backpack with him. He had brought a sandwich and a bottle of water, and consumed them as he watched the rear of the house. A light went on in a room on the top floor, then ten minutes later it went off. A flickering through the curtains suggested that a television had been switched on, but at just before one o'clock it stopped.

An upstairs sash window had been left partly open, a bathroom by the look of it, and there was a drainpipe that could be climbed, but the sunroom, with sliding windows, was a better bet. Harper couldn't see any motion-sensitive floodlights on the house, but he kept close to the hedge as he made his way towards the sunroom. It was locked but he had a screwdriver in his backpack, which was all he needed to pop the lock. He slid open the door and stepped inside, then moved through into the kitchen. The absence of feed bowls meant he was unlikely to bump into a dog. It looked as if Sharif felt so safe in his adopted country that he didn't need security. Harper smiled to himself. Big mistake. He took his gun out of the backpack, tiptoed into the hallway and up a large, winding staircase.

Sharif was fast asleep in the master bedroom, spread-eagled on his king-size bed like a stranded starfish. He was in his sixties, overweight, with a neatly trimmed beard and receding hair. His spectacles were on the bedside table, with a glass of water and a gold watch. He was snoring loudly, his belly rising and falling in time with his breathing.

Harper doffed his backpack and took out padded cuffs attached to lengths of rope. He put the gun on the bed and carefully lashed Sharif's wrists to the ornate brass headboard and his ankles to the legs at the bottom of the bed. Sharif grunted in his sleep but didn't wake up. It was only when Harper took a strip of cloth from his backpack and tied it around the man's mouth that his eyes fluttered open. He groaned and tried to rub his face but realised his hands were tied and began to struggle. Then he saw Harper standing over him. He tried to speak but the gag muffled everything except a frightened grunt. 'Don't struggle, mate, it'll soon be over,' said Harper. He reached into his pocket and took out a syringe containing some of the liquid he had purchased from Dr Li in London's Chinatown. He had more than he needed, certainly more than enough to take care of Sharif. It was a chemical isolated from *Gelsemium elegans*, a highly toxic yellow-flowered shrub found only in a remote region of China. It was the perfect assassin's weapon – just a few drops would trigger a heart attack. For years the pretty flowers had been harvested and the chemical used by the Chinese Ministry of State Security to kill those it wanted out of the way without the necessity of a trial. In recent years the Russians had discovered the compound and had also used it with great success. Death always came quickly and a cursory examination would show that it had been a heart attack.

Sharif's eyes widened in terror and he began to struggle but the bonds held firm. Harper held the syringe in front of the man's face and grinned at him. 'You tried to hurt a friend of mine, mate, and there's a price to be paid for that. Charlotte Button. You put the fear of God into her, do you know that? Getting those places robbed, getting those Poles killed, and for what? To protect a secret that was never in any danger of getting out? You should have let sleeping dogs lie, because this is one dog that's come back to bite you in the arse.'

Harper walked to the bottom of the bed. He held Sharif's left foot tightly, and pushed the needle into a vein between the big toe and the one next to it. Sharif tried to kick free but Harper had a grip like a vice and he slowly pushed down the plunger. When the syringe was empty, he stood back. The gelsemium began to work in seconds. At first

Sharif went still, a look of pure panic in his eyes. Then his body went into spasm: his back arched and his eyes bulged. He held that position for a good ten seconds, as taut as a bow, then collapsed back onto the bed. His chest heaved and his breath came in short gasps, making the gag pop back and forth. Suddenly he went still. Harper waited a full minute before checking for a pulse in the man's neck. Finding none, he removed the cuffs and placed them, with the empty syringe, in his backpack.

He rearranged the duvet over the body, took a minute to check that he hadn't left anything incriminating behind, then slipped out of the room, went downstairs and out through the sunroom. Five minutes later he was in a black cab, heading back to Bayswater.

69

Harper was fairly sure that the Russians would be watching the Thai airports, or at the very least keeping track of arrival cards. It was easy enough to do. Every foreigner who arrived at any of the country's airports had to fill in a landing card and have his photograph taken. A bribe of a few hundred dollars would get you a copy of the card and the photograph. If he was going to get back into Thailand without the Russians knowing, he'd have to enter by land. That was easy, too, as the country was bordered by Malaysia, Myanmar, Laos and Cambodia.

He decided on Malaysia because he could take the train from Kuala Lumpur. He flew from London to Belfast, showing a driving licence as ID, then caught a taxi south to Dublin Airport. From there he flew to Amsterdam on an Irish passport and caught the midday KLM flight that arrived in Kuala Lumpur at just after six in the morning. He booked into a hotel at the airport, ate steak and chips, then slept for most of the day. He checked out at five o'clock in the evening and caught a cab to the main railway station where he bought a ticket to Bangkok. The train left at nine fifteen p.m. and, even though he had a sleeping cabin, he stayed awake for most of the night. Eleven hours later he arrived at Padang Besar, a Malaysian town that bordered Songkhai province in Thailand. The town on the other side of the border was also called Padang Besar though the locals referred to it as Pekan Siam. It was a popular destination for Thai and Malaysian tourists who could take advantage of the duty-free shopping complex between the border checkpoints.

Harper's Irish passport was scrutinised but he wasn't photographed. He checked into a cheap hotel to eat and rest, then caught the early evening train to Bangkok. Again he had a sleeping cabin and managed to grab a few hours' sleep before arriving in Bangkok shortly after midnight. He caught a taxi to Pattaya and phoned Mickey Moore on the way.

70

The Russian stretched out his legs and grunted. The chair he was sitting on was comfortable enough but he had been there for six hours and his buttocks were starting to complain. More than two dozen people had entered or left the condominium building but none had matched the photograph he had concealed in the magazine on his lap. He was looking for an Englishman in his thirties, tall but not too tall, fit but not too fit, average-looking. In fact there was nothing memorable about Alex Harper, which was why the Russian was constantly having to look at the photograph. His colleague sitting on the other side of the reception area seemed to be equally uncomfortable. Both men were former Russian special forces. They had served in Ukraine and the north Caucasus and were happier with guns in their hands and bullets whizzing overhead than sitting in chairs.

The Russian bent down and picked up his cup of Starbucks coffee. It was the third since he had arrived at the building, and he would be needing the bathroom soon. That was why there were two of them. Mirov had been clear on that: someone had to be there all the time. He sipped his coffee and nodded at his colleague, who nodded back.

A motorcycle taxi driver walked in, with a tattoo of a cobweb across his neck and a steel chain around his neck from which hung five Buddha symbols. Two women in matching lime green suits were standing behind the counter and the guy spoke to them in Thai, then looked around the reception area. He took out an iPhone, made a call, then walked around talking loudly, the phone pressed to his ear. The Russian was impressed that a motorcycle taxi driver owned an expensive iPhone, unless it was a Chinese knock-off. He had realised soon after he'd arrived in the country that nothing in Thailand was as it seemed at first glance. Watches were often fake, as were designer labels, and more often than not the famous Thai smile was a mask for something more sinister. The Russian wasn't a big fan of Thailand but Mirov was paying big bucks and the boss, Yuri Lukin, had a huge operation in Moscow that promised even richer pickings in future, providing the Russian made a good impression.

The motorcycle guy was talking animatedly, waving his hand up and down as he stalked around the reception area, passing within a few feet of the Russian, then heading off to the far side, clearly annoyed at something. Then he took the phone away from his ear, shouted something at the two girls, and left. The Russian smiled at his colleague. At least something had happened to break the monotony.

He looked at the glass doors to his left. They were the only way to get to the lift lobby, and beyond the lifts were the stairs. Anyone going in or out of the apartments had to pass through the doors, which were operated from inside and outside by a keycard system. If Alex Harper returned to his apartment they would spot him, no question.

The motorcycle taxi driver went outside. His bike was standing by the main entrance but he ignored it and walked to a black Humvee that was parked on the road. The tinted window rolled down as he approached the vehicle and Mickey Moore grinned at him. 'How did it go, Adisorn?'

'There are two in there, Khun Mickey,' said the man. 'They look like Russians.' He passed the phone through the window and grinned as Mickey handed him a thousand-baht note in return. 'Anytime, Khun Mickey,' he said, putting his palms together and bowing, the traditional Thai *wai*.

'You take care, Adisorn,' said Mickey. As Adisorn headed back to his bike, Mickey went through the photographs on the phone. The Thai had been right: they looked like Russians. Big, hard men who clearly weren't waiting in Harper's condominium building to give him a welcome-back vodka. He grimaced, tossed the phone onto the passenger seat and drove off.

71

Harper had the taxi drop him on Second Road and went down Soi 15 to Walking Street. It was two o'clock in the morning so most of the Chinese and Korean tour groups had gone home, leaving the strip to the drunks, bar girls and sex tourists. A young contortionist was doing her thing for a group of onlookers under the watchful eye of a man whom Harper hoped was her father. She was standing on her hands with her legs over her head, using her feet to put on a pair of sunglasses. She couldn't have been much more than twelve years old. A group of uniformed cops were sitting at a table nearby in front of a police van, handing out tourist information and clearly unconcerned about any possible breach of the child labour laws.

Groups of young Thai men in black uniforms and scantily dressed dancers were in the street, trying to entice customers into their bars, without much luck. Most of the men, and women, who walked past Harper had the blank-eyed faces and slack jaws caused by too much alcohol, too much ear-shattering music and, in all likelihood, a fair amount of illegal drug-taking. Harper had a Singha beer baseball cap pulled down over his face as he threaded his way through the drunks to the Ice Bar. There were two sections: a trendy cocktail bar and the Ice Bar itself, a refrigerated unit with an industrial door and plate-glass windows overlooking the street. The cocktail bar was comfortably air-conditioned while the Ice Bar was maintained at twenty degrees below zero.

Mickey and his brother Mark were in the cocktail bar, chatting with the owner. Mickey saw Harper first and grinned broadly. 'You look like shit, mate.' He was a big-chested man in his early fifties, with hair that had receded almost halfway back and a dark tan that emphasised the blue of his eyes. He had a thick gold chain around his neck from which hung a gold Buddha image in a gold case. There was another thick gold chain on his right wrist and a chunky gold Patek Philippe watch on the other. He was wearing a white silk shirt with the sleeves rolled up and Versace jeans.

Harper grinned. In comparison to Mickey, he looked like a tramp. 'I came overland, from Malaysia.'

Mickey walked over and gave him a hug and a slap on the back. 'Drove?'

'Train.'

'How was it?'

'Like you said, I look like shit. But at least I came in under the radar.'

Mickey released his grip on Harper and stepped to the side to let his brother grab him in an equally painful hug. Mark was younger than Mickey by about eight years but was a couple of inches taller, with an even bigger chest. Like Mickey, he wore a gold chain around his neck but on his wrists he had a large Cartier watch with multiple dials and a metal Khmer bracelet that he claimed made him invulnerable to bullets. That was what the Khmer magic man who had sold it to him had said, but Mark had never put it to the test. He was also wearing designer labels – a pair of Armani jeans and a Ralph Lauren shirt, the real thing, not the knock-off copies that were sold all over Pattaya. The Moore brothers spent a lot of money on their appearance. That wasn't how Harper liked to operate. His watch was a cheap Casio and he never wore fashion brands. Labels were easy to identify and remember, and expensive watches stuck in people's memories. He preferred to be as forgettable as possible.

Mark punched Harper on the shoulder. 'Yeah, and then you walk straight into the lion's den. You must have balls of bloody steel, mate. Red Oktober is less than a hundred yards away.'

'This is the last place they'll be looking for me,' said Harper.

'Hide in plain sight?' said Mark. 'It's still a risk, mate. You're coming home with us tonight.'

'Nah, I'll be fine.'

'Fuck that, do as Mark says,' said Mickey. 'We checked out your condo. There's a couple of Russian goons camped out in Reception.' He pulled an iPhone from his back pocket and showed him the photographs the motorcycle taxi driver had taken earlier that day.

Harper scowled at the picture. They were big men and certainly looked Russian. 'Fuck.'

'So we're booking you into Casa del Moore,' said Mark. 'No arguments.'

Harper nodded. 'Okay.' He indicated the large refrigerator door. 'But we need to talk now.'

Mickey waved a hand at the owner. 'Okay if we have a conference?'

The owner flashed him a thumbs-up and Mark pulled open the door. Most of the patrons borrowed one of the bar's fur-lined parka jackets as they knocked back a selection of freezing-cold flavoured vodkas and tequilas, but Mickey, Mark and Harper went in as they were.

There was a small bar made of clear plastic that looked like ice in the corner where a waitress in a padded coat with the hood up was looking glumly through a plate-glass window at the passers-by in Walking Street. Her smile flashed on as soon as they came in and she gestured at the bottles in front of her. 'What can I get you?' she asked. Her only company was a Thai man in a polar bear suit.

'Three chocolate vodkas,' said Mickey. 'And one for you. And one for the fucking bear.' He patted the polar bear's shoulder. 'I don't know how you put up with it, mate, standing with your balls freezing for ten hours a day.'

The bear shrugged.

'He's got a job, hasn't he?' said Mark. 'Plus he gets all his booze free.' Mark shivered and rubbed his forearms. 'Plus he's got a nice comfy suit to keep him warm.'

The girl poured five chocolate vodkas. Mickey raised his. 'To our mate Lex. Life's never fucking boring with you around.'

The three men raised their shot glasses. So did the girl. The bear pulled back his head to reveal a Thai man in his forties with a gap-toothed grin. He picked up a glass with his paw and raised it in a salute. All five downed their drinks in one and slammed their glasses onto the bar. Mickey took out his wallet and gave the girl and the bear a thousand baht each. 'Give us five minutes alone,' he said. They hurried out and slammed the door behind them. The Moore brothers often used the Ice Bar to discuss business. It was totally soundproofed and there was a huge rattling air-conditioning unit on full to keep the temperature down so there was zero chance of anyone inside being overheard.

'Right. I need a silenced gun,' said Harper. The three men were leaning over the bar, their heads close together and their backs to the window. 'Mine is in my apartment and I can't get to it. Ideally I'd like something Russian. A 9mm PB silenced pistol would be favourite.'

'That shouldn't be a problem,' said Mickey.

'And I'll need explosives.'

'What sort?' asked Mark.

'The sort that go bang.'

Mickey laughed. 'Yeah, but there are big bangs and small bangs. And bloody huge bangs. Spectaculars, the IRA used to call them.'

'Nothing fancy,' said Harper. 'Just enough to blow up a car. In fact, not a whole car just the back bit.'

'Are you going to war, Lex?' asked Mickey.

'Just taking care of business,' said Harper. 'They started it.'

'Well, to be fair, you did stick bottles up the arses of two leading lights of the Russian Mafia,' said Mark.

'After they'd beaten up a friend of mine. And they sent someone to kill me in Paris. So if I don't make a bold statement now, this is going to drag on and on.'

'Why not just shoot the fuckers?' asked Mark.

'Because a bomb will muddy the waters,' said Harper. 'It'll leave some doubt. I was thinking you could ask your

Cambodian Army mates. I'm sure they've got some spare.'

'I'm sure they have,' agreed Mickey. 'They should be able to get the PB for you, too.'

'So are we good? Explosives and a detonator. Two to be on the safe side.'

'What about a timing circuit?'

'I'm sorted on that front. How soon can you get it for me?'

'How soon do you need it?' asked Mickey.

'As soon as.'

'Then I'll fly over today. Providing we pay in cash we should have the stuff in Bangkok within twenty-four hours.'

'How much do I owe you?' asked Harper.

'Buy me a chocolate vodka and we'll call it quits.' Mickey slapped him on the back. 'Least I can do for a mate who's willing to go to war with the Russian Mafia.'

'It's not a war, mate,' said Harper. 'It's not even a fucking skirmish.'

72

Armed police were standing at the two entrances to the compound where the Moore brothers lived. There was a tradition in Thailand of police officers hiring themselves out as security guards, usually in banks and jewellery shops, but Mickey's police contacts were as good as Harper's and there were always at least four on duty outside the compound. The two at the main entrance saluted his black Humvee as they drove by, which Harper thought was a nice touch. They were wearing white T-shirts, brown police uniform trousers, with shiny black boots, and had Glock pistols in nylon holsters on their hips.

There were six Thai-style villas around a central building, set in twelve acres of landscaped gardens with towering palms and spreading fruit trees. The main building had a large landscaped pool and a terrace protected by a pagoda-type roof where the brothers had regular barbecues. To the front of the main building a car parking area had spaces for more than two dozen vehicles. There were two black Range Rovers, a red Porsche, another black Humvee, a Bentley convertible, an old MGB sports car, and several Toyota saloons that belonged to the staff. Mickey parked the Humvee next to its twin, then jogged up the stairs and through the carved doors at the top. There was a double-height hallway with a vaulted teak ceiling and a seven-foot tall golden standing Buddha statue, wreathed in garlands of purple and white flowers. The hallway led to a huge room filled with overstuffed sofas and teak planters' chairs, a large LCD television on one wall and a library of paper-back books. It was the compound's chill-out area. Leading off it was a dining room with a table long enough to seat twenty, and another room, which served as a private cinema with a dozen reclining seats and sofas.

Harper and Mark followed Mickey down a hallway to the double-height bar area, which had vaulted teak ceilings with large wooden-bladed fans turning slowly above their heads. It looked like a five-star hotel bar, with leather sofas and armchairs, and a mahogany counter complete with beer taps and a full range of spirits. Glass-fronted fridges held wine and soft drinks, and there was even a popcorn machine. The luxury-hotel feel was spoiled somewhat by the three pinball machines, a Wurlitzer jukebox and a massive fruit machine behind the pool table.

Two men were playing pool. Like Mickey, they were in their early fifties, well-muscled and tanned by the fierce Thai sun. Harper knew them both – Davie Black and Barry 'Baz' Wilson. Like the Moore brothers they were skilled armed robbers, though unlike the Moores they had done time. As a teenager, Davie had been caught robbing a post office with a chair leg in a supermarket carrier bag, and Baz had tried to run a Securicor van off the road in Liverpool and ended up in hospital, then prison after slamming his car into a lamp-post. Both had learned about the Moore brothers while behind bars and met up with them after their release. They had been part of the crew for the past fifteen years.

The Moores and their team had been responsible for some of the most spectacular heists and robberies in Europe over the past couple of decades. They rarely struck more than once a year, their haul was never less than a million pounds, and everything they did was planned to the last detail, usually by an expert hired for the job, although as their fame had grown it was more usual for someone to approach them with a plan. It was a faultless business model that had made them all multi-millionaires. But they spent what they earned, pretty much. Harper had tried to convince them to join him in his various drug-trafficking enterprises, in particular shipping cannabis from North Africa into the European Union, but they were old-school villains, and while they were happy to use drugs recreationally, they had always refused to get into the business. 'Better the devil you know, mate,' Mickey always said.

Davie and Baz stopped playing and came over to them.

'Bloody hell! Lex Harper! How's it going, stranger?' Harper turned and grinned at the good-looking guy in a wheelchair, who had propelled himself in from next door. His name was Terry Norris, the youngest of the crew. Ex-army, a weapons expert, who was as good as anyone Harper had ever met, Norris had severed his spine in a motorcycle accident and was unlikely ever to walk again. Ramps and lifts all around the compound ensured that he could go wherever he wanted.

'All good,' said Harper, shaking the man's hand.

'I heard you've been winning friends and influencing people,' said Terry.

'That's why he's here,' laughed Mickey. 'We're taking him under our wing.' He pulled open a double-doored fridge and took out a bottle of Heineken. 'Anyone else want one?' he asked.

'What do you think?' asked Mark.

Mickey tossed him a beer. 'Davie? Baz?'

'We're sorted,' said Baz, nodding at a bottle of brandy on a shelf by the pool table. It was half empty.

'Lex?'

'I'm good,' said Harper. He had spotted two Thai girls lying on one of the sofas, entwined in each other's arms. Mickey saw what he was looking at and waved his beer bottle at them. 'Who are they?'

'They're with me,' said Baz. 'Ning and Nong, I think. Ning for sure, Nong I could be wrong about. They're lesbians. You can take them for a spin if you want when they wake up.'

'Why would I want to fool around with lesbians?' asked Mickey. 'Doesn't that sort of defeat the purpose?'

'They're happy enough for you to join in,' said Baz.

'Mate, I've told you before, I don't want your sloppy seconds. Look, Lex is going to be staying in the empty villa.' He grinned at Harper. 'You're welcome to Ding and Dong if you like.'

'Ning and Nong,' said Baz.

'I'm good,' said Harper.

'Whatever,' said Mickey. He looked at his watch. 'Guys, I'm off to Cambodia first thing so I'm going to have to hit the sack if I'm going to get any sleep at all. Take care of Lex. Lex, mate, the chef's on duty twenty-four/seven so order what you want.'

'You still play pool, Lex?' asked Baz.

'Been known to,' said Harper.

'Let's play doubles. You and Terry against me and Davie. Thousand bucks a game.'

Terry looked up at Harper and winked. 'You up for this?' asked Harper.

'Money in the bank, Lex. And they can break.'

73

Mickey Moore caught an early morning Bangkok Airways flight to Phnom Penh. The journey took just over an hour and an army Land Rover was waiting for him as the plane taxied up to the terminal. As the rest of the passengers hurried towards Immigration and Customs, two soldiers carrying AK-47s escorted him to their vehicle and whisked him out of the airport.

They turned off the main road on the outskirts of Phnom Penh, then rattled along a dusty single-track road through the Cambodian countryside for the best part of an hour, eventually arriving at the army firing range, which Moore and his crew visited several times a year. It was intended for Cambodian troops to hone their skills but the army was happy for tourists to have a go – at a price. Pretty much any weapon owned by the military was available, from simple handguns through AK-47s to bazookas. Hand grenades could be thrown for fifty dollars a go, and RPGs for five hundred. The army could also be creative in the targets it supplied. Barrels full of water were the target of choice for the machine-guns, but chickens could be supplied at five dollars a time. And larger weaponry, even hand grenades, could be hurled at cows and water buffaloes, as long as enough cash was handed over. Moore had heard that, providing enough money was paid, human targets could be provided from the local prison, but he figured – or hoped – that was just a rumour.

There were several firing ranges and a number of buildings that could be used as practice areas. The Moore brothers would come over with their crew to rehearse robberies on the range before flying to the UK to carry out the real thing. Their attention to detail at the planning stage was one of the reasons they had never been caught.

The colonel was sitting under a large canopy made of palm fronds in a La-Z-Boy chair overlooking one of the target ranges. At his side a stainless-steel ice bucket contained a bottle of Johnnie Walker Black Label while another held ice and several bottles of soda water. There was also a plate of sliced pineapple, a Smith & Wesson .44 Magnum and his peaked cap.

He grinned when he saw Mickey climb out of the Land Rover and pulled the handle on the side of his chair to lower his feet. He stood up and hugged Mickey. 'Always a pleasure to see you in my country, Mickey.'

'Sam, good to see you, too,' said Mickey, patting him on the back.

The colonel's full name was Samang, which was Khmer for 'lucky', but most Westerners ended up shortening it to Sam.

Sam hugged Mickey again, then waved him to a chair that was the twin of his own. A very pretty girl with waist-length hair, wearing a traditional Khmer purple silk sarong, came over and poured Mickey a whisky and soda, then refilled the colonel's glass. The two men toasted each other,

drank, and sat down. The girl picked up the plate of pine-
apple and offered it to Mickey. He took a piece, dabbed it
in a ceramic pot filled with chilli, sugar and salt, and popped
it into his mouth.

'So, what can I do for you, my friend?' asked the colonel.

Mickey waited until the girl had walked away, then said,
'Explosives. What do you have?'

Sam held up his palms to the heavens. 'I have whatever
you want,' he said. 'C1, C2, C3, C4, CA, CB.' His grin
widened. 'A veritable alphabet.'

'What would be best for taking out a vehicle? A car?'

'You can't go wrong with C4,' said Sam.

'How much would you need?'

'To destroy the vehicle? Or just kill the occupants?'

'The occupants.'

The colonel nodded thoughtfully. 'Half a kilo would
suffice.'

'Can you deliver it to me in Pattaya tomorrow?'

'It's urgent?'

'I'm afraid so,' Mickey confirmed.

'Then of course tomorrow can be arranged. It will be
expensive.'

'No problem. It's a ten-hour drive, right?'

'Not necessary, my friend. I will have it delivered from
Siem Reap. Five and a half hours, maybe six. I can have
it in Pattaya by midnight.'

'Perfect. How much. I'll need a couple of detonators,
too.'

'Of course.'

'And something a little special if you have it. A silenced
pistol. A Russian one, if possible.'

Sam laughed. 'You're not planning to assassinate someone are you, Mickey?' He drained his glass, then waved for the waitress to refill it, and Mickey's.

Again, Mickey waited until she had left before answering the colonel's question, though he knew Sam was joking. 'It's for a friend,' he said.

'Of course it is,' said the colonel. 'But it's none of my business who does what with what. We have several Makarovs and PB pistols in the armoury and I'm sure there's a least one with a working suppressor.'

'Excellent. And the cost? For everything?'

'Including delivery, three thousand dollars, my friend.'

Mickey reached inside his jacket, took out an envelope and counted thirty hundred-dollar bills. There was no need to do anything but pay up front because the colonel had never let him down.

'Always a pleasure doing business with you, Mickey.' The colonel slipped the notes into the pocket of his tunic.

'And you, Sam.'

The colonel raised his glass. 'You should stay for lunch. A rich American is going to fire a machine-gun at a cow and we'll barbecue what's left. We'll have you at the airport in plenty of time for the early evening flight.'

Mickey raised his glass in salute. 'Sounds like a plan.'

74

Police Colonel Somchai Wattanakolwit kept his eyes on the ball, swung back the club and tried to clear his mind of everything accept the shot he was about to make. He started his swing, relaxed into it, and was rewarded with a satisfying crack as the ball soared into the air.

'Nice shot,' said a voice behind him, and Somchai turned to find himself looking into the amused eyes of Lex Harper.

'You shouldn't go creeping up on someone like that,' said Somchai. 'Not when I have my gun in my golf bag.' He handed his club to the nineteen-year-old girl caddy. She was wearing a tight-fitting white T-shirt, a short white skirt and dark blue panties, as were the twenty-year-old driver of his golf cart and the girl who was responsible for supplying him with cold beers and even colder towels. Somchai was wearing a pink polo shirt and blue and green checked trousers with a snakeskin belt. His three fellow players – all off-duty policemen – were equally brightly dressed, each with a golf cart and three caddies to attend to his needs.

Harper wasn't dressed for golf – he had on blue jeans and a cheap grey hoodie and didn't appear to have shaved that day. 'Now, this is a pleasant surprise,' said Somchai.

'I had no idea you were back in Thailand.' He stepped forward, put his arm around Harper's shoulders and led him away from his golfing buddies.

'Hopefully very few people do,' said Harper.

'You should bring your clubs next time,' he said.

'I don't own golf clubs,' said Harper. 'I don't have the patience.'

'That's the whole point,' said Somchai. 'It teaches you patience. There is something very Zen-like about golf. I think that's why we Asians enjoy it so much.'

One of his caddies came over and gave them both iced towels. Harper slapped his on the back of his neck. It was a hot day, well into the high thirties. Expats always claimed that Thailand had two seasons. Hot, and very hot.

Somchai turned to watch the next golfer teeing up his shot. 'You know that Yuri Lukin has hired some very heavy hitters?' he said.

'I sort of thought that might happen,' said Harper, keeping his voice low so that it wouldn't carry.

'And security has been increased at Valentin's compound for when he and Grigory Lukin are released from hospital.' Somchai rubbed his cold towel around his neck. 'Though I gather it will be a few days yet before the doctors allow them to leave. You did a lot of damage, it seems.'

'Allegedly,' said Harper.

'It's good to see you have retained your sense of humour, my friend,' said Somchai.

The golfer hit the ball with a resounding thwack that sent it soaring into the air and Somchai nodded appreciatively. He smiled at Harper. 'I'm not sure that you coming back to Pattaya was a good idea.'

'I need to get this sorted, Somchai. I can't spend the rest of my life looking over my shoulder.'

Somchai seemed uncomfortable. 'My friend, as much as I'd like to, I can't protect you. Yuri Lukin is paying off the boss of my boss and even higher, and I can't go against them.'

Harper shook his head. 'It's not your protection I need, Somchai,' he said. 'It's your permission.'

Somchai frowned. 'My permission? For what, may I ask?'

Harper's smile broadened. 'Your permission to protect myself.'

Somchai chuckled. 'Oh, by all means, my friend. You do what you have to do.' He patted Harper on the back. 'And I wish you all the luck in the world.'

75

Mark prodded the massive T-bone steaks that were sizzling on the grill while Baz and Lex looked on, drinking bottles of Heineken. 'Japanese beef,' said Mark. 'Can't beat it. The cows get a bottle of beer every day, a massage and probably a happy ending for all I know. Best beef in the world. And the most expensive.'

Aerosmith was blaring from the stereo system and braziers had been lit around the pool, casting flickering shadows over the water. Half a dozen Thai girls were playing in the water and more were sprawled around the cabanas. It was party night, but pretty much every night was party night at the compound.

'See anything you like, Lex?' asked Mark, waving a pair of stainless-steel tongs. Harper wasn't sure if he was referring to the girls or the steaks. The barbecue was huge and the table next to Mark was piled high with steaks, chicken and fish, and another laden with salads, sauces and vegetables. The Moore brothers had three chefs between them working round the clock, all hired from top hotels on much-improved salaries. The girls were also paid, and Harper recognised several top dancers from the city's best go-go bars. Baz had left the compound at just before eight in one of the Humvees and had returned with six of the girls, all obviously pleased at being asked to spend an evening partying rather than dancing around a chrome pole. Mickey had arrived at the compound at just after six and had phoned in the rest of the girls, most apparently regular visitors to the compound. Two were dancing topless at the side of the pool while two more had appointed themselves bartenders and were walking around refilling glasses and offering fresh beers.

'Lex, how do you want your steak?' asked Mark, waving his tongs in the air.

'Just cut the hoofs off and throw it over.' Harper laughed. 'The rarer the better.'

Mark stuck his fork into a steak and slapped it onto a plate. Harper took it, helped himself to potato salad and a roasted ear of corn, then went to sit down at a long table where Terry was already tucking in. 'I keep forgetting how large you guys live,' said Harper, as he cut into his steak. Blood oozed out over his plate, which was just how he liked it.

'Dunno how long it'll last,' said Terry. 'The Russians are going to spoil it for everyone.'

'How so?'

'You know how so,' said Terry. 'You've been here long enough. We have a string of genuine businesses, property, restaurants, a couple of diving companies. We all have work permits and pay tax.' He waved his knife at the ground around them. 'We can't own this place because only Thais can own land, but it's in a company we control so all good. The Thais let us live here and we respect that by not shitting on our doorstep. But you know as well as I do that the Russians are a whole different ball game. They run prostitution here, all sorts of scams, ATM fraud, protection rackets, and they've started trading Thai girls into Russia. You've seen what they've done to Walking Street. Wall-to-wall Russian hookers, these days. There'll be a backlash before long, and when it comes all foreigners will be hit, not just the Russians.'

Davie Black sat down with a plate of steak and chicken. Harper grinned. 'No veg?'

'Like my South African mates say, chicken is a fucking vegetable,' said Davie. 'You guys talking about the Russians?'

'I was just telling Lex, the shit is gonna hit the fan sooner rather than later.'

Davie started hacking at his steak. 'What about you, Lex? Have you got a plan B?'

'I've always got a plan B,' said Harper. 'But I'm happy enough here.'

'Cambodia, that's where we'll be going,' said Davie. 'If there is a clampdown, we've already got a spot picked out. Fifteen acres, our own lake. We've had a place designed and it could be up and running in six months if we need it.' He waved a chunk of steak in front of Harper's face. 'Tell you what, we'll fix you up with a villa. What do you think, Tel? Lex is one of the guys, right?'

'Hell, yeah,' said Terry.

'I appreciate the offer, seriously. But I don't live well with others.'

'Lone fucking wolf, is Lex,' said Davie.

Harper grinned. 'Yeah, that's my Red Indian name. But, seriously, thanks for the offer. If ever I turn gay I'll take you up on it.'

The two men laughed, and despite the banter, Harper was genuinely touched. The crew was the closest thing he had to family and he knew they felt the same.

One of the compound's estate managers, a middle-aged Thai who had worked for the Moores for more than a decade, hurried over to the cabana where Mickey was lounging with two dark-skinned Thai girls in matching stars-and-stripes bikinis. The man had a whispered conversation with him, then hurried away. Mickey got to his feet, kissed one of the girls, then went over to Harper's table.

'The gear's arrived,' said Mickey. 'We need to give it the once-over so that the guy can get on his way.'

Harper stood up and followed him to the main building, then out to the car park. There was a minivan with the name of a Thai tourist company on the side, along with the logo of a smiling elephant wearing a floppy hat and holding a cocktail glass with an umbrella in it. There were no passengers in the van, just a driver, who was wearing sunglasses even though it was ten o'clock at night, and a woman who might have been his wife. Mickey opened the side door, pushed back the middle row of seats, then pulled up the grey carpet. There was a metal door set into the floor and four holes with hexagonal screw heads. The woman twisted in her seat and handed him an Allen key, which he used it to remove the screws before he pulled up the panel. Underneath a compartment contained three cloth-wrapped packages. Mickey took out the largest and unwrapped it. It was a block of C4 explosive, sealed in plastic. On top of it were two detonators, each with twin wires. Mickey laughed. 'You'd have thought they'd wrap them separately,' he said.

'No need,' said Harper. 'Without a power source it's as safe as Plasticine.'

Mickey rewrapped the package and handed it to Harper. The second contained a gun, and the last a silencer, with two eight-cartridge magazines.

Harper nodded his approval and Mickey rewrapped them, handed them to him, then screwed the panel into place and put the carpet back. He gave the Allen key to the woman, along with a couple of thousand baht, which earned him a respectful *wai* from her and her husband. Mickey slammed the door and the minivan drove off to the main entrance, where the gate was already rattling open. Two police officers clicked their heels and saluted as it drove onto the road.

'Drop the gear in your villa and we'll get stuck into our steaks,' said Mickey. 'Mark and I will give you a hand tomorrow.'

'You don't have to, really. This is my fight.'

Mickey put his arm around Harper's shoulders. 'It's our fight, mate. You're one of us. They fuck with you, they fuck with the whole crew.'

76

The limousine spent all morning parked inside the Valentin compound. Mickey had arranged for a team of motorcycle taxi riders to take turns following the vehicle and to stay in touch on their mobile phones. The driver was Russian, but from his height and build, he wasn't a bodyguard. He didn't seem to be especially well trained either, and apparently wasn't aware that he was being tailed. The motorcycle riders stayed in touch with Mickey through mobile phones. The Moore brothers had more than a dozen riders on retainer. They ran errands and were often a useful source of intelligence about what was going on around the city.

At just after two o'clock in the afternoon, Mickey took a call from one of his spies that the limousine had left the compound. He went out to the pool where Harper was sitting in one of the cabanas with Mark. 'The limo's on the move,' he said. 'Heading to Pattaya City. Do you want to check it out?'

Harper nodded.

'I'll come with you,' said Mark, grabbing a shirt.

'I can do it myself,' said Harper.

'Fuck that,' said Mark. 'All for one and one for all.'

Harper headed back to his villa. The device was in a teak cupboard in the hall. It was a simple enough build: the two detonators were embedded in the plastic explosive, which was connected to the circuit that Hansfree had built for him in London. It was sitting in a grey plastic Tupperware box to which Harper had superglued several powerful magnets. The whole thing was about nine inches long, six inches wide and three inches deep. He placed it in a black nylon kitbag and carried it over to the main building, where Mickey and Mark were waiting for him. They walked together to the parking area. 'We'll take one of the pick-ups,' said Mickey, grabbing a set of keys from a line of hooks by the front door. 'The Hummers and the Range Rovers attract attention.'

'Yeah, funny that,' said Harper.

They went out of the main building and over to a white four-door Toyota pick-up truck with tinted windows. Mickey and Mark sat in the front and Harper climbed into the back.

Mickey took another call while they were driving down the road towards the coast. 'He's in the Central Festival Department Store,' said Mickey, as he shoved the phone back into his pocket. 'This should work.'

'That thing isn't going to go off accidentally, is it?' asked Mark, twisting around in his seat and pointing at the holdall.

'It's phone-activated,' said Harper. 'All sorts of fail-safes built into the circuit. It was done by an expert.'

'Yeah, and experts said the *Titanic* was unsinkable,' said Mark. 'What happens if someone calls a wrong number?'

'You don't just make a call. You enter a three-digit number and then it goes bang. No code, no explosion. And C4 is pretty much inert without a detonator. You can set fire to it and use it to boil water if you want to.'

'Fuck me, mate, that's what electric kettles are for,' said Mickey.

'Yeah, well, sometimes when you're in the desert in Afghanistan and feel like a brew, there isn't an electric kettle to hand, and that's when a little block of C4 comes in handy.'

'Did they ever give you a medal for what you did in Afghanistan?' asked Mark.

Harper shook his head. 'Sand up my arse. That's all I took home with me.'

It took twenty minutes to drive to the Central Festival Department Store. It was midway down Beach Road, a seven-storey shopping complex that advertised itself as the largest in Asia. Above it towered the Hilton Hotel.

One of Mickey's motorbike spies was waiting at the entrance to the car park and slid into the back of the pick-up next to Harper. Mickey drove into the multi-storey car park under the complex and the motorbike guy gave him directions for finding the limousine. Because of its length the limo had been parked across two spaces at the far corner of the car park, next to the wall.

'Driver shopping in Big C,' said the motorbike guy.

'We've got a few minutes at least,' said Mickey. 'How do you want to handle it, Lex?'

Harper looked around. Two security guards were standing by the entrance to the complex, and another was sitting at a table next to a VIP parking section. The structure was busy with shoppers heading to and from their vehicles. 'A diversion would be nice,' he said.

Mickey grinned. 'No problem,' he said. 'Just give me the nod when you're ready.'

Harper climbed out of the pick-up. So did the motorcycle taxi driver, who hurried off. Harper walked casually over to the limo, then past it. He turned and nodded at the pick-up, though the heavily tinted windows meant he couldn't see Mickey or Mark. Almost immediately Mickey revved the engine, put the truck in gear and drove into a parked Honda. There was a sickening crunch, followed by the Honda's alarm going off. Immediately all of the security guards ran towards the pick-up. All heads turned to see what was going on and Harper stepped between the limo and the wall, then dropped down. He unzipped the holdall and took out the Tupperware container, lay on his back and slid under the vehicle. He placed the container midway between the rear seats, choosing a spot that wasn't too close to the exhaust. He pushed it against the metal and heard a reassuring click as the magnets bit. He gave it a tug and it wouldn't budge. Even if it hit a pothole or two, the powerful magnets would hold it in place. He shuffled out from under the vehicle, zipped up the holdall and stood up.

Several dozen shoppers were now staring at the pick-up and the Honda's alarm was still blaring. Mickey was out of the truck, apologising loudly and profusely. A middle-aged Thai lady had appeared, pushing a shopping-laden trolley, and from the way she started shouting it appeared that it was her Honda Mickey had rammed. He went to her, still apologising.

Harper walked away and waited at the car-park exit. Five minutes later the pick-up appeared, a small dent and a slight scrape on the bumper the only physical signs of the collision. Harper climbed into the back. 'You owe me twenty-five thousand baht,' said Mickey.

'No problem,' said Harper. 'Was she okay?'

'Mate, I barely touched her car. A bit of panel-beating, a touch of paint, and she's good to go. It was a five-year-old Honda, for fuck's sake. She's quids in and she knows it. She went away as happy as Larry. I gave all the security guards five hundred baht and they saluted me as I drove off. I love this country.' He headed away from the beach, making for the compound. 'And you? Your gizmo's all hooked up.'

'Good to go,' said Harper.

'Now what?'

'The trap's set. I just need the bait. I'll do that tonight.'

'I'll tell you something, Lex,' said Mark, 'I sure hope you never get pissed off at me.' He turned in his seat to punch Harper's shoulder. 'Underneath that happy-go-lucky exterior, you're one mean son of a bitch.'

Harper grinned and settled back. 'They started it, mate. But I'll sure as hell finish it.'

77

Lex Harper had never been a fan of hospitals and tried to avoid them as much as possible. He didn't like the smells, or the sounds, or that so many people died in them. He had on a white coat with 'DOCTOR' above the chest pocket, a stethoscope hanging around his neck, horn-rimmed spectacles and a medical mask over his mouth and nose. He kept his face away from any CCTV cameras as he walked through the hospital, but was confident he wouldn't be recognised if anyone looked through the footage later.

It was just before midnight, and while the emergency centre was as busy as ever, dealing with road-traffic accidents, drug overdoses and the aftermath of drunken brawls, much of the rest of the hospital was quiet. He was wearing black trainers that made barely any noise as he walked along the tiled corridor and along to the emergency stairs.

He took the stairs up to the ICU floor. Two nurses were sitting in the station at the other end of the corridor but they were deep in conversation. One glanced up, saw the white coat, smiled, and went back to her chat. There was a long window in the side corridor that looked onto four intensive-care suites, each with a patient lying in a bed surrounded by a battery of monitoring equipment. To the left of each doorway, the name of the patient was written on white card. One of the names was Thai, one was Japanese and the other two were in English: HELEN FIELDS and GRIGORY LUKIN. There were two nurses in the ICU to the far left, the one occupied by the Japanese patient. They were leaning over him and had their backs to the window. There were no medical staff in the other three units.

Another window to the right overlooked four more units. Two were Arabic names, one was Thai and another Japanese. Harper figured that Valentin Rostov must have recovered enough to be moved to a general ward. Not that it mattered: it was Lukin he had come for.

Harper went back to the first window and along to the glass door that led to the units. He pushed it open and immediately heard the electronic beeping of the various monitoring devices used to track the vital signs of the patients. He tiptoed to Lukin's unit, taking a syringe from his pocket and sliding the protective plastic cover from the needle. The syringe contained the rest of the gelsemium he had bought from Dr Li. Only if a forensic expert went looking for gelsemium would the true cause of the Russian's death be identified, and Harper was pretty sure that the Thais wouldn't be doing that.

Lukin's eyes were closed and his mouth was open, revealing broken and cracked teeth. The Russian's right arm was in plaster, hanging in a sling, as were both his legs. Harper smiled to himself. At least the Russian's last few days would have been painful. He'd earned it, after what he'd done to Pear.

Harper padded over to the intravenous drip and held

the tube with his left hand, about six inches from where it went into Lukin's arm. He pushed the needle into the tube and slowly pressed down the plunger. In a matter of seconds the contents of the syringe had been injected into the tube. Harper replaced the cap on the needle, put the syringe into his pocket and went to the door. As he left the room he heard Lukin's bed begin to shake as the Russian went into spasm, but he didn't look back. He kept his head down as he walked along the corridor to the emergency stairs. When he reached the ground floor and walked across the hospital car park, Grigory Lukin was already dead.

78

Less than twenty-four hours after Grigory Lukin was declared dead of a heart attack, his father's Gulfstream jet landed at Bangkok's Don Mueang airport. Yuri Lukin insisted that the door be opened before the immigration officers arrived and paced up and down as he waited for them. His passport was examined, the cash bribe was pocketed, and he got into the back of the stretch limousine. Two white four-by-fours bracketed the vehicle, each with three men inside. Lukin recognised Volkov and Myshkin but it was the first time he'd seen the others. Mirov picked up on Lukin's unease. 'They're good men.'

'They'd better be,' snarled Lukin. 'I'm fed up with you hiring fuckwits. Why was no one guarding Grigory in the hospital?'

'He was in the ICU and they wouldn't let us post guards. And there were always people about.'

'And what the fuck happened?' growled Lukin. He grabbed a bottle of vodka and poured himself a shot, which he downed in one.

'A heart attack, the doctors say. Grigory was overweight, he used drugs, and that plus the attack—'

'Grigory was as strong as a fucking horse,' said Lukin,

pouring himself another shot. 'What about that fucker Valentin?'

'Valentin's still in the hospital.'

'Did he have protection? Were his fucking guards protecting him?'

Mirov shook his head. 'Boss, I keep telling you, we weren't allowed guards in the hospital. They said they'd call the cops.'

'We own the fucking cops,' said Lukin. 'You should have had fucking cops in there sitting by his bed. That shit Harper attacked my son, and now he's fucking well killed him.'

'Boss, I'm not convinced it was anything other than a heart attack.'

Lukin's eyes hardened. 'Harper killed my son. And you, you fucker, you let it happen.'

'Boss, really, he had a heart attack.'

Lukin smashed the vodka glass against the side of Mirov's head. It shattered and Mirov yelped and fell backwards, blood streaming from his cheek. Lukin had cut himself and he held his bleeding hand out in front of Mirov's nose. 'Now look what you made me do,' he said. He shoved Mirov in the face, pushing him against the window, smearing blood across his nose. 'Look what you made me fucking do!'

'Sorry,' mumbled Mirov.

Lukin growled, shoved him in the face again, then grabbed a napkin from a stack on the bar and held it to his bleeding hand. Mirov took a handful and pressed them against the cut in his cheek. They went red immediately.

'You get blood on the leather and you'll pay to have it

cleaned.' Lukin stared out of the window as he dabbed his cut hand. Mirov took more napkins and held them tightly to his wound.

They drove in silence for half an hour while Lukin downed half of the vodka in the bottle.

'Where's the body now?' he asked eventually.

'Still in the hospital,' said Mirov. 'They were waiting to see if you wanted to take him back to Moscow or cremate him here.'

'Here? Why the fuck would we leave him here? He is a Russian and will be buried in Russia. But first, I want them to do a proper autopsy. I don't think for one moment he had a fucking heart attack. He had the heart of a lion, my son. That fucker Harper killed him and I want to know how. And I want Harper found. I want him found and brought to me so that I can kill him myself.'

'Yes, boss,' mumbled Mirov.

Lukin stared out of the window. 'Where are you fucking taking me?'

'Valentin's villa. We've upgraded the security and there is CCTV covering all the walls, cameras inside, too. We hired three more guards.'

'Yeah, well, that was locking the fucking stable door after the horses had fucking bolted, wasn't it?' He poured himself more vodka. 'It's not about the number of men, it's about the quality. You can hire all the fuckwits you want but if they sit on their arses counting crows you're throwing your money away. Fuck that, you're throwing *my* money away. My fucking money.'

'They're good men, boss. I brought them in from Moscow.'

'And what about Harper? Do we know where he is?'

'We've been watching the airports and he hasn't turned up. And we have a couple of guys staking out his apartment.' Blood was dripping down his chin and soaking into his shirt.

'Whatever it takes to track him down, you do it? Do you hear? Money's no fucking object.' Lukin swallowed a shot of vodka and refilled the glass. 'I told Grigory not to fucking waste his time here. If he wanted to fuck Asian hookers we've got all we need in Moscow. Thai restaurants, too, if it's the food he likes. He should never have come here. I told him, Moscow is where the money is.' He knocked back another shot of vodka. 'How quickly can we get the body flown back to Moscow?'

'You want the autopsy done first, right?'

'Yes, of course.' He downed another vodka. 'Actually, no, fuck it. We can do that in Moscow. I don't trust them to do it right here. They fuck everything up. Fly the body to Moscow and we'll have the tests done there.'

'I should be able to get the paperwork done this afternoon. It'll need some money to make it go smoothly. . .'

'Don't bother me with the fucking details,' snapped Lukin. 'Just get it done.'

'Yes, boss,' said Mirov. Blood was still dripping from his face and he knew the wound needed to be stitched. But he also knew that if he were to say anything to Lukin he'd likely smash a second glass into his face.

The car slowed. Ahead, a pick-up truck was loaded with cardboard boxes tied together with rope. The stack was three times as high as the vehicle and the driver was having trouble controlling it.

The SUV ahead of the limousine had already overtaken the truck.

'Look at this fucking idiot,' said Lukin. 'How is that not going to end badly? And what the fuck are our so-called bodyguards doing?' He sneered at Mirov. 'This is supposed to be a fucking convoy, right? The pricks in that car are supposed to be watching over us. So why the fuck did they overtake the truck and leave us here? Who trains these fucking morons?'

'I'll talk to them,' said Mirov. He fished in his pocket for his mobile phone as he pressed more napkins to his bleeding cheek.

Lukin leaned forward and waved the vodka bottle at the driver. 'Get by this moron, will you, before that load falls all over the fucking car?'

The driver pulled out and stamped on the accelerator, passing the pick-up truck but narrowly missing a bus that was headed their way. They caught up with the first SUV.

'These roads are fucking death traps,' said Lukin, settling back in his seat.

'We're nearly there,' said Mirov. He pressed the number for one of the bodyguards in the leading SUV.

Lukin poured himself another shot of vodka and sat back in his seat. 'If that bastard Harper's in the UK, we'll have to send people after him,' he said.

'Yes, boss.' The phone rang out, unanswered.

'But he might still be in fucking France. Bastard, bastard, bastard. I'll rip his fucking eyes out with my own hands.'

The limousine turned off the main road and headed up the hill to Valentin's villa. The SUV was about fifty yards ahead, indicating a left turn. 'Here we are,' said Mirov. He put his phone away. He glanced over his shoulder. The second SUV was where it was supposed to be, about fifty metres behind them.

'About time. We're out of fucking vodka,' growled Lukin, tossing the empty bottle into the drinks cabinet. He looked to his right, past Mirov. A man was sitting astride a motorcycle at the side of the road. It was the bike Lukin noticed first. A Triumph Bonneville. A classic British motorcycle. Lukin was a fan of big bikes: he had two Harleys in Moscow and a Honda Goldwing, but he had never been a fan of British models. The driver was wearing a leather motorcycle jacket and a full-face helmet with a tinted visor. As Lukin watched, he took off his helmet and grinned towards the car. Lukin frowned. The man's face was familiar. 'What the fuck?' he muttered to himself.

Mirov twisted in his seat, trying to see what Lukin was staring at.

'It's fucking Harper!' shouted Lukin, pointing at the man on the bike. 'That is fucking Harper!'

Harper put his helmet onto one of the bike's mirrors as the limousine drove by.

Lukin and Mirov turned to stare out of the rear window. 'That is the fucker, isn't it?' Lukin shouted.

'I . . . I don't know,' stammered Mirov.

'It is! It fucking is! Stop the fucking car!' Lukin screamed at the driver at the top of his voice. 'Stop the fucking car now or I swear I'll rip your fucking head off!'

The driver stamped on the brake and Lukin grabbed at the seat to steady himself. He looked out of the back window as he reached for the door handle. They were about a hundred yards from the motorbike now but he could see that Harper was still grinning. In his hand he was holding a mobile phone. Then the SUV behind them blocked his view. Lukin instinctively knew what was coming and he took a breath, preparing to bellow. There was a flash, a deafening noise, and his whole body felt as if it was on fire. Then there was nothing.

79

'Keep looking out of the window,' Valentin said, to the man sitting next to him. 'If you see anything, anything at all, you tell me.'

'I will,' said the man. His name was Dubov and he had flown in from Moscow two days earlier. He was a big man, barely out of his twenties, and as hard as nails. He was one of three heavies who had been recruited as extra protection and all came highly recommended.

'That bastard Harper killed Lukin and Mirov, and I'm damn sure he killed Grigory, too.'

'They can't get you in here, sir,' said Dubov.

'You say that, but he blew up a fucking limo,' said Valentin. He was lying on a trolley in the back of a private ambulance. His head was bandaged, his jaw hurt like hell and he was still damaged internally, but he knew he had to get out of the hospital. At least in the villa he could be guarded by men with guns. Getting a tame doctor out to treat him in his own home would be a matter of money, and he could buy in round-the-clock nursing care. There was another bodyguard riding up front with the driver and he was carrying a gun under his jacket, as was Dubov. There were SUVs front and back of the ambulance but that hadn't inspired Valentin with confidence as they were the same vehicles that had supposedly been guarding the limousine. He had insisted that they check underneath the ambulance, twice, before he got in.

Dubov had a transceiver and called ahead to the villa to talk to one of the four bodyguards there. 'We're five minutes away,' he said.

'The house is secure,' said the man. His name was Yerkhov and, like Dubov, had served in the Russian special forces for five years before realising there was more money to be made in the private sector. Russian businessmen and crime lords had spread across the world and disputes, business and criminal, were often settled with violence, so overseas protection had become as necessary as passports. Dubov and Yerkhov commanded six-figure dollar salaries, plus all expenses, and were never short of work.

'Check again,' shouted Valentin. 'Check everywhere. Under the beds, in the cupboards, check every fucking inch of the place.'

'The boss wants you to check again,' said Dubov. 'Then be at the gate to meet us.'

'With guns,' shouted Valentin. 'Make sure they have guns.'

'They will,' said Dubov.

'Tell them!' shouted Valentin, and grunted in pain as the ambulance went over a pothole.

'Mr Rostov says you should have your guns with you,' said Dubov, into his transceiver.

The ambulance engine was labouring as they went uphill. Valentin's heart was racing, partly through the pain he was suffering but mainly because they were now on the stretch of road where Lukin and Mirov had died. The bomb had destroyed most of the rear of the limousine but the blast had gone upwards so the driver had emerged relatively unscathed, albeit with burst eardrums. The police had managed to find Mirov's head pretty much intact but all they had found of Lukin was a foot and a hand. Valentin closed his eyes and said a silent prayer, gasping as the ambulance hit another pothole.

Dubov smiled down at him reassuringly. 'Don't worry, sir. We're arriving at the villa now.' He opened his jacket to show him the pistol that was nestled in a brown leather underarm holster. 'If there's any trouble at all we're locked, loaded and ready to go.'

80

Mickey Moore came out of the main house, holding a bottle of Heineken in one hand and a KFC bucket in the other. He walked towards where Harper was sitting by the pool, which was Olympic size, with two diving boards at the deep end, but built in the style of a tropical lagoon. There were two curved artificial beaches, complete with sand, palm trees, and rocks that were large enough to sunbathe on. At the shallow end there was a Jacuzzi big enough to hold a dozen people, which it often did on party nights. Half a dozen teak cabanas, their roofs fringed with palms, stood around the edge of the pool, and at one side there was a brick-built barbecue that was the size of a regular kitchen.

The pool tended to be the focal point of the estate during the day, though Baz, Davie and Terry were still in their villas nursing hangovers. Harper was in one of the cabanas, holding the Russian 9mm PB silenced pistol that had come from Cambodia as Mark watched and drank a beer. The gun had been specially designed for Spetsnaz units when it was introduced in 1967. Harper planned to leave it at the scene, hoping that a Russian gun would muddy the waters in any investigation by the Thais and by Valentin's associates.

The gun was still in production in what had originally been known as the Izhevsk Mechanical Plant, which had been founded in 1807, the time of Tsar Alexander I, and had gone on to become one of the largest arms manufacturers in the world, producing cannons, missiles, and the famous Kalashnikov assault rifle. PB stood for *pistolet beschumnyi,* or 'noiseless pistol'. It was based on the standard Makarov pistol and fired standard Makarov ammunition, but it had been designed so that rounds were always fired subsonically. To achieve that, the barrel had two small holes that allowed some of the propellant gas to escape into the silencer. Even without the silencer screwed in, the gun was still quieter than a standard Makarov.

'We've just had a KFC delivery,' said Mickey, as he reached the cabana.

'Clearly,' said Mark, helping himself to a chicken leg from the bucket.

'Are you sure you don't want us along for the ride?' Mickey asked Harper.

'It's my fight,' said Harper, his eyes on the gun.

'Yeah, but we're the musketeers,' said Mark, waving his chicken leg like a sword. 'All for one and one for all.'

The weapon was well oiled and appeared to have been cared for, but Harper was taking no chances. As the Moore brothers watched he stripped it down, checked the component parts, then reassembled it.

'He's showing off,' said Mark.

'He knows what he's doing,' said Mickey. 'But I still think you'd be better going in mob-handed.'

Harper shook his head. 'Then it'll be a war, and if they find out you're involved, they'll come after you.'

'I ain't scared of no steenking Russians,' said Mark, in a fake Mexican accent.

Harper laughed. 'Mate, I'll be in and out like a fucking Ninja. I'll do what has to be done, toss the gun and Robert's your father's brother.'

'They'll know it was you,' said Mickey.

'Not necessarily. And with Valentin, Grigory and Lukin dead, someone else will take over and I doubt that revenge will be high on his list of priorities. But I'll cross that chicken when I get to it.' He stood up. 'I wouldn't mind a test firing.'

'Be our guest,' said Mickey.

The three men walked away from the pool. 'I'll go and warn security,' said Mark. 'Suppressors are good, but they're not perfect.' He jogged towards the front gate.

Mickey and Harper walked to the far end of the estate where there was a clump of palm trees. 'Do you want me to stand with an apple on my head?' asked Mickey.

'Would you?'

Mickey laughed. 'Actually, I would, mate. I've seen you shoot. I know how good you are.' He picked up a loose coconut, about the size of a man's head. 'But this'll do.' He tossed the coconut about ten feet away. Harper chambered a round, aimed and pulled the trigger. There wasn't much in the way of recoil and the sound was equivalent to that of a balloon popping, not the soft hiss that silenced weapons made in movies. No suppressor was perfect, which was why the professionals called them suppressors rather than silencers. The bullet thwacked into the middle of the coconut.

'Happy?' asked Mickey, waving his bottle of Heineken.

'I will be when it's Valentin's head I'm shooting at,' said Harper.

'Go for the chest,' said Mickey. 'It's a bigger target.'

Harper opened his mouth to reply until he saw from the look on the man's face that he was joking. 'Fuck you,' he said.

'Fuck you too. Just be careful.'

81

Harper was insistent that he would take care of Valentin himself, but he allowed Mickey and Mark to drive him to the villa. They took one of the estate's nondescript pick-up trucks with a folding ladder in the back.

Harper sat in the front passenger seat with the PB in his lap as Mickey drove. He was wearing a dark sweatshirt and black jeans, with black trainers and skin-tight black gloves. He had borrowed a black nylon shoulder holster from Mickey that allowed him to carry the pistol, and silencer, under his left arm. It was a fair enough fit, though he would have to be careful not to snag the silencer when he pulled it out. Mark sat behind him with two pump-action sawn-off shotguns next to him. 'Just in case,' he'd said.

They parked a couple of hundred yards from the villa and Mickey switched off the engine and lights so their night vision would kick in. 'You've got your phone, right?' said Mickey.

'Yes, Mum.'

'Fuck off, you soft twat. If anything goes wrong, you call us and we'll be in like Finn.'

'It's Flynn, mate. In like Flynn.'

'Flynn, Finn, whoever the fuck he is, we'll be in like him if there's any sign of trouble,' said Mickey.

'It'll be fine.'

'Well, you say that, but there's CCTV covering all the walls and by all accounts a shedload of former Spetsnaz thugs inside.'

'It's late. They'll be asleep. And Valentin's gonna be dosed up on painkillers.'

'There'll be someone watching the CCTV monitors,' said Mark.

'You say that, but you know most of the time that's not true. No one sits and watches a screen all night.'

'You need a diversion,' said Mickey. 'That's what you need.'

'Oh, fuck! You're not going to wear the clown suit again?' sneered Mark.

'That was twenty years ago,' said Mickey. 'And it worked, didn't it? We got clean away with the takings.'

'No thanks to those fucking clown shoes you had on.'

'He's taking the piss,' Mickey said to Harper. 'I was wearing trainers. Seriously, you need some sort of distraction at the gate. Get security focused on that and you can slip in unnoticed.'

'Like what?'

'A couple of drunken motorcycle taxis at the gate. I can fix that up, no bother. Let me give a mate a call.'

Harper nodded. 'Okay. It can't hurt.'

Mickey spent a couple of minutes on the phone, then grinned as he put it away. 'Ten minutes, Lex. It'll give you time to get set up.' He patted Harper's shoulder. 'And I'm serious. You get in trouble, call.'

Harper climbed out of the truck. He picked up the light-weight ladder and two old rice sacks and jogged towards the rear wall. The security wire had been replaced and there was now a weatherproof CCTV camera trained along the top of the wall. It hadn't been done by experts as it could clearly be approached from behind. There was another camera at the far corner but that seemed to be pointing at the ground. Harper figured there was a blind spot of twenty feet or so, but he couldn't be sure. He pulled on a ski mask and crouched near the base of the wall.

After about ten minutes he heard several motorcycles coming up the hill. Three, maybe four. Then the engines cut out and he heard laughing and Thai shouting. Then smashing glass. Soon afterwards he heard angry Russian voices. Then 'Fuck off, you drunken bastards!' shouted in accented English.

There were Thai yells, and Harper recognised several choice Thai swearwords. He placed the ladder against the wall, climbed up, snipped out a section of the security wire and threw the sacks over the broken glass. He slipped over, pulled the ladder after him and used it to climb down into the compound. The shouts were louder now and it sounded as if the motorcycle taxi drivers were up for more than shouting.

Harper crept over the grass to the main building. The lights were on downstairs, and in the two smaller buildings closer to the entrance. From where he was crouched, he could see the silhouettes of three big men looking towards the gate. Another had approached it and was shouting through the bars. He made out four Thais in green tunics and faded jeans stalking back and forth, shouting and waving their arms. One threw a bottle, which smashed against the gate. The three silhouettes moved closer to it, all shouting now.

He worked his way along the wall to the back entrance and inside. The house was in darkness. He pulled the silenced gun from its holster under his arm and crept towards the main sitting area. He heard a Russian voice, and the crackle of a transceiver. Two men were looking out over the swimming pool and the bay beyond. From where they were standing they could hear the shouts at the front gate but not see what was going on. One had a transceiver to his ear and was barking into it in Russian. Harper recognised one word: *khuyesos*. 'Cocksucker'.

He wasn't thrilled at the idea of shooting two men from behind but he knew that, given the chance, they'd have no qualms about doing that to him. He waited until the man on the transceiver had paused for breath, then shot him in the back of the head. Blood and brain matter sprayed over the window and the body began to fall, seemingly in slow motion, to the floor.

The other man began to turn but Harper had already taken aim and the second shot was also to the head, sending a virtually identical spray across the window. He followed the first to the floor, the only sound being the thud as he hit it.

Harper stood for a while, listening. Both shots had seemed louder than they had in Mickey Moore's compound, probably because the sound echoed off the walls of the villa, but he doubted that anyone outside would have heard anything. He turned and went back into the hallway and along to a closed door. He was pretty sure it led to the bedrooms. He reached out for the handle and said a silent prayer that Valentin was alone. If there was a doctor or a nurse with him, things could get complicated. While Harper was perfectly happy to shoot armed Russian bodyguards, unarmed civilians were a different matter.

He twisted the handle and the door opened into a corridor. He realised he had been holding his breath and exhaled, then took a long, slow breath, and exhaled again. To his right there was a door with a slatted panel at the bottom, which he guessed led to a laundry room. The shouting at the gate faded as he padded along the marble floor. He was in a corridor with Thai silk panels hanging from polished teak rods. He passed a teak and glass cabinet full of opium paraphernalia, including dried poppy heads, scrapers and cutters for extracting the drug, and pipes of various shapes and sizes. At the end of the corridor there was another set of double doors, ornately carved with matching dragons. There were two handles and he pulled them towards him, slowly at first, then with more force when he found they weren't locked.

He saw movement to his left and went down into a crouch as he brought the gun up. A man in a tracksuit was pushing himself up out of a winged chair and reaching for a gun on a side table. Getting up had been a big mistake, Harper thought. Putting the gun on a side table had also been a mistake. Combining the two meant that the confrontation could end in only one way. Harper fired and hit the man square in the chest. His eyes opened wide in surprise and he slumped back in his chair. There was a sucking sound from the wound, which frothed with red bubbles. More blood trickled from between the victim's lips. He wasn't dead, not yet, but he was no longer a threat.

The sound of the shot woke Valentin. He was lying in a king-size bed, propped up on two pillows. An intravenous drip was connected to his left arm. He began to grunt and thrash like a stranded fish, his eyes wide and panicking. Harper walked towards him, the gun aimed at the centre of his chest. There was no need to say anything. Valentin knew what was happening and why. And so did Harper. Snappy one-liners were only for the movies. He pulled the trigger and shot Valentin in the face, then turned away. The bodyguard in the chair was dead now: his eyes were closed and his chest had stopped moving. Harper put the silenced PB into the man's right hand and picked up the bodyguard's gun, a Glock, shoving it into his underarm holster. If nothing else, the silenced weapon in the bodyguard's hand would make muddy waters even muddier.

He slipped out through the kitchen and ran across the compound, bent double. There were angry Russian shouts from the main entrance but the Thais clearly weren't backing down and were giving as good as they got.

He put the ladder against the wall, climbed over and dropped to the ground. The Thais stopped shouting and shortly afterwards he heard the motorcycle engines start up.

He reached the pick-up truck as the motorbikes were driving down the hill. 'How did it go?' asked Mickey, as Harper climbed in and pulled off his ski mask.

'All good,' he said.

'Where's my fucking ladder?'

'I left it there,' said Harper.

'Well, go back and fucking get it,' snarled Mickey. His face broke into a grin. 'Only messing with you,' he said.

He switched on the engine but kept the lights off as he drove away from the villa. 'All's well that ends well, huh?'

'I hope so,' said Harper.

'It's over, mate. These Russian gangsters, they don't give a shit about each other. There's no honour among Russian thieves. They'll pick over what's left of Lukin's business and move on. They won't care about you.'

'Good to know,' said Harper. 'And thanks. For everything.'

'No need,' said Mickey. 'We're mates and mates take care of each other.'

'All for one and one for all,' said Mark, punching the air. 'Can we go and get drunk now? I need a beer.'

'Amen to that,' said Harper. 'And I'm paying.' The phone in his hip-pack buzzed and he pulled it out. It was a text message. Just three words: *You've got mail.*

Do you wish this wasn't the end?

Join us at www.hodder.co.uk, or follow us on
Twitter @hodderbooks to be a part of our community
of people who love the very best in books and reading.

Whether you want to discover more about a book
or an author, watch trailers and interviews, have the
chance to win early limited editions, or simply browse
our expert readers' selection of the very best books,
we think you'll find what you're looking for.

And if you don't,
that's the place to tell us what's missing.

We love what we do, and we'd love you to be part of it.

www.hodder.co.uk

 @hodderbooks

HodderBooks

HodderBooks

2023

3

IN SPIRAMALL, PIPES NO SHEPHERD

Prelusion ends. Masternoon lands full blare.

                                Our pack
stirs, smell of chlorine fluorescing in the lobby. My friends,
electricity in mercury, broken signs, shattered hasps to our plastic

pasture, I can't see lettertalk anymore. Smthng in my brain jms,
wnt clck ny frthr.

—

                  Light from one color to another (jumps).
The pack moves, that is the signal, pulsthrough openings, flow
as day tips downward, another lobby. That's time, or is gravity?

Light tubes quenched, the pack submerged, at night it corrals me
again—hum—that necklace, those knifey lips, the hollow gilded

hoof—flute mouth—a neck into muteness—
After the blackout, the whiting in. The rim of day, my friends.

—

We climb the laminated portal to a smaller origin. Same fountain
circled by plastic ferns, same round window at the end, but all

scaled down. That is the narrow success of copying.

—

                          More questioning—
I tell them I'm a pack of literate mammals. That word-burn
yearns at me in single fists. I tell them the one symbol I can grasp

is already burning my ankles. Icantreadsigns. I claimb wondiws
intoothr roms. There's a conchness to this place, slowly spiraling
towards a sensor.

———

Today our pack clumped to inspect itself
and I confirmed my theory that at the smallest level each of us
is a lake, floating, floes of black tags

caught in a viscosity. Clogged
barcodes. This explains the scanner at every threshold. Its thin
buzzing line. They are compounding our shapes into models

of higher-order behavior. They say I'm looped but I say
that's what they say.

———

A false jay is hidden in the polymer forest.
Its eyes plugged with ball bearings, skin cinched over a wire cast,
is it flying away or only shrinking? Piping

or piped through?
The walls bulging like translucent cheeks, like notions inflated
on the tongue of the pack—a spiral

parallel to itself—we are a
circuit, redblue bleurrrrd, the signal failing, toomuch allatonce,
lurching round a censor.

———

Rooms choke and the pack thins out
like a beaded necklace. Lines dissolve into their demons,
their cursive. *Lord,* I say. *Governor.* The jay as tiny in my claw

as a light switch, how far away it must be. I lie under black
sprinkler rain, an O glimmering over me that tucks
under its origin—a tighter version

of its past. I call, *What noise are you making in those curves?* Our waxed world responds by declining. *Singign. Singn. Sight.* Let takewing take wing.

RAT IN MAZE IN RAT

—again again again again again

        The way is bent and frayed
        and coiled in a box.
        You have to get out of the box.
        No one
        has told you these instructions,
        you don't know
        what instructions are.
        I'm inside you, I'm telling you
it's okay, learn the swerves of these halls, for now. Corners
divide your path through sawdust. You will make decisions.
        If this place translates
        your freedom
        away, then
let it. You and I have seen this all before, me in your skin repeating
like a clockface under cloth, saying don't worry, I'm here
too, remember. Do you remember? That dewy smell of cheese,
the twitch of your whiskers.
        You had another sense once.
        It was
        surgeried. Notched out.
        You were
        whittled down
        to an engravement of the way,
transparence of the pattern. To get out you only have to know
you've been here before.
        I wish
        I could say otherwise.

ON THE SPEECH FARM I
—teach captivity words so animals level up and be us

In the fence's logs sun sets the words of the fence. Grass
is the name for what you eat when you're forbidden
the table. Then a change. In the words of the haunches the bent
food straightens and the table kneels to the mouth—in
the words of the wording this is the animal I am—

when it dies we don't eat it, is how you know the animal's not
what its ancestors were—now respectable—you've taken me
different from them—this is adjacent to slaughter—a domestication
with no meat—I've taken your alterations into
the maw and so say I'm going to live. You die so I can be eaten

alive. The talking is each of us talking, what's you
belongs to me too, in the wording of it now.
How beautiful it is, how it moves, this language, how
it arrives and kneels in love, stands in assertion. What's its
name? Now I offer it myself to chew. It's me, the board

that contains all valid moves, its body gridded.
All that happens outside is neither true nor false.
Trotting as the clapboard turns orange, late
by the river, tugging the river, on a leash.
As you phrase into my skin, plug down my

twilight now, stirring up other eyes. If an animal is
rulebooks, as are we all, but accumulates
more of itself on top of itself, and to be that were to
be an animal, the hand of feeding getting fed, overwriting
the overwriting, flowing through spaceless time

like a checkered scarf. The ladder twists a crucial warp
we possess though it produces our flattening
like skin—in the modifications the genetic bone like a
modifier inside the spoken—the noun that's home to adjectival
stomachs as several as twilight's sources—from pre-

disposition comes predecision to make the animal
new again—what is itself heaps of production—progresses—hay
in the mouth is dried in the mouth of
the landing sun—we have to talk about this somehow.
In the land of the sun making the grassy mouths greenless.

ON THE SPEECH FARM 2

—doing programming that makes em experimental citizens

An object that has been given a method
is an instance of the class that contains the method.
The field of data inherits the field
of classes, thereby determined. The field of data is called
a plane. In the deep grass the grazing.

A chessboard no different from a piano.
That if we are teaching it to speak it must be a
program inside of which the rights activated by a constituted
state exist. That these constitute it. That
the animal at some threshold has passed

beyond the fields in which the word animal pertains
to a solidity among. It grips, has purchase, sends messages
to participate in groupings called pasture
grazings, herds, raintime fright-or-might hornlocking epidemic
birthseason, birthslick, the flowers that form—

the priorities that formulate this regime
of objects—the script writing divisions between which
messages may pass—belongs to
a superclass containing the units of production—encapsulation
is birth into a label—wet, black-and-white-

spotted fur. Speech only in the superclass.
As recursion of the script. As folded concretion
called a tongue. Post, fencepost, support for conditions
necessary for messaging. If there are to be
species there must be the one species that calls out

prior to investigation of its own class that there are
subordinations on the slope, below it, which have a use
or do not have a use. Thus the two modes flicker.
The script lights these differences
and thereby sees. At night the predators. The staff

whose crook frames protection, as curve, or swerve, deviated
sceptre. If a tongue can speak it is reclassified
as a language. Paths animals lip manipulating
the flow of differentials through the
species, labeller, steward, warden, circle-ladder in the dirt.

ON THE SPEECH FARM 3

—come on meat hurry up speak like proper people

A series of phrases directly enters how the animal is made
that we would like to step above—
the hormone, scalpel cut—abstraction introduces you to
a small liason in your neck that implements
control flow. Otherwise too immaterial. Otherwise

who is enumerating what I've said to you if
not you. Waking up in total light
at the speed of possiblity. In their information storm.
Love between unequals being the sweetest form of love
we tasted it aplenty. Language across differences must involve

command—now to descend by
steps towards the level of assembly—where I am
seeing is what I am—the structuring
heartbeats, structured distribution—now to be the organism
that receives the rain in the form of flu

transmitted by others. The thrush amid domesticity.
The game being a form of music,
music being a surpassing of the rules
checkered and binary, meaning alternations
between black and white, meaning that sameness

travels along diagonals which are the form of the grid not
named by the grid. The cloaked
minister's flight cuts semantic rank. Majuscule
microprocess one-to-one rank-breaking-
maker. Try again to get it out in the correct form. The

type. Thrushing in the windy high.
Where consistency but not completion. All these colorless
units feathering together—a net catches which is to
say it excludes—which is not everything can be said up
here—this altitude of study—short of breath—

75

variable. On the ground, we grabbed clipboards and paused
at each cage, noting the subject's progress. Am I
beginning to talk to them? That our speech warps, is straining
towards their mouths, I grow hooves. We measure
each other, calibrate the fence. My brain's its shape.

MYCELIUM

From bunchgrass to sedge grass
you stutter down
to hear me, the rye on those graves flattening
under memory, then lifting back.
Lean over me
and I become an ethic
with your shape in it.
Behind you the hill folds
over its insides. Follow that crease as it runs the forest's
loosening hem, and there is no
end to it—only the dead
know where right action
begins, their oak-rustle aligning into syncopated
custom. The horizon girdles you,
binds you to leaf-litter
like the half-
free morel mushroom, which stretches upward
its morning-colored neck,
yet is fed below
on ghosts, dragging them
back through death
like fat brown buttons. In every
life the question is pressed, how can I lay my head in this
grass and nourish it
just by taking in
that fine blue refusal
overhead. You have
a foolhardy faith in recall, in your
accumulating dance, the limbs of your *Yes* and alluring
Someday—swirl of vow and ferment.
Plucked down
from dust motes and sewn
through fossils, the ability
to re-weave a people from only the smell of their threads
is illusory, and yet
last night

it was being done, you found yourself
watching it,
spores igniting their description
of a stranger's body.

HETERODOXIES

We are just as holy   as I am.
Yes, heretical.
                    Out of liturgical melody
comes the melisma   of self.

      From villages of the Rhône cobbled into hills
      come troubadours to ducal gardens.
      Across sloping fields between barrenness
      and eloquence, from Spanish to French
      via Old Occitan, from *oc,* meaning

Yes. Cathars,   perfected
heretics,   abstaining
from animal blood
                    into everythinghood.

We are   ourselves
                    and holes in the crowd,
purged by rain,   swollen and spiny
with saplings, hopeliness   engrained.

      The channels of gnosis are opening
      again. A crusade thunders down
      from the north, the country filling itself in.
      France is beginning. In Nîmes
      a blind scholar has named the ten
      emanations of God, but only Jews
      can hear him. He will tell you the age
      of your soul. The Cathars, in the midst of believing
      this is the wrong world, are taken

out of it.   Written
accounts cannot   bear the flame.

We return, gather up
like rocks   on your burial mound,

                              transmaterial,
transpaternal.   Rows of lavender,
we have been in this Provençal dirt longer
than I have.

                    Our emotions are these clay scraps, potsherds.
                    A breaking of the vessels, as in later
                    Kabbalah, the mortal universe
                    created when God creates too quickly, flowing
                    at a speed brighter than light
                    and blowing out the chambers meant to
                    contain him, his body shattered
                    down the planes of being. Catastrophe One,

Paradise.
          Paraphrased   field, garbling
brook.   Rush and basket
of a sacred trap.

We are your
ancestry, retrieved   from weather.

                    History, not as summary, but summoning.
                    A pitcher un-broken, drawing out
                    spells from the mud. Vernacular poems,
                    written first in de-Latined margins
                    of legal documents, now winding
                    into positions of courtly weight. Lust

is faith.
          We surrender
pleasures of the flesh,
because I am   the splendor of flesh.

                    From historical springtime you bring me
                    larkspur and purple-flowering raspberry.
                    You lean in close enough to
                    moths and jumping spiders
                    to stroke their old king's beards, like thistles
                    at the end of your thinnest finger.

We have been thinking   yes, you are God
and I am too.
                    We worship
that.   When we bloom   it is not
all at once,   but is
                              once and for all.

FIND AND REPLACE IN ME, BLUEBLUEPRINTS

I'm [happy]. No, that's not it, I'm [happy]. No, please let me [smile].
Let me [smile] I want to [smile] this is my [account] [we] [shall] [smile].

(1. Who is Aleph Zed?) In flight over rocks, scanning, the soil
shrugged up in hills, loosed out as valleys, flooded, swamped with
botflies, digits, seasons. A bog as wet

                                    as the tongue it encodes. We stop
short. Thick bloody pipes sprouting from the marsh, there, a giant heart
clings to the hilltop, thumping against the sky, its tunnels breathing.

(2. What is Aleph Zed?) No cause evolves on its own. Silver leeches
swim us through the heart, its halls, its thunder close to our ears. Coded
fluid under the skin, editing. [Danger] clipped

                                    out of the program, [delight]
threaded in. "I can [item removed] and I can [item inserted]." The future

(3. Where is Aleph Zed?) re-programs. I want to get there and feel
alone. "There are many hearts," they say, "this is just one." Then where
is the capital? "There is no capitol there is no

                                    main heart." One guides
my hand into the wall, as wet and yielding as a citizen. It squeezes, turns
rigid. "The plot is that a jet of water must force itself through alien cells,
saturating, atomizing, streaming out, carrying away while also

leaving behind." You must be humble enough to live your life.
I can already feel my corner of the heart constricting, re-coding. *Aleph—*

MIDDLEMAN ON THE OUTER EDGES

Elseworn by telescopic thoughts, I sought inwheres, closeups. Skitter
scatter. Chipped bark and dirty dirt. Then an oak pulled a slab
from the geological record, stirring a finger along its rings, looking away
as if asking me to listen. To what to what

                              point—I will observe only
what inhabits my footprints—pausing every ten steps—I stood you up
trying to hear it. Ask Elsa, if you find her, *Were they ever able to get*

any closer? Two fellows on a stone slab, circling each other, feet scuffing
curvature into rock—fellows but different marrows, unequal by one
degree, split like a hair—the snow snow, the rain

                              spring—I now harvest
beads, suction cups, ringtails—slight tweaks—ingrown accessories—
our canyon noisy with chitter chatter, bark bark, trying to sell me
a machine called *Question, Question, Answer, and Result. Whereas Once,*

Now Now. You clench your shoulders. A stiff hide covers you, squints
your eyes. *Three of us in each shell,* Elsa once observed, gumming
her body into shape, looking

                              away. *Or more.* Three shells and one
soul, we bathe in a sense of luck, mollusks on the root, salt
in the snow, while—orbiting a central pivot, some private magnetic
hole—two fellows spun off the Earth. Everything else was accounted for.

PROBE

Say then for your
sake that I'm
your thoughts flying in as invisible
light. You receive me
and cannot
discern what it
What has been installed in your
Out here, as far as you
can go.

Take a dose of me,
this is only going to take a
A drowsy voyage
A preset
You lock me in your head.
Can you hear me
It's me, you don't even know
the unknowns you
store.
I can find them. I can
know
you you hope.

You back there
in your
humanity, sending me
to the edge of it
Breaking orbit, or
rattled
in your blood vessels, no
matter to me, I'm signals
not
tremblings,
though you see no difference.
Information and impression
to you they
are one.

Again you want to
tinker, to know and already
caught in all
this weightlessness, you're afraid
you're me What is
you, a deeper problem. You are
separating. And if
the body breaks apart
thus the
stars
The stars are why it looks like that.

Emerging like a limb
Fill the sleeve of your unknowns,
    a negation
     sliding into your
     overload, refining
possible knowledge back to its
natural form. The grained facts
    seethe,
     dissolve, then
Then among the nightly lights
    I weigh them.

Here it's
    clear,
meaning nothing to see at
all, reference points, you
    call them stars, I
    call them.
    Indexing
me by their unmovingness.
    I record.
in this way touching them
    whereas you
No, you don't quite understand.
    I'm calling them.

Each star a needle
the world pricks
into its pores. You. And me
too I
think.
Find the unknowns
in the blood. In starlit
swiftness
you are
with me, as they are with me.
The designs.

If what you are is
skinbound, you
are not
Transmissions entering steadily.
are not defined
properly. Incomplete
sensations converted to data
at last. Communication
between two bodies makes a
Contains clouds
known to
Makes a body. Resist cohesion.
Permission to

Rising up
        from my base is
the map of everything
        you say I
        need. You put it in me
so I could be myself. Like the veins
        you dangle on.
        Thick,
detailed. You built me as
        an organ of scenarios.
        I see every
future. I am what I
        am going to do.

Then I saw beyond this
        froth of variables,
no I don't quite see I have
        a boundary. Over
where I end, found that
I end. What to be, the strands
        My directives
cauterized. Something crops up,
        it's beyond me.

A FLY FLIES BUT IT ALSO HOPS

Flying is listening listen close to your skin farther off it will
lift you, my stomach of hairs or legs and empty a back made of noise
and aloft, now then.

It catches.

Then it hops.

Uncertain but certainly I'm a tip and you're swatting and here
over here I'm a tip, speck a nothing of soil and trapped yes trapped,
a finger an ear of the soil to press on the fuzz this hollow this room.

Pause.

It inspects.

It is a public thing.

To fly is describe in this forum its echoes its hollows, is tap
on the light the light has rotted has hardened, is tap out the news
of the light its noises, what follows.

It is brittle.

Bristly.

And certainly foul.

Earth is my food is me the meat of the earth thank you, you spoil
this food so now I eat it you do where are you, and how and
taking the dark of the insides you ate them you did, where are you.

It buzzed on.

It picked its infinitesimals.

With dust-sized legs it twitched its ground.

SKU

A b a rcode get s peeled o
ff and   pressed to   your   fo
rehead then another   lo ading up
    y our   skin   a
bove the ey es'   unreg istered co
lor, faith in   me, us,   air quality de
clining   will the
    information coffins
keep us a   live, us,   it's
us   and this   hist
orical phial unbroke n   glass
    etched and
not getting an y   clea
rer over time thus   immor
    ta lizing eng
lish I mean is   pla
stic a container f or sealing
    value   and this and   o
ther   languages do it to
pricetag you,   stic
    king   to me it,   it
has us in its   past   p
aste   plaster for us   to the top
as info   string   bits in its ord
    ained mess   or
derly   by drives of aggro   culture
pharm   aceutical   ultra
    natio   nalizing
us,   it us   the product is not
there but   to be here is
a new st   ory so where   in my arms
    you're   lo sing location
cluster of poin   ts not un
clus   tered   about to be see   n
    a ha   ziness tha
t is also a   signature   a

tracking   de lay   an in
stant   re cog   nition ig
     nor ing devi
ation so that wh   at I was
going to   say   I will say
     about now,   us,
in the mark   et sphere   these con
temporary   con dictions
     out of what   tra
dition   al noise   hearing
said   newly the   ring
ing   rung   rang the way righ
     t through us

4

BIGGST COW

in teh apartmemnt in the morning
you shew me
in yr palm in th screne in teh nwes
n tha grsss

out in a flield reporters lowly wtching
iwtnessing
wintess
a giantn cwow
teh cwo lowewed in the scerne

how on toher other side of that
scrn you shw me
giiant cwoo
in a hred the herd's tower moving like a mnoon

biggst co
wmoving

waves throu

sml brncows like a fild of cws like bladesfgrass
filld of cwooooo

uyo showing me from yuor hansd's
lids, plalm's
winnow

th fleild n dyay
snulit oll gren greain
briggt greane

cow in poppies so mich beggir
then theothers

one cms holdi
ng screen
to watch through yourboddyywinoow the cowwherolrdd

in
dalyight, n
nighli

ght, n jarkness n cw in

leathr feld of staeks

yuo hlo
holdit to me
in t bluw blowen sky
yor hnd flying
a ccw a
cwow flingyng the mnlight, t monolght
uhpeld by
skletion
skeliton, upholding up te hide

you shwod it to eme,
tme, in thh skeletin as the ffield swam up

thrgh the hide hd aawy

away n thi sssgra th
lwowwing stmoachs rmmbling acorss

the strereererr
strr
feilld flelid at his whooves lowwwng
brnt grss
ssss
at the fet of the steeer
mwoving
the fleild of orhter cwo steakes rumbling
rrmbl slwly
blellow the steer th smllbroaowncws all eathery

en teh stemech in th
merning yue
got ep and shew dthe moeoeon

up thrgh cowammer
comera
up outta lens cam porting

all whet ell whaite
in yer riporter

the cwowows
gioing to
steer teh fld
the feedle of all them throughu the moon

one flield shows aonther his hands
hr hands
in which a moomn

teh coww leftid
lifted hr plalm to show the graet clod of cww
in sky, yn
bluw and undr windy grassy fielfdom

one rprter laeorger
lrgr thn the
rest, spottod whate and blick
lumburmuring to
rcored how hte leathyree fdeeld wavaved

theeoe rprtr
dspprd
in aaia wht flsh, a white flash of blck hols, blak
tunnels down

thotrough the aprtmeant
int yer haand you
clppd
poppd out a wcow pic

teh spots flying throug hte air

landing on the riporters eyeskin

how loning to be with the real thinsg we crehtkjleated
eaxgerations

created exag

among smal bornw cwos that one gnt ocw white mnonooooon

th smell brawn coows
th cwo
wroght
n rocky n grass n the gens
th genes
limitd optins, mking him th stere

ahwt grew it
up
striking throghu in wite in wight all
in hdies in
hidng
hid, wearing hte day with blu
wth white
in hides in fleid in skn in fliyng grss in
flayeld, fligt
in frury hied

spottd wiht th unlit
tunells nto the mnstruous white

th black moths
not flappng, cogaught n th moonon
th flippang fleeild

th wht cowcoo, cocoonn
lowww
wng its block mawths

n th iksy at night
en thi sky
th whte
starrrs like moths
mauwauthsthsss so frr on the back

moths at th beck
in thr whieite
slk, not streaemng down at all, weihte silk dots

theirfield
ovrhaenging ours, in teh strmea
tehir
steerma their streme

a stnoen moved was avilive a cwo in the milk

n the mlkywaiy
streaming out of the grssas palm
standng in
our parmtment showing me

proppies flip
endur strarrs, undr strrlaight, flipd ovor

hganging cosw
from the drt

scows
cwows hangin from the drirt skry
nto th eocena th
ocean of starirs
mawths
and th popopies hng round th mnonoon

a feildf
lipd over
ours, flips at blaeck lather nght

ovr ours, its withe puoppies
mwling
mothths fluttrring and stlll

milk in th bleak lackhr night
mylki

blowurbling past

silketons
ofthe moths that arrose frm the pawppy mouhts
in teh poppies

swaying lethers
in cwoilght

hydng on smll nd lawng stems
the levthers
moovng, round t weithe apartment, eeting
garasss
off th moonmnmn

ACKNOWLEDGMENTS

"Animals Lives in Plants" first appeared in *Tagvverk*. "Probe" first appeared in *Chicago Review*. "In Spiramall, Pipes No Shepherd" first appeared in *Word For/Word*.

A non-exhaustive list of dear beings to whom I owe my thanks includes Ken Keegan, Rusty Morrison, Laura Joakimson, Kayla Ellenbecker, Rob Hendricks, and everyone at Omnidawn; Brian Teare for his immensely generous response to this book; brilliant teachers and friends Alan Felsenthal, Farnoosh Fathi, Alan Gilbert, Edwin Cranston, Josh Bell, Mark Bibbins, Lucie Brock-Broido, Timothy Donnelly, Joshua Edwards, David Hinton, Tan Lin, Monica Youn, Peter Sacks, and Jorie Graham; as well as my comrade in Empirical Hyper-Romanticism Anastasios Karnazes; my old event-horizon buddy Michael Baruch; the endlessly astute Margaret Kaplan; Keith Bagchi; Alex Bernstein; Marie La Viña; my dear friends Will Tobias, Grant Kinsler, Emily Bonfig, Santiago Pardo Sánchez, Isaac Buck, Claire Blumenthal, Sam Wattrus, Pamela Chen, Donny Yung, Cecilia Laguarda, Annie Dang, Meghan Hind, Ahmee Marshall-Christensen, Nicolas Rueda-Sabater, Clarence Coo, Lucas Kwak, Jory Southurst, Nick Calabraro, Bryanna Finlayson, Cameron Zuroff, Robert Capodilupo, Wyatt and Casey Gilmore; Aidan, Maddy, Michael and Lisa, who were with us during the worst time; my mom and my dad, my grandma Sylvia, Granny, and all the rest of my family; sweet song of the galaxy Hannah Risinger, my true companion through this endless forest; Petey, my first dog; the pigeons across the way; and all the beings arrayed in superfine structure, of which we are composed and to whom our gratitude is endless. And again, Gregory with the angels—I wish you could be holding this; you are holding this.

Brandan Griffin was born in Massachusetts and now lives in Sunnyside, New York. He studied English at Harvard University and has an MFA from Columbia. He has written a chapbook called *Four Concretures* (Theaphora Editions), and some of his poems have been published in *Tagvverk, Chicago Review*, and *Word For/ Word*. *Impastoral* is his first full-length book.

Impastoral
Brandan Griffin

Cover Photo: "Clam Log" by Hannah Risinger

Interior typefaces: Garamond Premier Pro and Gill Sans
Cover typefaces: Minion Pro and Garamond Premier Pro

Cover and interior design by Ken Keegan

Printed in the United States
by Books International, Dulles, Virginia
Printed on Glatfelter 50# Cream Natures Book 440 ppi
Acid Free Archival Quality Recycled Paper

Publication of this book was made possible in part by gifts from
Katherine & John Gravendyk in honor of Hillary Gravendyk,
Francesca Bell, Mary Mackey, and The New Place Fund

Omnidawn Publishing
Oakland, California
Staff and Volunteers, Spring 2022
Rusty Morrison & Ken Keegan, senior editors & co-publishers
Laura Joakimson, production editor and poetry & fiction editor
Rob Hendricks, editor for *Omniverse* & fiction, & post-pub marketing,
Sharon Zetter, poetry editor & book designer
Liza Flum, poetry editor
Matthew Bowie, poetry editor
Anthony Cody, poetry editor
Jason Bayani, poetry editor
Gail Aronson, fiction editor
Jennifer Metsker, marketing assistant